James Skerret Shore Baird

The classical manual: an epitome of ancient geography, Greek and Roman mythology, antiquities, and chronology

Chiefly intended for the use of schools

James Skerret Shore Baird

The classical manual: an epitome of ancient geography, Greek and Roman mythology, antiquities, and chronology
Chiefly intended for the use of schools

ISBN/EAN: 9783337185046

Printed in Europe, USA, Canada, Australia, Japan

Cover: Foto ©Paul-Georg Meister /pixelio.de

More available books at **www.hansebooks.com**

THE

CLASSICAL MANUAL:

AN EPITOME OF

ANCIENT GEOGRAPHY,

GREEK AND ROMAN MYTHOLOGY,

ANTIQUITIES,

AND CHRONOLOGY.

CHIEFLY INTENDED FOR THE USE OF SCHOOLS.

COMPILED BY

JAMES S. S. BAIRD,

TRINITY COLLEGE, DUBLIN,
ASSISTANT CLASSICAL MASTER, KING'S SCHOOL,
GLOUCESTER.

NEW YORK:
SHELDON & COMPANY, PUBLISHERS,
498 & 500 BROADWAY.

1870.

TO THE

REV THOMAS EVANS, D.D.

HEAD MASTER OF KING'S SCHOOL, GLOUCESTER,

THIS LITTLE WORK

IS RESPECTFULLY DEDICATED,

BY

HIS OBLIGED AND FAITHFUL SERVANT,

JAMES S. S. BAIRD.

PREFACE.

MANY excellent works have recently issued from the press, which, either separately or in the form of dictionaries, treat of the subjects of the following pages: and yet the want of an Epitome has been recognized, which would contain, in the compass of a single volume, of small size and moderate price, as much information upon such points as is calculated to elucidate the Greek and Roman authors usually read in the junior forms of our schools. It has been the object of the compiler of the present manual to supply this deficiency by introducing into it such details as are most likely to be useful (indeed much of which is absolutely necessary to the classical student) in so small a space as to admit of its being thoroughly *mastered* and *retained*. Although at first the requirements of junior forms were chiefly contemplated, yet in the progress of the work so much additional matter has been supplied as, it is hoped, will render it not unacceptable to more advanced students.

In the compilation, the best and most recent authorities have been consulted, but particular obligations must be acknowledged to the following works: Dr. William Smith's

Dictionaries of "Greek and Roman Mythology and Biography," "Greek and Roman Antiquities," and "Classical Dictionary;" the Rev. T. K. Arnold's editions of the "Handbook of Ancient Geography and History," by W. Pütz, and the "Handbooks of Greek and Roman Antiquities," by Dr. Bojesen. The editor's best thanks are also due to the Rev. H. Haines, M. A., Second Master of the King's School, Gloucester, for his kind supervision of these pages while passing through the press, and also for the valuable assistance he has afforded in several parts of the work.

J. S. S. B.

Gloucester, January, 1852.

CONTENTS.

GEOGRAPHY.

EUROPE.

COUNTRIES, Seas, Gulfs, Straits, Rivers, Mountains, Lakes, Islands 13, 14
Hispania.—Boundaries, Mountains, Rivers, Promontories, Divisions, Tribes 15
    Tarraconensis, Lusitania, Bætica. Islands.... 16
Gallia. Boundaries, Mountains, Rivers, Lake, Divisions.. 17
    Narbonensis .... ib.
    Aquitania, Lugdunensis.. 18
    Gallia Belgica. Tribes, Islands................................ 19
Germania.—Boundaries, Mountains, Rivers, Divisions, Tribes 20
Vindelicia, Rhætia, Noricum, Pannonia, Illyricum.—Vindelicia. Boundaries, Rivers, Tribes, Towns 21
    Rhætia. Boundaries, Rivers, Tribes .... ib.
    Noricum. Boundaries... ib.
    Rivers, Towns 22
    Pannonia. Boundaries, Rivers, Lakes, Divisions, Towns .... ib.
    Illyricum. Boundaries, Mountains, Divisions........... ib.
    Towns, Islands... 23
Italia.—Boundaries, Gulfs, Strait, Mountains .... ib.
    Rivers, Lakes 24
    Capes, Divisions.. 25
    Liguria, Gallia Cisalpina or Togata .... ib.
    Venetia, Carni, Histria, Etruria.............................. 26
    Umbria, Picenum, Sabinum 27
    Latium, Samnium.. 28
    Campania, Apulia.. 29
    Lucania, Bruttium... 30
    Islands: Sicilia.. ib.
Mœsia.—Boundaries, Divisions, Tribes, Rivers, Towns.... 31
Dacia.—Boundaries, Rivers, Tribes................................. 32
Sarmatia.—Boundaries, Tribes, Towns .... ib.

CONTENTS.

Macedonia. — Boundaries 32
        Gulfs, Mountains, Rivers, Divisions, Cities 33
        Illyris Græca .... ib.
Thracia.—Boundaries, Straits, &c., Mountains, Rivers, Cities 34
Græcia. — Boundaries .... ib.
        Gulfs, Strait, Mountains, Rivers................................... 35, 36
        Lakes, Promontories, Divisions.. 37
        Thessalia... ib.
        Epīrus, Acarnania, Ætolia, Doris, Locris.......... 38
        Phocis, Bœotia 39
        Attica, Megaris (PELOPONNESUS), Achaia, Elis...... 40
        Messenia, Laconia, Argolis.. 41
        Arcadia, Corinthia, Sicyonia......................................,.. 42
Greek Islands. — In the Ionian and Ægean Seas............. 43
Britannia or Albion.—Boundaries, Rivers, Promontories,
    Divisions 44
        Tribes, Towns, Islands.. 45

ASIA.

Countries, Mountains, Seas and Gulfs, Rivers, Islands..... 46, 47
Asia Minor. — Boundaries, Gulfs, Mountains, Rivers........ 47
        Lake, Promontories, Divisions.. 48
        .Bithynia .... ib.
        Paphlagonia, Pontus, Mysia, Lydia or Mæonia 49
        Caria, Lycia, Pamphylia, Cilicia....................... 50
        Phrygia, Galatia, Cappadocia, the Six Dorian
           States, the Twelve Ionian States................... 51
        Ætolian League, "Seven Churches of Asia"..... 52
        Island: Cyprus... ib.
Syria, Palæstina. — Boundaries, Mountains, Rivers........ ib.
        Divisions: Syria, Phœnicia, Palæstinæ or Judæa.
           Tribes... 53
        Divisions: Galilee, Samaria, Judæa...................... 54
        Peræa and Batanæa, the Cities of Refuge, Seven
           Heathen Nations 55
Arabia. — Boundaries .... ib.
        Mountains, Divisions, Tribes, &c........................ 56
Countries between Pontus Euxinus and Hyrcanum
    Mare.—Sarmatia Asiatica, Colchis or Æa, Iberia ib.
    Albania.. 57
Armenia Propria vel Major. — Boundaries, Mountains,
    Rivers, Lake, Towns .... ib.
Mesopotamia... ib.
        River, Divisions, Towns.. 58
Babylonia and Chaldæa. — Boundaries .... ib.
Countries East of the Euphrates and Tigris: —
    Assyria, Media, Susiana or Susis................................. 59
    Persia or Persis 60

CONTENTS.

Countries South of the Oxus: —
  Hyrcania, Parthia, Aria, Bactriana.................. 60
  Carmania, Gedrosia 61
Countries North of the Oxus: —
  Sogdiana, Scythia .... ib.
India. —
  Boundaries, Rivers, Divisions, Towns, &c., Islands, &c. 62

AFRICA.

Boundaries, Bays, Strait, Rivers, Lakes 63
Ægyptus.—Boundaries, Divisions, Ægyptus Inferior or Delta, Heptanomis 64
  Ægyptus Superior vel Thebais 65
Northern Coasts of Africa.—Divisions................. ib.
  Libya, Tripolitana, Africa Propria................. 66
  Numidia, Mauritania, Islands 67

MYTHOLOGY.

The Twelve Olympian or National Deities of the Greeks and Romans 68–70
Minor Deities 70–75
Heroes, Mythical Persons, &c. 75–84

EARLY GRECIAN LEGENDS, &c.

The Argonautic Expedition............................. 85
Early Legends relating to Thebes 86
Story of Œdipus and War of the Seven against Thebes 86, 87
Early Kings of Troy 88
Legend of the Trojan War........................... 89, 91
Grecian Heroes, &c., connected with the Trojan War 91-94
Trojan Heroes, &c................................... 95–97

GREEK ANTIQUITIES.

Divisions of the Inhabitants of Attica and Sparta 98
Magistrates: —
  Archons, their number, functions, &c.......... 98, 99
  Inferior Magistrates............................. 99
  Ephori.. ib.
Assemblies.—The General Assembly, The Senate of the Five Hundred................................... 100
  Gerousia, the Senate at Sparta................. 101
Judges and Courts of Justice.—The Court of Areopagus ib.
  The Heliasts. The Diætetæ. The Forty........... ib.
  Court of the Ephetæ. Amphictyones.............. 102
Punishments. — Ostracism, Atimia, &c............ 102, 103
Temples, Priests, and Sacrifices................. 103, 104
Oracles. — Zeus at Dodona. Apollo at Delphi 104, 105
  Other Chief Oracles: of Zeus; of Apollo; of Heroes... 105

CONTENTS.

Festivals. — Adōnia, Anthestēria, Dionȳsia, Eleusinia, &c. 106–108
Public Games. — Principal Exercises used in 108, 109
  The Four National Games. Olympic Games 109
  Pythian Games. Nemean Games. Isthmian Games.... 110
Military Affairs. — Divisions of the Army and Classes of Soldiers 111
  Arms (defensive and offensive) .... ib.
  Officers. Minor Divisions of the Army 112
Naval Affairs. — Ships of Burden; War Galleys; Principal parts of the vessel, &c. Tackling, &c. 113
  Naval officers, &c. 114
Private Life of the Greeks. — Meals, Dress, Funerals 114–116
The Greek Theatre 116, 117

ROMAN ANTIQUITIES.

Divisions of the Inhabitants of the Roman Empire; Patricii, Plebei 118
  Equites, Nobiles, Ignobiles, Optimates, Populares, Servi, &c. 119
The Senate. — Members, Proceedings, &c. 119, 120
Assemblies. — Comitia Curiata, Comitia Centuriata........ 121
  Comitia Tributa 122
Magistrates and Chief Public Officers: —
  Ædiles, Apparitores .... ib.
  Censores, Consules, Curatores 123
  Dictator, Præfectus, Prætor 124
  Pro-Consul, Procurator, Pro-Prætor, Quæstores, Tribuni 125, 126
Judicial Proceedings, Punishments 126
Priests. — Pontifices, Augures or Auspices 127
  Fetiales, Haruspices, Decemviri, Curiones, Rex Sacrificulus, Flamines, Virgines Vestales 128
  Salii, Luperci, Galli, Fratres Arvales 129
Prayers, Sacrifices, Festivals 129, 130
Games. — Ludi Circenses, Gladiatorii 131
Classes of Gladiators, Scenic, or Stage Plays, Theatres 132
Military Affairs. — Conscription and Period of Service, Pay, &c. 133, 134
  Divisions of the Army; Arms 134, 135
  Officers: Legati, Tribuni, Centuriones; Encampment... 135
  Order of Battle, Standards, Military Engines 136
  Military Rewards and Punishments, Triumph, Ovation 136, 137
Naval Affairs 137
Private Life of the Romans. — Dress 138, 139
  Meals, &c. 139, 140

CONTENTS. xi

Private Houses, Baths, Amusements 140, 141
Funerals 142
Names, and their abbreviations 143

ANCIENT GREEK WRITERS.

Poets. — Epic, Tragic 144
    Comic, Lyric 145
    Pastoral 146
Prose Writers. — Historians 146, 147
    Orators, Medical Writers 147, 148
    Mathematicians, Geographers, Fabulist 149
    Satiric Writer, Critic, Philosophers 150, 151

ANCIENT ROMAN WRITERS.

Poets. — Epic 152
    Elegiac, Lyric 153
    Tragic, Comic, Didactic. Satirists 154
    Epigrammatist, Fabulist 155
Prose Writers. — Historians .... ib.
    Orator, &c. 156
    Epistolary Writers. Writers on Philosophical Subjects,
      Natural History 157
    Agriculture, Architecture, Medicine, Grammar and
      Criticism 158

SCHOOLS OF ANCIENT PHILOSOPHY.

The Ionic School 159
The Italic School .... ib.
TOPOGRAPHY OF ATHENS 160, 161
———————— ROME 162–164
GREEK AND ROMAN DIVISION OF TIME 165–167

MISCELLANEA.

Hills of Rome, Kings of Rome 168
Twelve Cæsars, Seven Wonders of the World, Seven Sages
  of Greece 169
Twelve Labours of Hercules, Nine Muses, Three Graces 170
Three Horæ, Three Fates, Three Furies, Three Judges of
  Hell, Five Rivers of Hell 171
The Winds 172
ROMAN CALENDAR 172, 173
GREEK CHRONOLOGY 174–180
ROMAN CHRONOLOGY 181–187
INDEX 189

ABBREVIATIONS.

- **Cap.** = Capital.
- **L.** = Lacus, Lake.
- **Mts.** = Mountains.
- **Prom.** = Promontorium.
- **R.** = River.
- **G.** = Gulf.
- **O. T.** = Old Testament.

GEOGRAPHY.

EUROPE.

COUNTRIES.—Hispānia, *Spain;* Lusitānĭa, *Portugal;* Gallia, *France* and *West of Switzerland;* Germānĭa, *Germany;* Cimbrĭca Chersonesus, *Denmark;* Scandinavĭa, *Norway* and *Sweden;* Sarmătĭa Europæa, *Russia* and *Poland;* Rhætĭa, *East part of Switzerland* and the *Tyrol;* Vindĕlĭcĭa, *Bavaria* S. of Danube; Pannŏnĭa, *Hungary;* Illўrĭcum, Illўris, Illўrĭca, *Croatia, Dalmatia,* and part of *Turkey;* Italia, *Italy;* Græcia, *Greece,* and part of *Albania* and *Roumelia* in *Turkey;* Macĕdŏnĭa, *Western part of Roumelia;* Thrăcĭa, *Eastern part of Roumelia;* Mœsia, *Servia* and *Bulgaria;* Dācĭa, *Transylvania, Wallachia,* and *Moldavia.*

SEAS.—N.: Mare Pigrum, vel Cronium, *Frozen Ocean;* Oceanus Germanicus, *North Sea.* W.: Atlanticum Mare, *Atlantic.* E.: Palus Mæōtis, *Sea of Azov;* Pontus Euxīnus, *Black Sea;* Propontis, *Sea of Marmora;* Ægeum Mare, *Archipelago.* S.: Mare Internum, *Mediterranean;* Mare Ionium, W. of *Greece;* Mare Infĕrum, Tyrrhēnum, vel Tuscum, *Tuscan Sea,* W. of *Italy;* Mare Hadriaticum, vel Superum, *Gulf of Venice.*

GULFS, STRAITS, &c.—Sinus Codānus, vel Mare Suevicum, *Baltic;* Fretum Britannicum, vel Gallicum, *Straits of Dover;* Oceanus Cantabricus, *Bay of Biscay;* Fretum Gaditanum, *Straits of Gibraltar;* Gallicus Sinus, *Gulf of Lyons;* Sinus Ligusticus, *Gulf of*

Genoa; Tergestīnus Sinus, *Gulf of Trieste;* Fossa, *Straits of Bonifacio;* Fretum Siculum, *Straits of Messina;* Hellespontus, *Straits of the Dardanelles;* Bospŏrus Thracius, vel Thrācĭcus, *Straits of Constantinople;* Bospŏrus Cimmerius, *Straits of Kaffa.*

RIVERS.—Flowing into the Baltic: Vistula, *Vistula;* Viădus, *Oder.* Flowing into the North Sea: Albis, *Elbe;* Visurgis, *Weser;* Scaldis, *Scheldt;* Rhēnus, *Rhine;* Tamĕsis, *Thames.* Flowing into the Atlantic: Sequăna, *Seine;* Liger, *Loire;* Garumna, *Garonne;* Durius, *Douro;* Tagus, *Tago;* Anas, *Guadiana;* Bætis, *Guadalquivir.* Flowing into the Mediterranean: Ibērus, *Ebro;* Rhodănus, *Rhone;* Arar, *Saone;* Arnus, *Arno;* Tibĕris, *Tiber;* Athĕsis, *Adige;* Padus, *Po.* Flowing into the Black Sea: Ister, *Danube;* Tyras, *Dniester;* Borysthĕnes, *Dnieper;* Tanăis, *Don.* Falling into the Caspian Sea: Rha, *Volga.*

MOUNTAINS.—Sevo Mons, *Dofrefield Mts.;* Pyrenæi Montes, *Pyrenees;* Alpes, *The Alps;* Apenninus Mons, *Apennines;* Carpates vel Bastarnicæ Montes, *Carpathian Mts.;* Hæmus Mons, *Hæmus,* or the *Balkan;* Hyperborei vel Rhipæi Montes, *Ural Mts.*

LAKES.—Lacus Lemānus, *L. of Geneva;* L. Brigantinus, *Boden See,* or *L. of Constance;* L. Verbānus, *Lago Maggiore;* L. Larius, *Lago di Como;* L. Benācus, *Lago di Garda;* L. Copais, *L. Topolias.*

ISLANDS.—In the Atlantic: Britănnia vel Albion, *Britain;* Hibernia, *Ireland;* Hebūdes vel Ebūdes, *Hebrides;* Orcădes, *Orkneys;* Thule, *Iceland* (?). In the Mediterranean: Pityusæ Insulæ; among these Ebusv *Ivica;* Baleāres Insulæ (vel Gymnesiæ), Baleā Major, *Majorca;* Baleāris Minor, *Minorca;* Sardin vel Sardo, *Sardinia;* Corsica vel Cyrnos, *Corsica;* Æthălĭa vel Ilva, *Elba;* Trinacrĭa vel Sicilia, *Sicily;* Melīta, *Malta.* In the Ionian Sea: Corcȳra, *Corfu;*

Leucădĭa vel Leucas, *Santa Maura;* Ithăca, *Thiaki;* Cephallēnia, *Cephalonia;* Zacynthus, *Zante;* Cythēra, *Cerigo.* In the Ægean Sea: Creta, *Candia;* Cyclădes, *Cyclades;* Eubœa, *Negropont.*

HISPANIA.
Spain and Portugal.

BOUNDARIES.—N., Oceănus Cantabrĭcus, *Bay of Biscay,* and Pyrenæi Montes; E. and S.E., Mare Internum, *Mediterranean;* W., Mare Atlantĭcum, *Atlantic.*

MOUNTAINS.—N., Pyrenæi Montes, *Pyrenees;* Mons Idubĕda, *Sierra D'Oca* and *Sierra Molina;* Mons Herminius, *Sierra d'Estrella;* Marianus Mons, *Sierra Morena;* Orospeda Mons, *Sierra Segura.*

RIVERS.—Falling into the Atlantic: Minius, *Minho;* Durius, *Douro;* Tagus, *Tagus;* Anas, *Guadiana;* Bætis, *Guadalquivir.* Falling into the Mediterranean: Ibērus, *Ebro* (which receives from the N. Cinga, *Cinca,* and Sicŏris, *Segre,* and from the S. Salo, *Xalon);* Turia, *Guadalaviar;* Sucro, *Xucar;* Tader, *Segura.*

PROMONTORIES.—Artabrum Prom., *Cape Finisterre;* Magnum Prom., *Cape La Roca;* Sacrum Prom., *C. St. Vincent;* Junōnis Prom., *C. Trafalgar;* Calpe, *Rock of Gibraltar* (which, with Abўla on the African coast, formed the Pillars of Hercules); Scombraria Prom., *C. de Palos;* Dianium Prom., *C. La Nao;* Prom. Pyrenæum, *Cape Creux.*

DIVISIONS.—Hispania Citerior or *Hither,* afterwards called Tarraconensis; and Hispania Ulterior or *Further,* divided into Lusitania, *Portugal,* in the West, and Bætica, *Andalusia,* in the South.

TRIBES.—In Tarraconensis: Callaĭci, Astures, Cantabri, Vaccæi, Vascones, Arevāci, Jacetāni, Vescitani, Lacetani,

Ilergētes, Cosetāni, Arevāci, Carpētāni, Celtibēri, Edetāni, Ilercaŏnes, Oretāni, Contestāni, Bastitāni. In Lusitania: Lusitāni, Vettōnes, Celtĭci. In Bætica: Turdŭli, Turdetāni, Bastuli, Pœni.

TARRACONENSIS.— *Cities.*— On the Ebro: Cæsar Augusta, *Saragossa.* On the Salo: Bilbĭlis (the birth-place of Martial). On the E. coast: Tarrăco, *Tarragona,* the Capital; Saguntum, *Murviedro* (its destruction by Hannibal, B.C. 219, gave rise to the second Punic war); Valentia, *Valencia.* Near Scrombraria Prom., *Cape Palos:* Carthāgo Nova, *Carthagena* (taken by Scipio Africanus B.C. 210). On the Tagus: Toletum, *Toledo.* Near the source of the Douro: Numantia (destroyed by Scipio the Younger, B.C. 133). At the mouth of the Douro: Calle, *Oporto.*

LUSITANIA.— *Cities.*— Salamantĭca, *Salamanca,* on a tributary of the Douro; Norba Cæsarea, *Alcantara,* on the Tagus; Olisĭpo, *Lisbon,* near the mouth of the river; Emerĭta Augusta, *Merida,* on the Anas, *Guadjana* (colonized by Augustus with the veterans (*Emeriti*) of the fifth and tenth legions).

BÆTICA.— *Cities.*— Illiturgi, on the Bætis (destroyed by Scipio, B.C. 210); below it, Cordŭba, *Cordova,* surnamed Patricia (the birth-place of the two Senecas and Lucan); Italĭca, *Sevilla la Vieja* (the birth-place of the Emperors Trajan and Hadrian); Hispălis, *Seville;* Tartessus, on the coast; Gades, *Cadiz,* on a small island, one of the chief seats of commerce of the Phœnicians; Munda, *Monda,* on the South coast (battle B.C. 45, Cæsar defeated the sons of Pompey).

ISLANDS.— In the Mediterranean: Pityusæ Insulæ, comprising Ebusus, *Iviça,* and Ophiūsa; Baleāres (*or* Gymnesiæ) Insulæ, *Balearic Isles,* comprising Major Insula or *Majorca* (Cap. Palma, *Palma*), and Minor Insula, *Minorca,* Cap. Mago, *Port Mahon.*

GEOGRAPHY. 17

GALLIA.
France, Belgium, and West of Switzerland.

BOUNDARIES.— N.: Oceănus Britannicus, *English Channel;* Fretum Gallĭcum, *Straits of Dover;* and Oceănus Germanĭcus, *German Ocean.* E.: Rhēnus, *Rhine,* and Alpes, *The Alps.* S.: Mare Internum, *Mediterranean,* and Pyrenæi Montes, *Pyrenees.* W.: Atlanticum Mare, *Atlantic.*

MOUNTAINS.— Pyrenæi Montes, *Pyrenees;* Alpes, *Alps.*

RIVERS.—Falling into the North Sea and English Channel: Rhēnus, *Rhine* (with its tributaries, Mosella, *Moselle,* and Mosa, *Meuse);* Scaldis, *Scheldt;* Samăra, *Somme;* Sequăna, *Seine* (with its tributaries, Matrōna, *Marne,* and Axŏna, *Aisne,* Isăra, *Oise*). Falling into the Bay of Biscay: Liger, *Loire* (and its tributary, Elāver, *Allier);* Garumna, *Garonne,* with Durānĭus, *Dordogne,* and Aturus, *Adour.* Falling into the Mediterranean: Rhodănus, *Rhone* (with its tributaries, Arar, *Saone,* Isăra, *Isere,* and Druentia, *Durance*).

LAKE. — L. Lemānus, *Lake of Geneva.*

DIVISIONS. — Gaul was originally divided among the BELGÆ (between the Rhine and Seine); CELTÆ (between the Seine and Garonne); and AQUITANI (between the Garonne and the Pyrenees). About B.C. 120, Gaul was divided by the Romans into Provincia, or Gallia Braccata, and Gallia Comata; and again, B.C. 27, into, I. Provincia, or Gallia Narbonensis, in the S.E.; II. Aquitania, in the S.W.; III. Gallia Celtica, or Lugdunensis, in the N.W.; IV. Gallia Belgica, in the N.E.

NARBONENSIS, divided into *Narbonensis Prima, Narbonensis Secunda, Viennensis, Alpes Maritimæ,* and *Alpes*

2*

Graiæ et *Penninæ.—Towns.*—In Narbonensis Secunda and Viennensis: Massilia, *Marseilles*, on the coast (founded about B.C. 600, famous for its literature and commerce); Aquæ Sextiæ, *Aix* (Marius defeated the Teutoni, B.C. 102); Telo Martĭus, *Toulon*, on the coast; E. of which Forum Julii, *Frejus* (the birth-place of Agricola); Genēva, *Geneva*, on L. Lemānus; Vienna, *Vienne*, on the Rhone (the chief town of the Allobroges); Cularo, *Grenoble;* Valentia, *Valence;* Dea, *Die;* Arausio, *Orange* (a Roman colony); Avenĭo, *Avignon;* Arelāte, *Arles* (a Roman colony, founded by the soldiers of the sixth Legion). In *Narbonensis Prima:* Nemausus, *Nismes;* on the coast, Agătha, *Agde;* Narbo Martius, *Narbonne*, the Capital of Gallia Narbonensis. On the Garonne: Tolōsa, *Toulouse* (surnamed Palladia, a large and wealthy city). On the coast: Ruscino, near *Perpignan.*

AQUITANIA, divided into *Novempopulana*, S.; *Aquitania Prima*, E.; *Aquitania Secunda*, W.

Towns.—In *Novempopulana:* Climberris, *Auch.* In *Aquitania Prima:* Albĭga, *Albi;* on the Dordogne, Uxellodūnum, *Puech d'Issola;* near the Elaver, *Allier*, Gergōvia; West of this, Augustorītum, *Limoges;* in the N., Avarīcum, *Bourges.* In *Aquitania Secunda:* on the Garonne, Burdigăla, *Bordeaux* (the birth-place of Ausonius); in the N., Limōnum, or Pictavi, *Poitiers:* Mediolānum, or Santones, *Saintes.*

LUGDUNENSIS, divided into *Lugdunensis Prima, Secunda, Tertia,* and *Quarta.*

Towns.—In *Lugdunensis Prima:* Lugdūnum, *Lyons*, the capital, at the junction of the Rhodănus and Arar, *Saone* (the birth-place of the Emperor Claudius); N. of this, Bibracte, or Augustodūnum, *Autun*, and Alēsĭa, *Alise* (destroyed by Cæsar, B.C. 52). In *Lugdunensis Quarta:* on the Sequana, *Seine*, Augustobŏna, or Tricasses, *Troyes;* Agendĭcum, *Sens*, the Capital of the Senones; and Lutetĭa, or Parisii, *Paris;* Genăbum, Cenăbum, or Aureliani, *Orleans*, on the Liger, the Cap. of the

Carnutes. In *Lugdunensis Secunda:* Rotomăgus, *Rouen.* In *Lugdunensis Tertia:* on the Loire, Cæsarodūnum, *Tours,* Cap. of the Turones; in the N.W., Brivātes Portus, *Brest.*

GALLIA BELGICA, divided into 1. *Belgica Prima;* 2. *Belgica Secunda;* 3. *Germania Prima;* 4. *Germania Secunda;* 5. *Maxima Sequanorum.*

Towns.—On the Mosella: Tullum, *Toul;* Divodūrum, *Metz;* Augusta Treverōrum, *Treves.* On the Matrona, *Marne:* Durocatalaunum, *Chalons;* N. of this Durocortŏrum, *Rheims,* the Cap. of the Remi. On the Axona, *Aisne:* Augusta Suessionum, *Soissons.* On the Samara, *Somme:* Samarobrīva or Ambiāni, *Amiens.* On the coast: Gesoriăcum or Bonōnia, *Boulogne,* and Itĭus Portus (from which Cæsar set sail for Britain). On the Scaldis: Turnăcum, *Tournay.* On the Rhine: Argentorātum, *Strasburg* (Julian defeated the Alemanni, A.D. 357); Borbetomăgus, *Worms;* and Mogontiăcum, *Alentz;* at the junction of the Rhēnus and Mosella, Confluentes, *Coblentz.* On the Rhēnus: Colōnĭa Agrippīna, *Cologne;* Noviomăgus, *Nimeguen;* Lugdūnum Batavōrum, *Leyden.* On the Dubis, *Doubs:* Vesontio, *Besançon;* S.E. of this Aventicum, *Avenche.*

TRIBES.—In Narbonensis: Salўes or Saluvĭi, Allobroges, Volcæ Arecomĭci, Volcæ Tectosăges. In Aquitania: Biturĭges Cubi, Lemovices, Arverni, Pictones, Santones, Biturĭges Vivisci. In Gallia Lugdunensis: Ambarri, Ædui, Lingones, Senones, Carnutes, Veneti, Osismii. In Gallia Belgica: Treveri, Mediomatrĭci, Leuci, Remi, Suessiones, Bellovĭci, Atrebātes, Nervii, Morini, Helvetii (people of Switzerland), Sequāni, Rauraci, Ubii, Tungri, Menapii, Batavi.

ISLANDS.—On the W. Vindĭlis, *Belleisle;* Uxantis, *Ushant;* Cæsarēa, *Jersey;* Sarnia, *Guernsey;* Ridūna, *Alderney.*

GERMANIA.

Germany and Prussia.

BOUNDARIES.—N., Codānus Sinus and Marc Suevicum, *Baltic*, and Oceănus Germanicus; E., Vistula, *R. Vistula*, and Carpātes Montes, *Carpathian* Mountains; S., Danubius, *R. Danube;* W., Rhenus, *R. Rhine.*

MOUNTAINS.—Hercynĭi Montes, *all the mountains in the south and centre of Germany.* In the centre: Hercynĭa Silva, an immense forest which took Cæsar nine days to cross.

RIVERS.—Falling into the Baltic: Vistula, *Vistula;* and Viădrus, *Oder* (with its tributary Varta, *Wartha*). Falling into the German Ocean: Albis, *Elbe* (and its tributary Sala, *Saale*); Visurgis, *Weser;* Amăsia, *Ems;* Rhēnus, *Rhine* (with its tributaries Nicer, *Neckar;* Mœnus, *Main;* Lupĭa or Luppia, *Lippe*); Ister or Danubĭus,.*Danube.*

DIVISIONS.—1. Vindeli or Suevi, N. of the Elbe to the Baltic; 2. Hermiones, N. of the Danube; 3. Istævōnes, E. of the Rhine.

TRIBES, &c.—Among the Vindeli or Suevi: Lemovii, Longobardi, Burgundiōnes, Gothones, Semnŏnes. Among the Hermiones: Cherusci, Catti, Hermunduri, Boii, Marcomanni. Among the Istævones: Frisii, Chauci (divided into Minores and Majores), Bructĕri, Marsii, Sicambri, Tenctĕri, Mattĭăci, Sedusii, Marcomanni, Alemanni, in the S. Decumates Agri, whose inhabitants paid a tithe of their produce to the Romans.

N. of Germany: Saxones, Angli and Cimbri, inhabiting Cimbrica Chersonesus, *Jutland;* Hilleviŏnes, Sui-.ones, and Sitŏnes, inhabiting Scandinavia or Scandia, *Norway* and *Sweden.*

N. B. The Teutones, probably dwelt in the N. of Germany, on the coast of the Baltic.

VINDELICIA, RHÆTIA, NORICUM, PANNONIA, ILLYRICUM.

Bavaria; East of Switzerland, Tyrol; Austria, South of the Danube; Hungary; Illyria, Croatia, Dalmatia, and part of Turkey.

VINDELICIA.
Bavaria.

BOUNDARIES.—N. and W., Danubius, *R. Danube;* E., R. Ænus, *Inn;* S., Ænus, Fl. Rhætia, and Brigantinus Lacus, *Lake of Constance.*

RIVERS.—Isărus, *Iser;* Licus, *Lech.*

TRIBES.—Brigantii, Genauni, Estiōnes.

TOWNS.—Augusta Vindelicōrum, *Augsburg;* Brigantia, *Bregentz;* Regīnum, *Ratisbon.*

RHÆTIA.
East of Switzerland and the Tyrol.

BOUNDARIES.—N., Brigantinus Lacus, R. Ænus, and Vindelicia; E., Noricum; S., Gallia Cisalpina; W., the Helvetii.

RIVERS.—Rhēnus, *Rhine;* Ænus, *Inn;* Addua, *Adda;* Ticīnus, *Ticino;* Athěsis, *Adige* (all these rise in Rhætia).

TRIBES.—Lepontii, Cap. Oscela; Sarunētes, Cap. Curia, *Coire;* Brenni, Vennones, Tridentini.

NORICUM.
Austria, South of the Danube.

BOUNDARIES.—N., Danubius; E., Mons Cetius and Pannonia; S., Illyricum, R. Savus, *Save,* and Alpes Carnicæ; W., Rhætia and R. Ænus.

GEOGRAPHY.

RIVERS.—Juvāvus, *Salza;* Anĭsus, *Enns;* Murus, *Muhr;* Dravus, *Drave* (all these rise in Noricum).

TOWNS.—Juvāvum, *Saltzburg;* Boiodurum, near *Passau,* on the Danube, and Lauriăcum, the station of a Roman fleet; Norēĭa, *Neumarkt,* near the centre (battle B.C. 113, the Consul Carbo defeated by the Cimbri); S.E. Celēĭa, *Cilly.*

PANNONIA.

Hungary, Slavonia, and part of Croatia and Turkey.

BOUNDARIES.—N. and E., Danubius Fl.; S., Illyricum; W., Noricum.

RIVERS.—Arăbon, *Raab;* Dravus, *Drave;* Savus, *Save.*

LAKES.—Volcĕa Palus, *Platten See;* Peiso L., *Neusiedler See.*

DIVISIONS.—Pannonia Superior and Inferior.

TOWNS.—On the Danube: Vindobona, *Vienna;* Carnuntum (E. of Vienna); Acincum or Aquincum, *Buda;* Contra Acincum, *Pesth;* Pætovia, near *Pettau,* on the Drave; Mursa, *Esseck,* near the junction of the Drave and Danube. On the Save: Siscĭa, *Sissek;* and Sirmĭum.

ILLYRICUM.

Illyria, Dalmatia, Croatia, and part of Turkey.

BOUNDARIES.—N., Noricum;· E., Pannonia and Mœsia; S.W., Mare Hadriaticum and Histria.

MOUNTAIN.—Albius Mons.

DIVISIONS.—N. 1. Liburnia (inhabited by the Liburni and Japўdes); 2. Dalmatia. The Liburni were famed as bold and skilful sailors, their vessels were remarkable for their swiftness; hence, vessels after their models were ter · ed *Liburnicæ Naves.*

GEOGRAPHY. 23

TOWNS.—Æmōna, *Laybach;* Scardōna, *Scardona,* the Cap. of Liburnia; Salōna, *Spalatro* (the birth-place of Diocletian); Narōna, on the Naro, *Narenta;* S. of which Epidaurus, *Old Ragusa;* Scodra, *Skutari,* on Labeātis Palus, *Lake of Skutari;* S. of this, Lissus, *Alessio.*

ISLANDS.—W. of Illyricum: Scardona, *Isola Grossa;* Pharus, *Lesina;* Corcȳra Nigra, *Curzola;* Melīta, *Melida.*

ITALIA.

HESPERIA, ŒNOTRIA, AUSONIA, SATURNIA.

Italy.

BOUNDARIES.—N. and N.W., Alpes, *The Alps;* E., Hadriaticum Mare vel Superum, *Adriatic Sea,* or *Gulf of Venice;* S., Mare Internum, *Mediterranean;* W., Mare Tyrrhenum, Tuscum, vel Inferum, *Tuscan Sea.*

GULFS.—E., Tergestīnus Sinus, *Gulf of Trieste:* S., Tarentīnus Sinus, *Gulf of Taranto;* Scylacius Sinus, *Gulf of Squillace:* W., Terinæus Sinus, *Gulf of St. Eufemia:* Laus Sinus, *Gulf of Policastro;* Pæstūnus Sinus, *Gulf of Salerno;* Cumānus vel Putĕŏlānus Sinus, *Bay of Naples;* Cajetanus Sinus, *Gulf of Gaeta:* S. of Liguria, Ligustīcus Sinus, *Gulf of Genoa.*

STRAIT.—Fretum Sicŭlum, *Straits of Messina.*

MOUNTAINS.—Alpes, *The Alps,* in the North, divided into three principal chains.

I. THE WESTERN: Alpes Marĭtīmæ, *Maritime Alps;* Alpes Cottiæ, *Mt. Cenis,* and *Mt. Genèvre;* Alpes Graiæ, *Alps of Savoy,* including *Little St. Bernard* and *Mt. Blanc.* II. THE CENTRAL ALPS: Alpes Penninæ, *Alps of Valais,* including *Great St. Bernard, Mt. Rosa,* and *St. Gothard;* Alpes Lepontiæ, *Alps of the Grisons;* Alpes Rhæticæ, *Alps of Tyrol.* III. THE EASTERN ALPS: Alpes Noricæ, *Alps of Styria;* Alpes Carnicæ, *Carnic Alps;* Alpes Juliæ, *Julian Alps.*

GEOGRAPHY.

Appenninus Mons, *The Apennines,* running the whole length of Italy. *Principal Elevations:* Mons Soracte, *S. Oreste,* in Etruria; Mons Sacer, in Sabinum; Mons Albānus, in Latium (on which the Feriæ Latinæ were celebrated); Algĭdus Mons, in Latium; Mons Massĭcus, in Campania, near the coast (famous for its wines); Vesuvĭus, the celebrated volcanic mountain (the first eruption occurred Aug. 24, A.D. 79, which destroyed Pompeii and Herculaneum); Gargānus, *Mte. Gargano,* in Apulia; and Mons Vultur.

RIVERS.—In Gallia Cisalpina: Pădus, or Erĭdānus, *Po;* it rises in Mons Vesŭlus, *Monte Viso,* flows east, and falls into the Adriatic. Chief tributary streams from the N.: Duria Major, *Dora Baltea;* Tĭcīnus, *Ticino* (Hannibal defeated P. C. Scipio, B.C. 218), from L. Verbanus, *Lago Maggiore;* Addua, *Adda,* from L. Larius, *Lago di Garda;* and Mincius, *Mincio,* from L. Benācus, *Lago di Garda.* From the S.: Tanărus, *Tanaro;* Trebia, *Trebia* (Hannibal defeated the Romans, B.C. 218). Athĕsis, *Adige,* N. of the Po; Rubicon, *Fiumicino,* between Cisalpine Gaul and Umbria; Metaurus, *Metauro,* in Umbria (Hasdrubal defeated, B.C. 207); and Aufĭdus, *Ofanto,* in Apulia, all fall into the Adriatic. Running into the Tuscan Sea: Arnus, *Arno,* in Etruria; Tibĕris, *Tivere*—it receives, on the left, Clanis, *Chiano,* and Cremĕra (300 Fabii destroyed, B.C. 477); on the right, Tinia, *Tinia,* and its tributary Clitumnus, *Clitumno;* Nar, *Nera,* and Velīnus, *Velino,* its tributary; Allia (Gauls overcome the Romans, B.C. 390); and Anio, *Teverone.* In the S. of Latium: Līris, *Garigliano.* In Campania: Vulturnus, *Volturno;* Silărus, *Silaro* (victory of Crassus, B.C. 71).

LAKES.—In Cisalpine Gaul: L. Verbānus, *Lago Maggiore;* L. Larĭus, *Lago di Como;* L. Benācus, *Lago di Garda.* In Etruria: L. Trasimēnus, *Lago di Perugia* (Hannibal's third victory, B.C. 217); L. Vulsiniensis, *L. Bolsena.* In Sabini: L. Fucīnus, *Lago di Celano.*

In Latium: L. Regillus, *Lago di Regillo?* (battle B.C. 498); L. Albānus, *Lago di Albano.* In Campania: L. Avernus, *Lago Averno,* and L. Lucrīnus, famed for its oysters.

CAPES.— In' Etruria: Populonium Prom. In Latium: Circēium Prom., *Monte Circello.* In Campania:, Misēnum Prom., *Cape Miseno,* and Minervæ Prom., *Cape Campanella.* In Lucania: Palinūrum Prom., *Cape Palinuro.* In Apulia: Gargānum Prom., *Cape Gargano;* Iapygium vel Salentīnum Prom., *Cape Leuca.* In Bruttii: Lacinium Prom., *Cape Colonne;* Herculeum Prom., *Cape Spartivento;* Leucopētra Prom., *Cape Armi.*

DIVISIONS. — NORTH: I. Ligurĭa; II. Gallia Cisalpina, vel Togāta; III. Venetia, Carni, and Histria. MIDDLE: IV. Etruria, vel Tuscia; V. Umbria; VI. Picenum; VII. Sabinum; VIII. Latium; IX. Samnium; X. Campania. SOUTH: XI. Apulia; XII. Lucania; XIII. Bruttii.

LIGURIA.—*Nice, Genoa,* and part of *Piedmont.*—*Boundaries:* N., R. Padus, *Po,* and Gallia Cisalpina; E., Gallia Cisalpina; S., Sinus Ligustĭcus, *Gulf of Genoa;* W., Alpes Marītīmæ and Gallia.

Cities.—Genua, *Genoa,* at the N. of the Gulf of Genoa; Pollentia, *Polenza,* on the Tanărus.

Tribes.—N. of Apennines: Vagienni, Statielli, Friniates, Montani, Ligŭres. South: Intemelii, Ingauni, Apuani.

GALLIA CISALPINA, VEL TOGATA.—Part of the kingdom of *Sardinia, Lombardy, Parma, Modena,* and part of *States of the Church.*

Divisions.—I. GALLIA CISPADANA, inhabited by the Boii and Lingŏnes.

Cities: Placentia, *Placenza,* near the junction of the Po and Trebia, (founded by Romans, 219 B.C.); Mutīna, *Modena* (M. Antony defeated, B.C. 43); Ravenna, *Ravenna;* Bonōnia, *Bologna.*

GEOGRAPHY.

II. GALLIA TRANSPADANA, inhabited by the Taurini, Salassi, Insŭbres, Cenomāni.

Cities: Augusta Taurinǫrum, *Turin*, on the Padus: Vercella, *Vercelli*, near which Raudi Campi, (where Marius defeated the Cimbri, B.C. 101); Ticīnum, *Pavia*, on the Ticinus; Mediolānum, *Milan*, the capital of the Insŭbres; Comum, *Como*, on L. Larius; Cremōna, *Cremona*, on the Po, (founded by Romans, B.C. 219); Mantua, *Mantua*, on the Mincius, (near which Virgil was born, B.C. 70).

VENETIA, CARNI, ET HISTRIA.—Eastern part of *Venetian Lombardy* and *Istria*.

Boundaries.—N. and N.E., Alpes Carnicæ, vel Juliæ, and Rhætia; E., Liburnia; S., Mare Hadriaticum and R. Pădus; W., R. Athĕsis, *Adige*, and Gallia Transpadāna.

Cities.—Verōna, *Verona*, on the Athĕsis; E. of Verona, Patăvĭum, *Padua*, (Livy born, B.C. 59); Aquilēĭa, *Aquileia*, near the coast, (destroyed by Attila, king of the Huns, A.D. 452); E. of Aquileia, Tergeste, *Trieste*.

ETRURIA, TUSCIA, VEL TYRRHENIA.—*Tuscany*, and part of *States of the Church*.

Boundaries.—N., R. Macra, *Magra*, and Apenninus Mons; E. and S., R. Tiber; W., Tuscum Mare.

Cities.—Pisæ, *Pisa*, and Florentia, *Florence*, both on the Arnus. Luca, *Lucca*, on the Auser, *Serchio*. Fæsŭlæ, *Fiesole;* Pistoria, *Pistoia*, (Catiline defeated, B.C. 62); Portus Herculis, Labronis, vel Liburni, *Leghorn;* on the coast. Popŭlonium, or ia, the chief seaport of Etruria. Centum Cellæ, *Civita Vecchia;* on the coast, with a fine harbour.

The following were probably the twelve confederate cities of Etruria Proper.

Volaterræ, *Volaterra*. Vetulōnii, to the E. of Populonia. Rusellæ, on the Umbro. Tarquinii, *Corneto*. Agylla, or Cære, *Cerveteri*, (where the Vestal Virgins took refuge on the destruction of Rome by the Gauls, B.C. 390). Veii, *Isola*, on the Cremĕra, twelve miles from

Rome, (the most powerful city of Etruria). Falĕrii, or Ium, (taken by Camillus, B.C. 394), near Mt. Soracte. Vulsinii, *Bolsena*, on L. Volsiniensis, (the birth-place of Sejanus, the favourite of Tiberius). Clusium, *Chiusi*, near the Clanis, (the residence of Porsena). Perusia, *Perugia*, E. of Clusium, on the Tiber. Cortōna, *Cortona*, N.W. of Trasimene Lake. Arretīum, *Arezzo*, (the birth-place of Mæcēnas).

UMBRIA. — *States of the Church.*
  Boundaries.—N., Gallia Cispadāna; E., Mare Hadriaticum and Picenum; S., Sabini; W., R. Tiber. It was inhabited in the N. by Galli Senōnes.
  Cities.—Arimīnum, *Rimini;* Sēna Gallica, *Senigaglia*, on the coast; in the interior, Sentīnum, (battle, B.C. 294, Samnites defeated); Spolētīum, or Spolētum, *Spoleto*, in the South.

PICENUM. — Part of *States of the Church.*
  Boundaries.—N., R. Æsis, *Esino;* E., Mare Hadriaticum; S., Vestini, in Sabinum; W., Umbria and Sabini.
  Cities.—Ancōna, *Ancona*, in the N.; Ascŭlum Picēnum, *Ascoli*, (taken, B.C. 89, in the Marsic or Social War).
  Tribe.—Prætutii, in the South.

SABINUM. — Part of *States of the Church*, and part of *Naples.*
  Boundaries.—N., Umbria and R. Nar; E., Apenninus Mons and Hadriaticum Mare; S., Samnium; W., Latium and R. Tiber.
  Cities.—Reāte, *Rieti*, in the W.; Cures, *Correse*, (the native city of Numa, and capital of the Sabines); Fidēnæ, *Castel Giubileo*, and Crustumĕrium, between the Anio and Tiber; Amīternum, in the E., on the borders of the Vestini, (Sallust born, B.C. 86); Alba Fucentīa, *Alba*, N. of L. Fucinus; Marrŭvium, chief city of the Marsi; Sulmo, *Sulmona*, in the country of the Peligni, (Ovid born, B.C. 43); Corfīnium, the chief city of the Peligni.

Tribes. — Æqui, Marsi, Peligni, Marrucini, Vestini.

LATIUM. — *States of the Church.*

Boundaries. — N., R. Tiber and Anio; E., Samnium and Campania; S. and W., Mare Tuscum.

Cities. — Rōma, *Rome*, on the Tiber, (founded by Romulus, B.C. 753, on the Palatine Mount); built on seven hills, Palatinus, Capitolinus, Quirinalis, Viminalis, Esquilinus, Cælius, and Aventinus, to which were afterwards added Janiculum, Vaticānus, and Collis Hortulorum (Public Buildings, &c., vide Topography). Ostia, *Ostia*, at the mouth of the Tiber. Laurentum, on the coast. Lavinium, built by Æneas. Ardea, the city of Turnus. Antium, *Porto d'Anzo*, on the coast. Tibur, *Tivoli*, on the Anio, (a favourite residence of the Roman nobles). S. of this Gabii. Tusculum, near *Frascati*, surrounded by numerous villas. Alba Longa, on the border of L. Albanus, founded by Ascanius (a legend). Præneste, *Palestrina*. Velitræ, *Velletri*, (the native city of the Octavian family). Corīŏli, (which gave to C. Marcius the surname Coriolānus). Aquīnum, *Aquino*, (birth-place of Juvenal). Anagnia, *Anagni*, the capital of the Hernici. Eastward: Arpīnum, *Arpino*, (birth-place of Cicero and Marius); Anxur, or Tarracīna, *Terracina;* Suessa Pometia, (stormed by Tarq. Superbus). Cajēta, *Gaeta;* Formiæ, *Mola*, (famous for its wine); and Minturnæ; on the coast.

Tribes. — Latīni, Æqui, Hernīci, Rutŭli, Volsci.

SAMNIUM. — Part of *Naples.*

Boundaries. — N., Sabinum and Mare Hadriaticum; E., Apulia; S., Campania and Lucania; W., Campania and Sabinum.

Cities. — Beneventum, *Benevento*, (Pyrrhus defeated, B.C. 275). S.W. of Beneventum: Caudium, near which the pass called Furculæ Caudinæ, or Caudine Forks (where the Roman army, overcome by the Samnites,

passed under the yoke, B.C. 321); Bovīānum, *Bojano*, (chief city of the Pentri).
Tribes.—N., Frentāni; Middle, Pentri; S., Hirpīni.

CAMPANIA.—Part of *Naples*.
Boundaries.—N., Latium and R. Līris; E., Samnium; S., R. Silărus; W., Tyrrhenum Mare.
Cities.—On the coast: Cumæ, the most ancient Greek colony in Italy; Baiæ, (famed for its baths); Misēnum, the principal station of the Roman fleet in the Tyrrhene Sea; Pūtĕŏli, or Dicæarchĭa, *Pozzuoli;* Neāpŏlis, *Naples,* founded on the site of the ancient Parthĕnŏpe; Herculanĕum (over which stand *Portici* and *Resina*), Pompēii, and Stabiæ, (destroyed, A.D. 79, by an eruption of Vesuvius); Salernum, *Salerno*. In the Interior: Venāfrum, *Venafro*, (noted for its olives); Capua, *Capua*, (which espoused the cause of Hannibal, and, when taken by the Romans, B.C. 211, suffered the vengeance of the conquerors); Nola, *Nola*, (here Augustus died, A.D. 14). In the N.: Mons Massĭcus and Falernus Ager, both noted for wine (Massic and Falernian).
Tribes.—N., Aurunci; S., Picentīni.

APULIA.—Part of *Naples*.
Boundaries.—N. and E., Mare Hadriaticum; S., Tarentinus Sinus; W., R. Bradanus, *Brandano*, and Samnium.
Divisions.—Daunia, Peucĕtĭa, Messāpia or Iapȳgĭa, Calabria.
Cities.—Lucĕria, *Lucera*, (noted in the Samnite wars); Argȳrĭpa or Arpi, *Arpi.* On the Aufĭdus: Canŭsĭum, *Canosa*, and Cannæ, *Canne*, (battle, B.C. 216, Romans defeated by Hannibal); Ascŭlum Apŭlum (Romans defeated by Pyrrhus, B.C. 279); Venŭsĭa, *Venosa*, (the birth-place of Horace, B.C. 65). In Calabria: Brundŭsĭum, *Brindisi*, (the usual port of embarcation for Greece); Hydruntum or Hydrus, *Otranto;* Tarentum or Taras, *Taranto*, (a flourishing and opulent city).
Tribes.—Pediculi, Salentini.

LUCANIA. — Part of *Naples*.

Boundaries. — N., Campania, Samnium and Apulia; E., Tarentinus Sinus; S., Bruttii and R. Laus; W., Tyrrhenum Mare.

Cities. — In the E.: Metapontum; Hēraclēa, on the Aciris; Sybăris (proverbial for the luxury of its inhabitants); Thurii, (founded by the Athenians, B.C. 443, with whom were Herodotus, and Lysias the orator). In the W., also on the coast: Pæstum, vel Posīdōnia, (noted for its roses); Elĕa, Helĭa, or Velĭa, (the birth-place of Zeno and Parmĕnīdes, the founders of the Eleatic School of Philosophy). In the Interior: to the E., Pandŏsia; Potentia, *Potenza*.

BRUTTIUM. — Part of *Naples*.

Boundaries. — N., Lucania; E., Ionium Mare; S., Mare Siculum; W., Tyrrhenum Mare.

Cities. — On the East: Croton, *Cotrone*, (the residence of Pythăgŏras, who here founded his school, and of Milo, the most famous athlete of antiquity); Scylacĭum, *Squillace;* Locri Epizephyrii, (the city of Zaleucus, the law giver). On the West: Consentia, *Cosenza*, the Capital; Temesa or Tempsa. On the coast further South: Rhēgĭum, *Reggio*, N. of Rhegium, the Rock Scylla, opposite to Charybdis on the Sicilian coast.

ISLANDS.

SICILIA or **TRINACRIA**, *Sicily*, (inhabitants the Sicani) *Mountain.* — Ætna, *Monte Gibello*. *Rivers.* — Symæthus, *Giaretta*, in the E.; Himĕra, *Salso*, in the S. *Capes.* — Pelōrum Prom., *Cape Faro;* Pachўnum Prom., *Cape Passaro;* Lĭlўbæum Prom., *Cape Boeo*. *Cities.*—E. Messāna, *Messina;* Tauromĕnĭum, *Taormina;* Catăna, *Catania;* Syracūsæ, *Syracuse* or *Siragossa*, consisting of five towns, 1. Ortўgĭa, (or Nasos, the Island), 2. Achradīna, 3. Tyche, 4. Neapŏlis, and 5. the superb Epipŏlæ: in the S. Agrigentum, *Girgenti*, (famed for its temple of Zeus Olympius); Selīnus; *ruins:* in .the W. Lilybæum,

GEOGRAPHY. 31

Marsala; Drepănum, *Trapani:* in the N. Segeste or
Ægesta, near *Alcamo;* Panormus, *Palermo.* Hımĕra,
(battle, B.C. 480): in the centre Henna or Enna, *Castro
Giovanni,* (from which Pluto carried off Proserpine).
North from Sicily, Æŏlĭæ vel Vulcānĭæ Insulæ,
Lipari Islands, the largest of which Lipăra; Strongvle.
Stromboli: W. Ægātes Insulæ, (battle, B.C. 241, Carthaginians defeated): S. Cossȳra, *Pantelearia;* Melĭta,
Malta; Gaulus, *Gozzo.* W. of Etruria: Ilva vel Æthālĭa.
Elba, (famed for its iron-mines); Corsĭca. *Corsica. Chief
Towns.*—Mariana, and Alalia or Alērĭa. a Roman colony
S. of Corsica: Sardinia vel Sardo, *Sardinia,* Cap. Ca
rălis, *Cagliari,* in the S.

MŒSIA.

Servia and Bulgaria.

BOUNDARIES.—N., R. Danubius or Ister; E., Pontus Eux
inus, *Black Sea;* S., Hæmus Mons; W., Illyricum and R
Drinus, *Drino.*

DIVISIONS.—W., Mœsia Superior, including Dacir
Aureliani; E., Mœsia Inferior, including Scythir
Parva.

TRIBES.—Mœsi, Scordisci, Dardăni, Triballi.

RIVERS.—Drinus, *Drino;* Margus, *Morava;* Œscus,
Isker; Iatrus, *Iantro;* all tributaries of the Danube.

TOWNS.—In Mœsia Superior: Singidūnum, *Belgrade;*
Margus, near the Margus; Naissus, *Nissa,* on the Margus. In Mœsia Inferior: Sardĭca on the Œscus, S.E. of
which Tauresium, (the birth-place of Justinian). On
the Danube: Nicopolis, *Nicopoli,* built by Trajan. On
the borders of the Pontus Euxinus, *Black Sea:* Tomi, (to
which Ovid was banished by Augustus), to the South of
this Odessus, *Odessa,* W. of which Marcianopŏlis,
founded by Trajan.

DACIA.

Transylvania, Wallachia, Moldavia, Bessarabia.

BOUNDARIES.—N., Mons Carpătes vel Bastarnĭcæ, and R. Tyras, *Dniester;* E., Pontus Euxinus, *Black Sea,* and Sarmatia; S., R. Danubius; W., R. Tibiscus, *Theiss.*

RIVERS.—Tibiscus, *Theiss;* Aluta, *Aluta;* Ardiscus, *Argish;* Ararus, *Sereth;* Porata or Hierasus, *Pruth,* all falling into the Danube.

TRIBES.—Getæ vel Daci, (chief city Sarmizegethusa or Ulpia Trajāna); Jăzўges, in the West.

SARMATIA.

Part of European Russia.

BOUNDARIES.—E., R. Tanăis, *Don;* S., Palus Mæotis, *Sea of Azov,* and Pontus Euxinus; W., R. Tyras, *Dniester.*

TRIBES.—Bastarnæ, Jazўges, Roxolāni, Hamaxobii, Alāni, Venĕdi, &c. &c.

TOWNS, &c.—Olbia, near the junction of the Borysthenes, *Dnieper,* and Hypănis. S. of Sarmatia: Chersonēsus Taurica, *Crimea;* on the W. coast of which, Chersonēsus; on Bosporus Cimmerius, *Straits of Kaffa,* Panticapæum, *Kertsch,* the residence of the Greek kings of the Bosporus.

MACEDONIA.

Part of the Roumelia in Turkey.

BOUNDARIES.—N., Mœsia; E., Thracia; S., Mare Ægeum and Thessalia; W., Illyris Græca, included in Macedonia under the Romans.

GEOGRAPHY. 33

GULFS.—S. Thermaīcus Sinus, *Gulf of Saloniki;* Torōnāīcus Sinus, *Gulf of Cassandra;* Singitīcus Sinus, *Gulf of Monte Santo;* Strȳmonīcus Sinus, *Gulf of Contessa.*

MOUNTAINS.—N., Mons Orbēlus, Scardus Mons, separating Macedonia from Mœsia; S.W. of the Peninsula Acte, Mons Athos, *Monte Santo.*

RIVERS.—Strȳmon, *Struma* or *Carassou,* flowing into Strymonic Gulf; Axius, *Vardari* (with its tributary Erĭgon), and Hălĭacmon, *Vistriza,* flowing into the Thermaic Gulf.

DIVISIONS.—S., Piĕrĭa, Elymiōtis, Æmathia, Chalcĭdīce, with the Peninsulas Pallēne, Sithōnĭa, and Acte; E., Mygdonia and Sintīca. In the centre: Pelagonia; N., Pæŏnia; W., Lyncestæ and Eordæa.

CITIES.—Pydna, *Kitron,* near the Haliacmon, (battle, B.C. 168; Æmilius Paulus routs Perseus, the last king of Macedonia); Pella, *Alaklisi,* the Capital; Thessalonīca or Thermia, *Saloniki,* on the Thermaic Gulf; Potidæa, *Pinaka,* on the Isthmus of Pallēne; Olynthus, *ruins,* on the Toronaic Gulf, (destroyed by Philip II., B.C. 347); Amphipŏlis, at the mouth of the Strymon, (taken from the Athenians in the Peloponnesian War by Brasidas, B.C. 424); Eastward Philippi, *Philippi,* (battle, B.C. 42; Brutus and Cassius defeated and slain by Antony and Octavianus).

The tract of country called ILLYRIS GRÆCA (bounded N. by Drinus, R. *Drino;* E., Macedonia; S., Epirus; W., Hadriaticum Mare); inhabited by various tribes of Illyrian origin, was incorporated with the Roman province of Macedonia. *Chief Towns.*—On the coast: Epidamnus vel Dyrrachium, *Durazzo,* (the usual landing-place for persons who crossed over from Brundusium, in Italy). Inland: Apollōnĭa, (celebrated as a place of commerce and learning; here Augustus for some time studied literature and philosophy).

THRACIA.

Roumelia.

BOUNDARIES.—N., Hæmus Mons and Mœsia; E., Pontus Euxīnus and Bosporus Thracīus; S., Propontis, Hellespontus and Ægeum Mare; W., Macedonia.

WATERS OF THRACE.—Hellespontus, *Dardanelles;* Propontis, *Sea of Marmora;* Pontus Euxinus, *Black Sea;* Bosporus Thracius, *Straits of Constantinople;* Melas or Melănes Sinus, *Gulf of Saros.*

MOUNTAINS.— N., Hæmus, *Balkan;* W., Pangæus, *Pangea,* east of which Rhŏdŏpe, sacred to Bacchus.

RIVERS.—In the W. Nestus, *Nesto,* rising in the N.W. and flowing S. into the Ægean Sea; Hebrus, *Maritza.*

CITIES.—Abdēra, at the mouth of the Nestus, (the birthplace of Democritus); Adrianopolis, *Adrianople,* on the Hebrus; Chersonēsus, in the S. between the Gulf of Saros and the Hellespont, (colonized by Athenians under Miltiades); Lysimachïa, *Eksemil,* at the Isthmus; S. of this Sestos, (between which and Abydos, Xerxes formed a bridge of boats); Ægos Potamos, (near which Lysander defeated the Athenian fleet, B.C. 405); Byzantĭum, *Constantinople,* on the Thracian Bosporus, (made the Capital of the Roman empire under Constantine, A.D. 330).

GRÆCIA—HELLAS.

Greece.

BOUNDARIES. — N., Macedonia and Illyria; E., Ægeum Mare, *Archipelago,* and Myrtŏum Mare; S., Mare Internum, *Mediterranean;* W., Ionium Mare, *Ionian Sea.*

GEOGRAPHY.

GULFS.—E., Thermaĭcus Sir.us, *Gulf of Saloniki;* Pagasœus Sinus, *Gulf of Volo;* Maliăcus Sinus, *Gulf of Zeitoun;* Sarōnĭcus Sinus, *Gulf of Ægina;* Argolĭcus Sinus, *Gulf of Napoli.* S., Laconĭcus Sinus, *Gulf of Colokythia;* Messēnĭăcus Sinus, *Gulf of Koron.* W., Cyparissius Sinus, *Gulf of Arcadia;* N. of Achaia and Corinthia, Sinus Corinthĭăcus, *Gulf of Lepanto;* S. of Locris, Crissæus Sinus, *Bay of Salona;* S. of Epīrus, Ambracĭus Sinus, *Gulf of Arta.*

STRAIT.—Eurīpus, *Channel of Negropont,* between Bœotia and Eubœa.

MOUNTAINS.—In THESSALIA: N., Cambūnii Montes, *Bolutza Mts.;* W., Olympus, *Elymbo;* Ossa, *Kissovo;* Pēlĭon, *Plesnia;* S., Othrys, *Othrys;* W., Pindus, *Pindus.*

In EPIRUS: N.W., Acroceraunii vel Ceraunii Montes, *Chimera.*

In PHOCIS: N., Œta Mons, *Katavothra;* W., Parnassus, *Lyakouri.*

In BŒOTIA: S.W., Helĭcon, *Zagora,* (a haunt of the Muses). On the borders of Attica and Megăris, Cithæron, *Cithæron.*

In ATTICA: N., Parnēs Montes, *Nozia;* N.E., Pentĕlĭcus, *Pentele,* (celebrated for its marble); S.E. of Athens, Hymettus, *Telovuni;* at the S. extremity of Attica, Laurium, (famed for its silver-mines).

On the Borders of ACHAIA: Cyllēne, *Zyria,* (Mercury born).

In LACONIA: Taÿgĕtus, West of the Eurōtas.

In ARCADIA: in the S.W., Lycæus Mons; in N.W, Erўmanthus, (here Hercules slew the wild boar); towards the S., Mænŭlus, *Roino;* Parnōn, *Malevo.*

RIVERS.—In THESSALIA: 1. Penēus, *Salambria,* from Mt. Pindus, flowing through the lovely vale of *Tempe,* falls into the Thermaicus Sinus, *Gulf of Saloniki;* it receives on the

North the Titarēsĭus, on the South the Enīpeus and Apidănus. 2. Sperchēus, *Ellada,* from the West, falls into Sinus Maliăcus, *Bay of Zeitoun.*

In EPIRUS: 1. Aracthus, *Arta,* from the N., falls into Sinus Ambracĭus, *Gulf of Arta.* 2. Achĕron, and its tributary Cocȳtus, fall into the Glykys Portus or Harbour. Northward, Thyămĭs, *Kalamas,* falls into the Ionian Sea, opposite to Corcyra, *Corfu.*

In ACARNANIA: Achĕlōus, *Aspro Potamo,* from Mt. Pindus, flows southward, divides Ætolia from Acarnania, and falls into the Gulf of Patras.

In ÆTOLIA: Evēnus, *Fidhari,* from Mt. Œta, falls into the Gulf of Patras.

In DORIS: Cephīsus Major, *Mavronero,* flows through Phocis and Bœotia, and falls into Copais L., *Lake Topolias.*

In BŒOTIA: Asōpus, *Asopo,* falls into the sea opposite to Eubœa, the island *Negropont.* Ismēnus, into which the brook Dīrce flows, falls into L. Hylĭca. Permessus and Hippocrēne, or "fountain of the horse," falls into Copais L.

In ATTICA: Cephīsus Minor, from Mons Pentĕlĭcus, and Ilissus, from Mons Hymettus, flow South into Saronĭcus Sinus.

In ACHAIA: Crathis, *Crata,* (into which the Styx flows), and Selīnus, *Vostitza,* fall into the Corinthian Gulf. Pīrus, *Kamenitza,* falls into the Gulf of Patras.

In ELIS: Penēus, *Iliaco,* from Mons Erymanthus, falls into Ionium Mare. Alpheus, *Rouphia,* rising in *Arcadia,* and receiving from the North the Ladon and Helisson, falls into the Ionian Sea.

In MESSENIA: Pamīsus, *Pirnatza,* from Mt. Lycæus, and Nĕda, *Buzi,* between Elis and Messenia, fall into the Ionian Sea.

In LACONIA: Eurōtas, *Basilipotamo,* from the N., falls into Laconicus Sinus, *Gulf of Kolokythia.*

In ARGOLIS: Inăchus, *Banitza,* falls into Argolicus Sinus, *Gulf of Napoli.*

GEOGRAPHY. 37

LAKES. — Copāis L., *Lake Topolias*, in Bœotia, (famed for its eels, and subterranean communication with the Eubœan Sea); Acherūsĭa L., in the S.W. of Epīrus; L. Trichōnis, in Ætolia; L. Bæbēis, in the East of Thessaly; L. Stymphalis, in the North of Arcadia.

PROMONTORIES. — S.E. of Thessalia, Magnēsĭæ Prom., *Cape St. George;* S.E. of Attica, Sunīum Prom., *Cape Colonna;* S.E. of Argolis, Scyllæum Prom., *Cape Skillo;* S.E. of Laconia, Malĕa Prom., *Cape Maleo* or *St. Angelo;* S.W. of Laconia, Tænărum Prom., *Cape Matapan;* S.W. of Messenia, Acrītas Prom., *Cape Gallo;* N.W. of Elis, Chelonātas Prom., *Cape Tornese;* N.W. of Achaia, Araxus Prom., *Cape Kologria;* N. of Achaia, Chīum Prom., *Castello di Morea,* opposite to this in the S. of Ætolia, Anti-Rhīum Prom., *Castello Rumeli;* N.W. of Acarnania, at the entrance of the Ambracian Gulf, Actīum Prom., *La Punta,* (battle, B.C. 31, Augustus defeats Antony and Cleopatra.)

DIVISIONS. — NORTHERN GREECE.—1. Thessălĭa; 2. Epīrus. CENTRAL GREECE. — 1. Acarnānia; 2. Ætōlĭa; 3. Doris; 4. Locris; 5. Phocis; 6. Bœōtĭa; 7. Attica; 8. Mĕgăris. SOUTHERN GREECE or PELOPONNESUS, *Morea.* —1. Achaia; 2. Elis; 3. Messenia; 4. Lacōnĭa; 5. Argŏlis; 6. Arcadia; 7. Sicyōnĭa; 8. Corinthĭa.

THESSALIA. — *Boundaries.* — N., Macedonia; E., Ægeum Mare; S., Phocis, Doris, Ætolia; W., Epīrus.

Divisions. — N., Pelasgĭōtis; E., Magnēsĭa; S.E., Phthĭōtis; S., Ænĭānes; S.W., Dŏlŏpia; N.W., Hestĭæōtis;-in the Centre, Thessaliōtis.

Cities. — Larissa, *Larza,* the Capital, on the Penēus. Pharsālus, *Pharsa,* (battle, B.C. 48, Cæsar defeated Pompey). Cynocĕpĭ ălæ, (battle, B.C. 197, Philip defeated by Cons. Flaminius). Antĭcўra, at the mouth of the Spercheus. Phĕræ, *Valestino;* noted for its tyrants. Lamĭa, *Zeitoun;* near the mouth of the Sperchēus, (war between Antipăter and the Athenians, B.C. 323). Iolcos,

4

N. of the Pagasæus Sinus, (the city of Pelias and Jason, from which the Argonauts sailed in quest of the Golden Fleece).

EPIRUS. — *Boundaries.* — N., Illyria; E., Macedonia and Thessalia; S., Acarnania; W., Ionium Mare.

Divisions. — N.W., Chaonia; S.E., Molossis; S.W., Thesprōtĭa.

Cities. — Ambracĭa, *Arta*, (the residence of Pyrrhus), on the Aracthus. Nĭcŏpŏlis (built by Augustus, in memory of his victory at Actium). Dōdōna, on the borders of Molossis and Thesprōtĭa, (famed for its oracle of Zeus, the most ancient in Greece).

ACARNANIA. — *Boundaries.* — N., Ambracĭus Sinus and Epirus; E., River Achĕlōus; W., Ionium Mare.

Cities. — Stratus, on the Achĕlōus, the Capital. Actium, on a promontory of the same name, (near which Augustus defeated Antony and Cleopatra in a naval engagement, B.C. 31).

ÆTOLIA. — *Boundaries.* — N., Thessalia and Epīrus; E., Doris and Locris; S., Sinus Corinthĭăcus; W., R. Achĕlōus.

Cities. — Therma vel Thermum, the place of meeting of the Ætolian league. Călȳdon, the city of Tydeus and Diomēdes, (in the vicinity of this city the celebrated Calydonian hunt took place).

DORIS.—*Boundaries.*—N., Thessalia; E., Phocis; S., Locris; W., Ætolia.

Cities. — Four small cities which gave the name of Tetrapolis to the country, Erĭnĕus, Boium, Pindus, Cytinĭum.

LOCRIS was divided into two districts, inhabited by three tribes.

DISTRICT I.—*Boundaries.*—N., Doris; E., Phoçis; S., Sinus Corinthĭăcus; W., Ætolia. Inhabited by OZOLIAN LOCRIANS. *Chief Cities.* — Amphissa, *Salona;* Naupactus, *Lepanto.*

GEOGRAPHY. 39

DISTRICT II.—*Boundaries.*—N., Thessaly; E., Eubœan Sea and Malian Gulf; S., Phocis; W., Doris and Phocis. Inhabited S. by OPUNTIAN LOCRIANS. *City:* Opus, *Talanda.* Inhabited N. by EPICNEMIDIAN LOCRIANS as far as Thermŏpўlæ, (a celebrated pass, where Leonidas and 300 Spartans fell, after a gallant defence against the mighty army of Xerxes, B.C. 480). *Cities:* Phrŏnīum, *Romani,* Nīcæa, and Scarphīa.

PHOCIS.—*Boundaries.*—N., Locri Epicnēmĭdii and Doris; E., Bœotia; S., Sinus Corinthĭăcus; W., Locris.

Cities.—Delphi, or Pytho, *Castri,* on the western declivity of Mt. Parnassus, between its two peaks, (famed for the "infallible" oracle of Apollo, and celebrated as the place of meeting of the Amphictyons, and of the celebration of the Pythian games); Crissa, or Crisa, S.W. of Delphi; Elatēa, *Elephta,* N. of the Cephissus; Antĭcўra, *Aspra Spitia,* in the South, on the coast, (famed for its hellebore, the cure for madness among the ancients).

BŒOTIA.—*Boundaries.*—N. and E., Euboĭcum Mare; S., Mountain-chain of Parnes and Cithæron, separating Bœotia from Attica; W., Phòcis.

Cities.—Thebæ, *Thibai* (founded by the Phœnicians under Cadmus, thence called Cadmea; it was destroyed by Alexander, B.C. 335). Orchŏmĕnus, *Scripu,* near the Lake Copais, with a temple of the Graces, (victory of Sulla, B.C. 86). Platææ, or Platæa, *Kokla,* near Mt. Cithæron, (battle, B.C. 479, Mardonius defeated). Thespiæ, at the foot of Mt. Helicon, sacred to the Muses. Leuctra, *Lefka,* S.E. of Thespiæ, (battle, B.C. 371, Thebans overcame the Spartans). Tanăgra, *Grimada,* E. of Thebæ, (battle, B.C. 457, Athenians defeated). Dēlĭum, *Dilessi,* on the E. coast, (battle, B.C. 424). Haliartus, *Mazi,* on Lake Copais, (battle, B.C. 395; destroyed by the Romans, B.C. 171). Corōnēa, S.W. of Lake Copais (Bœotians overcame Athenians, B.C. 447; Agesilaus defeated allied Greeks, B.C. 394). Chærcnēa, *Capurna,* on the Cēphissus, (battles, B.C. 447; Philip conquers the Greeks, B.C. 338, Sulla's victory, B.C. 86). Ascra, near Mt. Helicon, the birth-place of Hesiod.

ATTICA.—*Boundaries.*—N., Bœotia; E., Ægeum Mare; S., Sarōnĭcus Sinus; W., Megăris.

Cities.—Ath ēn æ, *Athens*, between the rivers Cēphissus and Ilissus, the most celebrated city of antiquity for learning and the liberal arts; it consisted of two parts, viz.:— 1. The City; 2. Its three ports, Pirænus, *Pirœus*, Phalērum, and Mūnychĭa, united to the city by two long walls, called "Longi Muri," sixty feet in height (vide "Topography" for an account of Public Buildings. &c.) Eleusis, *Lepsina*, N.W. of Athens, famous for its temple and mysteries of Dēmēter or Cēres. Marăthon, *Marathona*, N.E. of Athens, (celebrated battle, Athenians and Platæans, under Miltiades, routed the Persians, B.C. 490). Phÿle, *Fili*, N.W. of Athens, (here Thrasybŭlus assembled the Patriots opposed to the thirty Tyrants, B.C. 404). Sūnĭum, *Colonna*, on a prom. of the same name in the extreme S. of Attica.

MEGARIS.—*Boundaries.*—N., Bœotia; E., Attica and Sarōnĭcus Sinus; S., Corinthia; W., Sinus Corinthĭăcus.

Cities.—Megara, *Megara;* Nisæa, on the coast.

PELOPONNESUS.

ACHAIA.—*Boundaries.*—N., Sinus Corinthĭăcus; E., Corinthĭa; S., Arcadia and Elis.

Cities.—Hĕlĭce, on the north coast, the ancient Capital, (engulphed by an earthquake, B.C. 373), Ægĭum, *Vostitza*, (here the meetings of the Achæan league were held); Patræ, *Patras*, a sea-port.

ELIS.—*Boundaries.*—N., Achaia; E., Arcadia; S., Messēnia; W., Ionium Mare.

Divisions.—1. Elis Proper, N.; 2. Pisātis with Olympia, Middle; 3. Triphÿlia, South.

GEOGRAPHY. 41

Cities.—Elis, on the Penēus. N.W., Cyllēne, on the coast. Pisa, on the Alphēus, (near this the plain of OLYMPIA, where the Olympian games were celebrated. Here was the sacred grove "Altis," which, with the neighbourhood, were adorned with temples, statues, &c. The "Altis" was inclosed by a wall; it contained the following temples: I. The Olympiēum, in which was the famous statue of Zeus, by Phidias, made of ivory and gold; II. The Heræum, or Temple of Juno; III. The Metrōum. Public buildings: The Thesauri of the states; The Prytaneum, in which the Olympic victors dined; The Bouleuterion, or council-hall, in which all the regulations were made. The chief buildings without the Altis were the Stadium, for gymnastic exercises, and the Hippŏdrŏmus, for racing). Pylos, in Triphȳlia.

MESSENIA.—*Boundaries.*—N., Triphȳlia and Arcadia; E., Laconia; S., Messenīacus Sinus; W., Mare Ionium.

Cities.—Pȳlos, *Navarino,* in the S.W., (the city of Nestor); Ithōme, in the centre, on a hill of the same name; near which was Messēne, *ruins,* the Capital, built by Epaminondas; Ira, in the N., (which Aristŏmĕnes defended against the Spartans for eleven years).

LACONIA.—*Boundaries.*—N., Arcadia and Argŏlis; E., Myrtoum Mare; S., Lacōnĭcus Sinus; W., Messēnia.

Cities.—Lacedæmon, or Sparta, *Sparta,* on the Eurōtas, the Capital of the most powerful state in Greece, (the city of Lycurgus, the lawgiver); S. of Lacedæmon, Amȳclæ, with a temple to Apollo; Hĕlos, near the mouth of the Eurōtas, (its inhabitants, the Helots, were reduced to slavery by the Spartans); Sellasĭa, (battle, B. C. 222, Athenians, under Antigonus Doson, defeated Cleomĕnes, king of Sparta).

ARGOLIS.—*Boundaries.*—N., Corinthia and Sarōnĭcus Sinus; E., Myrtoum Mare; S., Argolĭcus Sinus and Lacōnĭa; W., Arcadia.

4*

Cities.—Argos, *Argos*, on the Inachus, one of the most ancient cities in Greece; S.E. of Argos, Nauplĭa, *Napolı di Romania*, the port of Argos; N. of Argos, Mycēnæ, *ruins*, (the city of Agamemnon, noted for its Cyclopean walls; destroyed by Argives, B.C. 468); Tīryns, *ruins*, S.E. of Argos, (Hercules educated here, hence called Tĭrynthĭus); Němĕa, *ruins*, N.W. of Mycēnæ, (Hercules killed the lion, vide first labour; triennial games celebrated in consequence); Epidaurus, *Epidauro*, in the district of Epidauria, on the Saronic Gulf, (famed for a temple of Æsculapĭus); Trœzēne, *Demala*, in the district Trœzēnia, in the S.E. of Argolis; Hermĭŏne, *Kastri*, in the district Hermĭŏnis, in the South.

ARCADIA.— *Boundaries.*— N., Achaia; E., Corinthĭa and Argŏlis; S., Lacōnĭa and Messēnĭa; W., Tryphȳlĭa and Elis.

Cities.—Mantinēa, *Paleopoli*, in the East, (battle, B.C. 418, Athenians defeated; battle, B.C. 362, Epaminondas slain); Těgěa, *Piali*, S. E. of Mantinēa; Měgalŏpŏlis, *ruins*, on the Helisson, founded, by the advice of Epaminondas, B.C. 371, (the birth-place of Polybius).

CORINTHIA. — *Boundaries.*—N., Měgăris and Sinus Corinthĭăcus; E., Sarōnĭcus Sinus; S., Argŏlis; W., Achaia.

Cities.— Corinthus, *Corinth*, the Capital, built at the foot of a steep mountain, on which stood the Acro-Corinthus, the strongest citadel in Greece, the key of the Peloponnesus; (destroyed by Mummius, the Roman Consul, B.C. 146). At the narrowest part of the Isthmus stood Fānum Neptūni, a temple of Neptune, near which the Isthmian games were celebrated (vide Antiq.). On the Asōpus: Phlīus, the Capital of the independent state, Phliasia.

SICYONIA.— *Boundaries.*—N., Sinus Corinthĭăcus; E., Corinthĭa; S., Arcadia; W., Achaia.

City.— Sicyon, *ruins*, on the north coast, at the mouth of the Asōpus.

THE GREEK ISLANDS.

IN THE IONIAN SEA.—Corcȳra, *Corfu;* Cap., Corcȳra. Leucadia, *Santa Maura;* Cap., Leucas. Ithăca, *Theaki;* Cap., Ithaca. Cephallēnia, *Cephalonia. Cities.* — Cephallenia and Same. Zacynthus, *Zante;* Cap., Zacynthus. Teleboides Insulæ, between Leucadia and Epirus. Cythĕra, *Cerigo,* (sacred to Venus).

IN THE ÆGEAN SEA.—I. In the *Western part.* Hydrĕa, *Hydra.* Calauria, *Calauria,* (Demosthenes poisoned himself, B.C. 322). Ægīna, *Egina.* Salamis, *Colouri,* (battle, B.C. 480, Persian fleet defeated by Athenians, under Themistocles). Eubœa, *Negropont,* Artemisium Prom., in the N., (battle, B.C. 480); *Cities:* 1. Chalcis, *Negroponte,* the Capital; 2. Eretrīa. Scyros, *Skyro.*

II. In the *Northern part.* Lemnos, *Lemno,* (sacred to Vulcan, who is said to have fallen on this island, when hurled from heaven by Zeus). Imbros, *Imbro.* Samothrāce, *Samothraki.* Thasos, *Thaso,* anciently famous for its gold-mines. Tĕnĕdos, *Tĕnĕdos,* near the coast of Troas.

III. In the *Eastern part.* Lesbos, *Mytilene,* (noted for its wine); *Cities:* 1. Mitȳlēne (the birth-place of Sappho, Alcæus, Pittacus, &c.); 2. Methymna. Chios, *Skio,* (famed for its wine). Samos, *Samo;* Cap., Samos; (sacred to Juno, the native city of Pythagoras). Icăros, or -ĭa, *Nikaria,* which, with the adjoining sea, derived its name from Icărus, the son of Dædalus (vide Mythol.). Patmos, *Patino* or *Patmos,* (to which St. John was banished). Leros, *Lero.* Cos, *Kos,* (the birth-place of Hippocrătes the physician, and Apelles the painter) Rhŏdus, *Rhodes;* Cap., Rhodes, in the port of which stood the Colossus. Carpathus, *Scarpanto,* whence Carpathium Mare.

IV. In the *Southern part,* THE CYCLADES. Delos, *Delo,* in the Centre, with Mt. Cynthus, (the birth-place of Apollo and Diana); Naxos, *Naxo* or *Naxia;* (sacred to

Bacchus); Paros, *Paro,* (famed for its white marble).
N.: Andros, *Andro;* Tenos, *Teno;* Ceos, *Zea;* Cyth-
nos, *Thermia;* Syros, *Syra;* Myconos, *Myconi;* Scrī-
phus, *Serpho.* S.: Melos, *Milo;* Siphnus, *Siphno;*
Ios, *Nio;* Amorgus, *Amorgo;* Thera, *Santorin;* Asty-
palæa, *Stampalia.* The name SPORADES was applied
to those islands not lying round Delos, but scattered apart.

V. *South of the Cyclades.* Creta, *Candia;* Cap., Gnos-
sus, (the residence of Minos); N.W., Cydōnia, *Khania,*
(famed for its archers); S.W. of Cnossus, Gortȳna. Mons
Ida in the centre of the island; E., Mons Dicte, in a cave
of which Jupiter was brought up.

BRITANNIA or ALBION.
Great Britain.

BOUNDARIES.—N., Mare Pigrum, *North Sea;* E., Germanicus Oceanus, *German Ocean;* S., Fretum Gallicum,
Straits of Dover, and Oceanus Britannicus, *English Channel;* W., Oceanus Hibernicus, *Irish Sea,* and Verginium
Mare, *St. George's Channel.*

RIVERS, &c.—Tamĕsis, *Thames;* Sabrīna, *Severn;* An-
tona, *Nen;* Trivona, *Trent;* Abus, *Humber;* Tina,
Tyne; Itūna, *Eden;* Deva, *Dee.* In Scotland: Bodo-
tria, *Forth;* Glotta, *Clyde;* Tavus, *Tay;* Metaris
Æstuarium, *The Wash;* Bodotriæ Æst., *Firth of
Forth;* Glottæ Æst., *Firth of Clyde;* Itunæ Æst., *Solway Frith.*

PROMONTORIES.—Ocellum Prom., *Spurn Head;* Can-
tium Prom., *North Foreland;* Ocrīnum Prom., *Lizard
Point;* Bolerium Prom., *Land's End.*

DIVISIONS.—S., Britannia Prima; Centre, Flavia
Cæsariensis; W., Britannia Secunda, *Wales;* N.,

GEOGRAPHY. 45

Maxima Cæsariensis; N. of the Wall of Severus, Valentia, *South part of Scotland;* N. of the Wall of Antoninus, Caledonia, *North part of Scotland.*

TRIBES.—S. of the Thames: Cantii, *Kent;* Regni, *Surrey* and *Sussex;* Belgæ, *Hants, Wilts,* and *Somerset;* Atrebatii, *Berks;* Durotrīges, *Dorset;* Dumnonii, *Devon* and *Cornwall.* N. of the Thames: Trinobantes, *Middlesex* and *Essex;* Simēni, vel Icēni, *Suffolk* and *Norfolk;* Cattieuchlāni, *Herts, Bucks,* &c.; Dobuni, *Oxon* and *Gloucester;* Silūres, *South Wales;* Ordovīces, *North Wales;* Cornavii, *Cheshire, Salop, Stafford, Worcester, Notts,* &c.; Coritāni, *Lincoln* and *Leicester;* Brigantes, *York, Durham, Cumberland,* and *Westmoreland.*

TOWNS.—S. of the Thames: Durovernum, *Canterbury;* Rutupiæ, *Richborough;* Venta Belgarum, *Winchester;* Regnum, *Chichester;* Aquæ Solis, *Bath;* Uxela, *Exeter.* N. of the Thames: Londinium, *London;* Verulamium, *St. Alban's;* Glevum, *Gloucester;* Corinium, *Cirencester;* Isca Silūrum, *Caerleon;* Lindum, *Lincoln;* Deva or Deona, *Chester;* Eborācum, *York.*

Hadrian's Wall, between the mouth of the Tyne and the Solway Frith; erected A.D. 121. Wall of Severus; erected A.D. 209. Rampart of Antoninus, between the Friths of Forth and Solway; erected A.D. 140.

ISLANDS.—Orcădes, *Orkneys;* Ebūdes, *Hebrides;* Thule, *Shetland Isles* (?); Mona (of Cæsar), *Man;* Mona (of Tacitus), *Anglesey;* Cassiterīdes, *Scilly Isles,* (famous for their tin); Vectis, *Isle of Wight;* Hibernia, *Ireland,* Cap., Eblana, *Dublin.*

ASIA.

COUNTRIES — Asia Minor, *Anatolia, Roum,* and *Kara mania;* Syria, *Syria* and *Palestine;* Arabia, *Arabia;* Sarmatia Asiatica, *S.E. part of Russia in Europe;* Colchis, *Guriel, Mingrelia,* and *Imeritia;* Ibēria, *Georgia;* Albānia, *Shirvan* and *part of Daghistan;* Armenia, *Armenia* and *part of Georgia;* Mesopotamia, *Algesira;* Chaldæa, *Irak Arabi;* Assyria, *Kurdistan;* Mēdĭa, *N.W. part of Persia;* Susiana, *Khuzistan;* Persia, *S.W. part of Persia;* Hyrcānia and Parthia, *part of Turkistan;* Aria, *E. part of Khorassan* and *N. part of Afjhanistan;* Bactriāna, *Bokhara;* Carmānia, *Kirman;* Gedrōsia, *S. part of Beloochistan;* Sogdiāna, *part of Turkistan* and *Bokhara;* India, *Hindostan, &c.;* Scythia, *Tartary.*

MOUNTAINS. — Caucasus, (between Pontus Euxinus and Caspium Mare); Taurus Mons, in Asia Minor; Emōdi Montes, *Himalayah Mountains* in the N. of India.

SEAS, GULFS, &c. — Mare Hyrcanum vel Caspium, *Caspian Sea* and *Sea of Aral(?);* Sinus Arabĭcus, *Red Sea;* Erythræum Mare, *Arabian Sea;* Sinus Persĭcus, *Persian Gulf;* Gangetĭcus, *Bay of Bengal;* Indĭcus Ocĕanus, *Indian Ocean.*

RIVERS. — 1. Rha, *Volga* (flowing into the Caspian Sea); 2. Euphrates and Tigris, falling into the Persian Gulf, 3. Oxus, *Jihon,* 4. Jaxartes, *Sihon,* falling into the Sea

GEOGRAPHY. 47

of Aral, (but supposed by the ancients to fall into Mare Caspium); 5. Indus, *Indus*, with its five tributaries; 6. Ganges, *Ganges*.

ISLANDS.—Cyprus, *Cyprus*, in the Mediterranean; Taprobăna, *Ceylon*, S. of Hindostan.

ASIA MINOR.

Anatolia, Roum, and Karamania.

BOUNDARIES.—N., Pontus Euxinus, *Black Sea*; E., Euphrates and Syria; S., Mare Internum, *Mediterranean*; W., Ægeum Mare, and Propontis, *Sea of Marmora*.

GULFS.—N., Amisēnus Sinus. W., Adramyttēnus Sinus, *Gulf of Adrymitti;* Smyrnæus Sinus, *Gulf of Smyrna;* S., Glaucus Sinus, *Gulf of Macri;* Issĭcus Sinus, *Gulf of Scanderoon.*

MOUNTAINS.—Olympus, a chain extending from N.W. to N.E., passing through Galatia, Bithynia, and Paphlagonia; Ida in Troas; Dindỹmus in Phrygia, sacred to Cybĕle, (hence called Dindỹmēne); Tmōlus in Lydia (famed for its saffron and wine); S.W. of this Mycăle, (near which the Persian fleet was defeated by the Greek, B.C. 479); Crăgus in Lycia; Taurus, extending through Asia Minor, from W. to E., to the countries beyond the Euphrates; Mons Argæus, *Erdgish Dagh,* in Cappadocia.

RIVERS.—Flowing into Pontus Euxinus: 1. Thermōdon, *Thermeh;* 2. Iris, *Teshel Irmak;* 3. Halys, *Kisil Irmak:* 4. Parthenius; 5. Sangarius, *Sakariyeh.* Flowing into the Propontis: 1. Rhyndăcus, *Edrenos;* 2. Granīcus, (battle, B.C. 334, Alexander defeated the Persian Satraps). Flowing into the Ægean Sea: 1. Scamander or Xanthus, *Mindereh*, (joined by the Simoïs); 2. Hermus, *Ghiediz-Chai*, (with its tributary Pactōlus, famed for its golden sands); 3. Caÿstrus, (abounding in swans); 4. Mæander, *Mendereh*, (proverbial for its windings). Flowing into the Mediterranean: 1. Xạnthus, *Echen-Chai;* 2. Cestrus, *Ak-Su;* 3. Eurymĕdon, *Kapri-Su*, (battle, B.C. 469, Cimon defeated the Persians); 4. Calycadnus, *Giuk-Sooyoo;* 5. Cydnus, *Tersus-Chai*, (famed for the clearness and coolness of its water); 5. Sarus, *Sihan;* 6. Pyrămus, *Jihan.*

LAKE.—Tatta Palus, *Tuz Göl*, in Phrygia, a great salt lake.

PROMONTORIES.—N., Carambis Prom., *Cape Karempe*. At the entrance of the Hellespont: Rhœtēum and Sigēum Prom. W., Trogilium Prom., *C. St. Mary*, near which was the PANIONIUM, or place of assembly for the twelve Ionian states; Triopium Prom., *C. Krio*, with a temple of Apollo, (surnamed Triopius), the place of meeting for the six Dorian states, or "Hexapolis," afterwards reduced to five, "Pentapolis." S., Sacrum Prom., and Anemurium Prom., *C. Anamur.*

DIVISIONS. — N., Bithynia, Paphlagonia, Pontus; W., Mysia, Lydia, Caria; S., Lycia, Pamphylia, Cilicia; Central, Phrygia, Galatia, Cappadocia.

BITHYNIA. — *Cities.*—Heraclēa Pontica, *Harakli*, near which Acherusia Chersonesus, (with a cave through which Hercules is said to have descended to the infernal regions to drag up Cerebus). On the Thracian Bosporus: 1. Chrȳsŏpōlis, *Scutari;* 2. Chalcēdon, (or the city of the blind, so called from its founders having overlooked the more delightful situation of Byzantium). On the Propontis: 1. Libyssa, *Geibuzch*, (where was the tomb of Hannibal); 2. Nicomēdīa, *Izmid*, the Capital of the kings of Bithynia, (here Hannibal died, B.C. 183). On L. Ascanius, *L. of Iznik:* Nicæa, *Iznik*, (first Christian œcumenical council held, A.D. 325).

GEOGRAPHY. 49

PAPHLAGONIA. — *Cities.* — On the N. coast: Sinōpe, *Sinoub* or *Sinope,* (the birth-place of Diogenes, the Cynic philosopher); Cȳtōrus, *Kydros,* famous for its box-wood.

PONTUS.—*Cities.*—On the coast: 1. Trapēzus, *Trebizond;* 2. Cerăsus, *Kheresoun,* (from which the cherry-tree was first introduced into Italy, by Lucullus); 3. Polemonium, *Polemon;* 4. Themiscȳra, *Thermeh*(?) (founded by the Amazons); 5. Amïsus, *Samsun,* (the residence of Mithridātes). Inland: Zēla, *Zilleh,* (battle, B.C. 47, Cæsar conquered Pharnăces; an account of this battle Cæsar sent to the Senate in three words, viz., Veni, Vidi, Vici); Amăsia, *Amasiah,* (the birth-place of Mithridātes and Strabo the geographer); Magnopŏlis, (built by Mithridātes and Pompey).

MYSIA, with TROAS and ÆOLIS or IA.—*Cities.*—In the N.: Cȳzĭcus, *BalKiz,* (on an island of the same name, unsuccessfully besieged by Mithridātes, B.C. 75). On the Hellespont: 1. Lampsăcus *Lapsaki,* (celebrated for its wine, and one of the cities assigned to Themistocles for his maintenance); 2. Abȳdos, Nagara; 3. Dardănus, from which arose the modern name Dardanelles. At the foot of Mt. Ida, Troja or Ilium, *Troy,* with its citadel Pergăma; at the head of a bay of the same name, Adramyttium or ēum, *Adramytti.* Inland, on the Căĭcus: Pergamus (on or os), *Bergama,* (celebrated for its library, where parchment (Pergamenæ chartæ) was first used in writing; the library was afterwards added to that at Alexandria).

LYDIA or MÆONIA with IONIA.—*Cities.*—On the coast: 1. Phocæa, a colony from which was founded Massilia, *Marseilles;* 2. Smyrna, *Smyrna,* (one of the seven cities which claimed the honour of being the birth-place of Homer); 3. Tēos, (the birth-place of Anacreon); 4. Colŏphon, (famed for its cavalry); 5. Ephĕsus, *Ayasaluk,* at the mouth of the Caÿster, (famous for its temple to Diana, one of the seven wonders). Inland: Magnēsĭa, (battle, B.C. 190, Scipio defeated Antiochus); Sardes, *Sart*, on the Pactōlus, (the Capital of Crœsus, king of Lydia, taken by Cyrus, B.C. 546).

CARIA with DORIS.— *Cities.*— On the Mæander: Myus. On the coast: 1. Milētus, (one of the chief cities of Asia Minor, the birth-place of Thales, Anaximander, and other great men); 2. Hălĭcarnassus, *Budrum*, (the birth-place of Herodotus the historian, and Dionysius the rhetorician, and celebrated for the tomb of Mausolus. Opposite to the island Cos: Cnĭdus), (battle, B.C. 394, Pisander, the Spartan admiral, defeated by Conon, the Athenian).

LYCIA.— *Cities.*— On the coast: Telmessus, *Mŭrri*, (inhabitants famed for augury). On the Xanthus: Xanthus, *Gunik*. Near the mouth of the river: Patăra, *Patura*, (with a famous temple and oracle of Apollo). On the East: Phasēlis, (the head-quarters of the pirates before its destruction by P. Servilius Isauricus).

PAMPHYLIA with PISIDIA and ISAURIA.— *Cities.*— On the S. coast: Attalĭa. Inland: Perga, (the birth-place of Apollonius the mathematician); Selga, the chief city in Pisidia; Isaura, chief city in Isauria, (taken, B.C. 75, by P. Servilius, who thence received the surname Isauricus).

CILICIA.—Divided into Cilĭcia Trachēa or Aspera and Cilĭcia Campestris. *Cities.*— In C. Aspera.— On the coast: 1. Selīnus, *Selenti*, (where the Emperor Trajan died, A.D. 117); 2. Seleucia, *Selefkeh;* 3. Corўcus (famed for its excellent saffron). In C. Campestris: 1. Soli, also called Pompeiopŏlis; 2. Tarsus, *Tersus*, on the Cydnus, the Capital of Cilicia, (the birth-place of the Apostle Paul and many distinguished philosophers, celebrated for the study of philosophy and the liberal arts); 3. Issus, *ruins*, on the Issic Gulf, (battle, B.C. 333, Alexander defeated Darius).

GEOGRAPHY. 51

PHRYGIA with LYCAONIA. — *Cities.* — In the S.W. — On the Lycus: 1. Cŏlossæ, (to the inhabitants of which St. Paul addressed an epistle); 2. Laodicēa; 3. Apamēa Cibōtus. Near the centre: 1. Ipsus (battle, B.C. 301, Antigonus and Demetrius defeated by Lysimachus and Seleucus, the two other generals of Alexander); 2. Synnăda (famed for its marble). In Lycaonia: 1. Iconium; 2. Lystra; 3. Derbe (vide Acts xiv.).

GALATIA. — *Cities.* — On the Sangarius: 1. Gordium (the ancient Capital of Phrygia, where Alexander cut the famous "Gordian knot," on which its destinies were supposed to depend); 2. Pessīnus (the chief seat of the worship of Cybele, whose image was removed to Rome to satisfy an oracle in the Sibylline books). Near the centre: Ancȳra, *Angora,* (the Capital of the province in the time of Augustus).

CAPPADOCIA with ARMENIA MINOR. — *Cities.* — Near the centre, at the foot of Mons Argæus: Cæsarēa or Mazăca, *Kesarieh,* the chief city; S.W. of this, Tyăna, in the district Tyanītis, (the city of Apollonius the impostor). In Armenia Minor: 1. Nicopolis, *Devriki;* 2. Cabīra or Sebaste, *Sivas.*

THE SIX DORIAN STATES ("Hexapolis"), which met at the temple of Apollo at Triopium Prom., in Doris (vide Caria), were, 1. Lyndus; 2. Ialyssus; 3. Camīrus (in Rhodes); 4. Cos (in the island of Cos), 5. Cnidus; 6. Halicarnassus (in Caria); the last city was afterwards excluded from the number, the remaining five being termed "Pentapolis."

THE TWELVE IONIAN STATES, which held their meetings at the Panionium, near Mt. Mycăle, in Ionia (vide Lydia), were, 1. Miletus; 2. Myus; 3. Priēne (in Caria), 4. Ephesus; 5. Colophon; 6. Lĕbĕdos; 7. Teos; 8. Erythræ; 9. Clazŏmĕne; 10. Phocæa (in Lydia); 11. Chios, and 12. Samos; Smyrna from the Æolian colony increased the number to thirteen.

THE ÆOLIAN LEAGUE ("Panæoli͜m") possessed twelve cities, which met at Smyrna: 1. Cȳme; 2. Larissæ; 3. Neontīchos; 4. Temnus; 5. Cilla; 6. Notium; 7. Ægirūssa; 8. Pitane; 9. Ægææ; 10. Myrina; 11. Grynēa; 12. Smyrna (which subsequently became an Ionian colony).

THE "SEVEN CHURCHES OF ASIA."—1. Ephesus; 2. Smyrna; 3. Pergamos; 4. Thyatira; 5. Sardis; 6. Philadelphia; 7. Laodicea.

Island.

CYPRUS (sacred to Venus), separated from Asia Minor by Aulon Cilĭcius. *Towns.*—On the W. coast: 1. P a p h o s, *Baffa;* A m ă t h u s, *Limasol;* 2. C i t i u m (the birth-place of Zeno the Stoic philosopher); E., S a l ă m i s, (said to have been founded by Teucer); N., L a p ē t h u s and S o l i. Inland: 1. T a m ū s u s (famed for its copper-mines); 2. I d ă l ī u m (sacred to Venus). *Mountain.*—O l y m p u s.

SYRIA—PALÆSTINA.

BOUNDARIES.—N., A m ā n u s M o n s, and T a u r u s M o n s; E., R. E u p h r a t e s and A r a b i a; S., A r a b i a; W., M a r e I n t e r n u m, *Mediterranean.*

MOUNTAINS.—C a s i u s M o n s, *Jebel Okrah;* L e b ă n o n (famed for its snowy summits and its cedars), divided into L i b ă n u s on the W. and A n t i l ī b ă n u s on the E., to the E. Mt. H e r m o n. On the seá-coast: C a r m e l. Inland, in Galilee: Mt. T a b o r, Mt. H e r m o n, and Mt. G i l b o a. In Samaria: Mt. E b a l and Mt. G e r i z i m; (on the latter the Samaritans erected a temple to rival that at Jerusalem.) In Peræa: Mt. N e b o and Mt. A b a r i m.

RIVERS.—Falling into the Mediterranean: 1. O r o n t e s, *El Asy,* from the S.; 2. L e o n t e s. J o r d ā n e s, *Jordan,* from Hermon, flowing S., through, 1. S e m e c h ō n ī t i s L a c u s,

GEOGRAPHY.

Waters of Meron; 2. L. Tiberias vel L. Gennesăret, *Lake Chinnereth* or *Sea of Galilee,* falls into 3. Lacus Asphaltītes vel Mare Mortuum vel Salsum, *Dead Sea* or *Salt Sea.*

DIVISIONS.—1. Syria; 2. Phœnicia; 3. Palæstina.

SYRIA.—*Cities.*—On the coast: Seleucĭa Pieria, Capital of the district; Laodĭcēa, *Ladikeyeh.* Inland, on the Orontes: 1. Antiochīa, *Antioch,* the Capital, (where the disciples were first called *Christians);* 2. Epiphanēa, (O. T. Hamath), *Hamah;* Heliopŏlis or Balbec, near the source of the Leontes; (with a magnificent temple of the sun); to the S.E., Damascus, one of the most ancient cities in the world; E. of Antioch, Chalўbon or Berœa, *Aleppo.* In the Desert: Palmўra or Tadmor, (the city of Zēnŏbĭa, with whom Longinus the philosopher resided, destroyed A.D. 273). On the Euphrates: 1. Samosăta, *Someisat,* (the birth-place of Lucian); 2. Zeugma; 3. Thapsăcus, (famed for its ford, by which Cyrus in his expedition, Darius in his retreat, and Alexander previous to the battle of Arbela, crossed the Euphrates).

PHŒNICIA.—*Cities.*—On the coast: 1. Tripŏlis, *Tarabulus* or *Tripoli;* 2. Byblus, *Jebeil;* 3. Berytus, *Beirout;* 4. Sidon, *Saida,* (famed for its commerce and manufactures of glass); 5. Sarepta, for some time the residence of Elijah; 6. Tyrus, *Tyre* or *Sur,* (celebrated for its maritime wealth, enterprise, commerce, and colonizing activity: taken, B.C. 332, after a siege of seven months, by Alexander); 7. Ptolemais, *Acre,* one of the oldest Phœnician cities.

PALÆSTINA vel JUDÆA.—In Scripture called *Canaan, The Land of Promise, The Land of Israel,* and *The Holy Land.*

TRIBES.—W. of the Jordan: 1. Asher; 2. Naphthali; 3. Zebulon; 4. Issachar; 5. a half tribe of Manasseh;

GEOGRAPHY.

6. Ephraim; 7. Dan; 8. Simeon; 9. Benjamin; 10. Judah; E. of the Jordan: a half tribe of Manasseh, 11. Gad; 12. Reuben. After the death of Solomon the land was divided into the kingdoms of Israel and Judah

DIVISIONS.—1. N., Galilæa (divided into Galilæa Superior, *Galilee* of the *Gentiles*, and Galilæa Inferior *Lower Galilee*). 2. Centre: Samaria. 3. S.: Judæa. 4. Batanæa; 5. Peræa, both beyond the Jordan.

GALILEE.—*Cities.*—In the N.: Dan; E. of this, Cæsarēa Philippi vel Panēas, *Banias.* On the borders of the Sea of Galilee: 1. Capernaum (our Saviour's usual place of residence); 2. Bethsaida (the city of Peter, Andrew, and Philip); 3. Tiberias (built by Herod Antipas, in honour of Augustus Cæsar). W. of the Lake: Dio Cæsarea vel Sepphōris, *Sefurieh;* 2. Cana (where our Lord wrought his first miracle at the marriage-feast). S. of Cana: 1. Nazăreth (the residence of Joseph and Mary); 2. Nain, where the widow's son was restored to life.

SAMARIA. — *Cities.* — Near the centre: Samaria, aft. Sebaste, (founded by Omri, king of Israel; it was the Capital of the ten tribes until taken by Shalmaneser, king of Assyria, B.C. 721). S. of this, 1. Shechem or Sychar. afterwards Neapŏlis, *Nablous;* 2. Shiloh, (where Joshua erected the tabernacle); S.E., Archĕlāis, founded by Archelaus, son of Herod. On the coast: Cæsarēa, or Turris Stratonis, *Kaisariyeh,* (the residence of the Roman Procurators).

JUDÆA. — *Cities.* — On the coast: Joppa, *Jaffa,* a very ancient maritime city; in the N., Bethel, S.E. of this Jerĭcho or Hierĭchus, (taken and destroyed by Joshua); S. of Bethel, Emmaus, afterwards Nicopŏlis. W. of the northern extremity of the Dead Sea: Jerusălem vel Hiĕrŏsŏlўma (originally Jebus, the city of the Jebusites), the Capital of the Jewish nation from the time of

David, B.C. 1048; destroyed by Titus, A.D. 70; the city was situated on four hills, 1. Zion (or the Upper City), on which a fortress was erected by David; 2. Acra (or the Lower City); 3. Moriah, on which the temple was built; 4. Bezetha; at the foot of Mt. Moriah was the brook Kedron, which flowed into the Dead Sea; N.E. of Jerusalem, Bethany and the Mt. of Olives; S. from Jerusalem, 1. Bethlehem, the birth-place of David and of Our Blessed Saviour; 2. Hebron, the burial-place of Abraham, Isaac, and Jacob.

Five principal cities of the Philistines: 1. Gath; 2 Ekron or Accăron; 3. Azōtus or Ashdod, famed for its temple to Dagon; 4. Ascălon; 5. Gaza.

PERÆA and BATANÆA.—In Peræa: 1. Heshbon; 2. Ramoth Gilead; 3. Bethabara, on the Jordan. In Batanæa and N. of Peræa: DECAPOLIS, comprising, 1. Canatha; 2. Hippus; 3. Gadara; 4. Capitolias; 5. Abila; 6. Scythopolis; 7. Pella; 8. Gerasa; 9. Dium; 10. Philadelphia.

THE CITIES OF REFUGE.—W. of the Jordan: 1. Kedesh; 2. Shechem; 3. Hebron. E. of the Jordan: 4. Golan; 5. Ramoth Gilead; 6. Bezer.

SEVEN HEATHEN NATIONS.—1. The Hittites; 2. Girgashites; 3. Amorites; 4. Canaanites; 5. Perizzites; 6. Hivites; 7. Jebusites.

ARABIA.

Arabia.

BOUNDARIES.—N., Syria and Chaldæa; E., Sinus Persicus; S., Erythræum Mare, *Arabian Sea;* W, Ægyptus, *Egypt;* Sinus Arabicus, *Red Sea* or *Arabian Gulf;* Diræ, *Straits of Babel Mandel.*

MOUNTAINS. — In the N., between the two branches of the Red Sea: Mt. Sinai and Mt. Horeb; Mt. Hor, near Petra.

DIVISIONS. — N.W., ARABIA PETRÆA; W. and S., ARABIA FELIX; E. and in the interior, ARABIA DESERTA.

TRIBES, &c. — N., Idumæa; W., Nabathæi; S., Sabæi, Cap. Saba or Mariaba, O. T. Sheba. In Arabia Petræa: Petra. O. T. Tribes bordering on Palestine: Ammonites, Moabites, Midianites, Edomites, Amalekites.

COUNTRIES BETWEEN PONTUS EUXINUS, *Black Sea*, AND HYRCANUM MARE, *Caspian Sea.*

I. SARMATIA ASIATICA, *Circassia,* and S. E. part of *Russia* in *Europe.* — *Boundaries.* — N.E., R. Rha, *Volga;* S. E., Caspium Mare, *Caspian Sea;* S., Caucasus Mons; W., Pontus Euxinus, *Black Sea,* and R. Tanais, *Don.*

II. COLCHIS or ÆA, *Guriel, Imeritia,* and *Mingrelia.* — *Boundaries.* — N., Mons Caucasus; E., Iberia; S. Armenia; W., Pontus Euxinus.

Chief River. — Phāsis, *Faz* (which has given its name to the pheasant, said to have been first brought to Greece from its banks).

Towns. — On the Phasis: Cyta, (where Medēa was said to have been born). On the N. W. coast: Dioscūrĭas, *Iskuria,* (a considerable trading city).

III. IBERIA, *Georgia.* — *Boundaries.* — N., Caucasus; E., Albania; S., Armenia; W., Colchis (*inhabitants,* Ibēres or Ibēri).

Chief River. — Cyrus, *Kour,* (tributaries, Cambȳses and Alason).

Tribe. — W., Moschi.

IV. ALBANIA, *Shirvan* and part of *Daghistan.*—*Boundaries.*—N., Sarmatia Asiatica; E., Hyrcānum Mare; S., R. Cyrus, *Kour;* W., Iberia.
Mountain.—Caucasus Mons.

ARMENIA PROPRIA, vel MAJOR.
Armenia and part of Georgia.

BOUNDARIES.—N., Colchis, Iberia, and Albania: E., a point at the junction of the Araxes and Cyrus; S., Mēdĭa, Assyria, and Mesopotamia; W., R. Euphrates.

MOUNTAINS.—Mons Arărat, Imbarus Mons, Niphātes Montes.

RIVERS.—1. Araxes, *Aras* (rising in the country of the Chalȳbes), with its tributary, Harpăsus, falls into the Caspian; 2. Euphrātes, formed by two branches from the N. and E., and flow S., into Sinus Persicus, *The Persian Gulf;* 3. Tĭgris, with its tributaries, Nymphæus and Nicēphŏrius.

LAKE.—Arsissa Palus, *Lake Van.*

TOWNS.—On the Araxes: Artaxăta. On the Tigris: Amīda. On the Nicephorius: Tigranocerta (founded by Tigranes, son-in-law of Mithridātes, king of Pontus).

MESOPOTAMIA.
Algesira.

MESOPOTAMIA, so named from its position between the rivers Euphrates (W.) and Tigris (E.), was bounded on the N. by Masius Mons, Armenia, and Taurus Mons; S, by Babylonia.

GEOGRAPHY.

RIVER.—Chabŏras or Aborrhas, *Khabour* (a branch of the Euphrates).

DIVISIONS.—N.W., Osroēne; N.E., Mygdŏnĭa.

TOWNS.—On the Euphrates: 1. Nīcēphōrium, *Rakkah* (built by order of Alexander); 2. Cunaxa (battle, B.C. 401, Cyrus the Younger defeated and slain by Artaxerxes his brother. The Greek auxiliaries of Cyrus commence their return to Greece, usually called the retreat of the Ten Thousand). Between the two rivers: 1. Edessa, (O. T. Ur), *Urfah*, the Capital of Osroëne; 2. Charræ, the Haran of the O. T., (death of Crassus, and defeat by the Parthians, B.C. 53); 3. Nisĭbis, Cap. of Mygdonia, and a very important place as a military post.

BABYLONIA AND CHALDÆA.

Irak Arabi.

BOUNDARIES.—N., Mesopotamia; E., R. Tigris; S., Persicus Sinus; W., Arabia.

Cities.—Băbўlon, *ruins*, on the Euphrates, founded by Nimrod, about B.C. 2000, and taken by Cyrus, B.C. 538; it was built in the form of a quadrangle, on both sides of the Euphrates, and was distinguished for its extent and magnificence. Its chief buildings were: 1. The Tower of Belus; 2. The Old Royal Palace; 3. The New Palace, with the hanging gardens (*i.e.* gardens laid out in the form of terraces over arches). S. of Babylon: Borsippa (the chief residence of the Chaldæan astrologers), and Seleucĭa, on the Tigris, for a long time the Capital of W. Asia

COUNTRIES East of the EUPHRATES and TIGRIS.

I. ASSYRIA, *Koordistan.* — *Boundaries.* — N., Armenia; E., Media; S., Susiana; W., R. Tigris.

Rivers.—Flowing into the Tigris: Zabătus vel Lycus, *Zab;* Delas or Silla, *Diala.*

Divisions.—N., Aturia; Centre, Adiabēne; S., Sittacēne.

Cities.—On the Tigris: 1. Ninus or Nineveh, *near Mosul,* (the Capital of the great Assyrian monarchy, destroyed by the Medes and Babylonians, B.C. 606); 2. Ctesiphon (the usual winter residence of the Parthian monarchs). E. of the Tigris: Gaugamēla, (the scene of the last and decisive battle between Alexander and Darius, B.C. 331, usually called the battle of Arbēla, from its proximity to that town).

II. MEDIA, *North-west part of modern Persia, Irak.* — *Boundaries.* — N., Armenia, R. Araxes, and Caspium Mare; E., Hyrcānia and Aria; S., Persia and Susiana; W., Assyria.

Divisions.—N., Atropatēne; *Chief Town,* Gaza. S., Media Magna.

Chief Towns.—Ecbătăna, *Humadan,* (near Mt. Orontes, the residence of the Median, and latterly of the Persian kings. The city was built without walls, on the slope of a hill, on the summit of which stood the royal castle, surrounded by seven walls, with battlements). N.E. of Ecbătăna: Κάσπιαι πύλαι, a mountain-pass; near this the Nicæan plains, famed for the breed of white horses.

III. SUSIANA or SUSIS, *Khuzistan.* — *Boundaries.* — N., Assyria; E., Persia; S., Sinus Persicus; W., R. Tigris.

Rivers.—Choaspes, *Kerah;* Coprātes, *Abzal;* and Pasi-Tigris, *Karoon* (?), fall into the Tigris.

Tribes.—Cossæ, Elamītæ.
Capital.—Susa (O. T. Shushan), on the Chŏaspes (the winter residence of the Persian monarchs).

IV. PERSIA or PERSIS, *Persia.*—*Boundaries.*—N., Media; E., Carmania; S., Sinus Persicus; W., Susiāna.

Cities.—Persepŏlis (the burial-place of the Persian kings); Pasargăda (founded by Cyrus the Great, in memory of his victory over Astȳăges, the last king of Media, B.C. 559).

COUNTRIES SOUTH OF THE R. OXUS, *Jihon.*

I. HYRCANIA, *Astrabad.*—*Boundaries.*—N. and E., Parthia; S., Media; W., Caspium Mare.

II. PARTHIA, *Khorassan* (inhabited by a very warlike people).—*Boundaries.*—N., Scythia; E., Aria; S. and S.W., Media; W., Hyrcania.
Capital.—Hecatompȳlus (founded by Arsaces).

III. ARIA or ARIANUS, East part of *Khorassan* and N. of *Afghanistan.*—*Boundaries.*—N., Parthia; E., Bactriana and Indo-Scythia; S., Gedrosia; W., Carmania and Media.
Divisions.—N., Margiana (famed for its wine); Centre, Drangiana (*River:* Etymandrus, flowing into Aria Palus, *Lake Zurrah*); S., Arachosia.
Tribe.—Paropamisădæ (at the foot of Paropamisus Mons vel Caucasus, *Hindoo-Koosh.*
Capital.—Aria vel Artacoana, *Herat.*

IV. BACTRIANA or BACTRIA, *Bokhara.*—*Boundaries.*—N., Oxus, *R. Jihon;* E. and S., Paropamisus Mons, *Hindoo-Koosh;* W., Aria.

GEOGRAPHY.

Capital. — Backtra, *Balk* (the winter-quarters of Alexander, B.C. 329).

V. CARMANIA, *Kirman.*—*Boundaries.*—E., Aria and Gedrosia; S., Sinus Persicus; W. and N.W., Persia.
Divisions.—Carmania Propria and Carmania Deserta.
Capital.—Caramāna, *Kirman.*

VI. GEDROSIA, *Beloochistan.* — *Boundaries.* — N., Aria; E., Paropamisus Mons, *Hala Mts.;* S., Erythræum Mare, *Arabian Sea;* W., Carmania.
Mountains.—Parsici Montes, near the centre.
Tribes.—Ichthyophagi, Oritæ, and Arabitæ, on the coast.
Capital.—Pūra.

COUNTRIES NORTH OF THE OXUS.

I. SOGDIANA, part of *Turkestan* and *Bokhara.*—*Boundaries.*—N., R. Jaxartes, *Sihon* or *Sirr;* E., Imaus Mons; S., R. Oxus, *Jihon* or *Amou;* W., Sea of Aral (unknown to the ancients.)
Cities.—Maracanda, *Samarkand* (the Capital); Cyropolis, on the Jaxartes (founded by Cyrus).

II. SCYTHIA (*Independent Tartary* and *Mongolia*), the name given to the large tract of country N. of the Caspian Sea, R. Jaxartes, and Emōdi Montes, *Himalaya Mts.*, and E. of Sogdiana and Bactriāna. Scythia was divided by Imaus Mons, *Altai Mts.*, into Scythia intra Imaum, on the N.W., and Scythia extra Imaum, on the S.E.
Tribes, &c.—Săcæ and Massăgĕtæ; E. of Scythia extra Imaum, Serica, *N.W. part of China*, inhabitants the Sēres, famous for their manufactures of silk (the country was regarded as the native region of the silk-worm.)

INDIA.

Hindostan, Birmah, Siam, Cochin China, and Malaya.

BOUNDARIES.—N., Emŏdi Montes, *Himalaya Mts.*, and Scythia; S., Gangetĭcus Sinus, *Bay of Bengal*, and Indicus Oceanus, *Indian Ocean;* W., Erythræum Mare, *Arabian Sea*, and Paropamisus Mons, *Hala* and *Soliman Mts.*

RIVERS.—I. N.W., Indus, *Indus*, with its five tributary streams: 1. Hydaspes, *Jelum;* 2. Acĕsines, *Chenaub;* 3. Hydraōtes, *Ravee;* 4. Hyphăsis, *Gharra* or *Beeas;* 5. Zaradrus, *Sutlej.* II. Ganges, *Ganges.* III. Dyardanes or Œdones, *Burrampooter.*

DIVISIONS.—W. of the Ganges, India intra Gangem; E. of the Ganges, India extra Gangem.

TOWNS, &c.—On the Indus: Taxĭla, *Attock* (near which Alexander crossed the river). On the Hydaspes: Bucephăla, *Jelum* (built by Alexander, in memory of his favourite horse Bucĕphălus, which died and was buried here, B.C. 327). Malli, a tribe on each side of the Acĕsines, *Chenaub;* their Capital is supposed to have been on the site of the fortress of Moultan. On the Ganges: Palĭbŏthra, *Patna*, the Capital of the Prasii.

ISLANDS, &c.—Taprobăne vel Salice, *Ceylon;* Jabadii Ins., *Sumatra;* Aurea Chersonēsus *Malaya;* E. of which, Magnus Sinus, *Gulf of Siam.*

AFRICA.

BOUNDARIES.—N., Mare Internum, *Mediterranean;* E., Arabia, Sinus Arabicus, *Red Sea,* and Erythræum Mare, *Arabian Sea;* W., Mare Atlanticum, *Atlantic Ocean.*

BAYS.—Syrtis Major, *Gulf of Sidra;* Syrtis Minor, *Gulf of Cabes.*

STRAIT.—Fretum Herculeum vel Gaditānum, *Straits of Gibraltar.*

RIVERS.—Nilus, *Nile,* remarkable for its periodical inundations; some few miles below Memphis the river divided into three branches, but now into two, E., Ostium Phatnitĭcum, at *Damietta,* W., Ostium Bolbitīnum, at *Rosetta,* which flows through a low land, called from its shape (resembling the fourth letter of the Greek language) "Delta," and fell into the Mediterranean. The seven ancient mouths, from E. to W., were: 1. Pelusiac; 2. Saitic; 3. Mendesian; 4. Phatnitic, or Bucolic; 5. Sebennytic; 6. Bolbitic; 7. Canopic. Of these the fourth and sixth were artificial.

LAKES.—Near the western mouth of the Nile, L. Mareotis; S. of this, L. Mœris. E. of the Nile, L. Sirbōnis.

ÆGYPTUS.

Egypt.

BOUNDARIES.—N., Mediterranean; E., Arabia and Sinus Arabicus, *Red Sea;* S., Æthiopia; W., Libya.

DIVISIONS.—1. N., Ægyptus Inferior or Delta; 2. Middle: Heptanŏmis; 3. S., Ægyptus Superior vel Thebāis.

ÆGYPTUS INFERIOR vel DELTA.—*Cities.*—Between L. Mareotis and the Sea, Alexandria, with two harbours (the Capital of Egypt under the Ptolemies, founded by Alexander, B.C. 332, and famous for its learning and commerce; the library is said to have contained 400,000 volumes). Opposite to Alexandria: the island Pharos, with a famous light-house, built by Ptolemy Philadelphus, B.C. 283. E. of Alexandria: Canōpus, near *Aboukir* (its inhabitants were proverbial for their luxury). In the Delta: 1. Naucratis, founded by the Milesians, the only place in Egypt where Greeks were permitted to settle and trade); 2. Sais (the ancient Capital of Lower Egypt—it contained the palace and burial-place of the Pharaohs); 3. Busīris, with the temple of Isis; 4. Būto (with an oracle of the Egyptian goddess Buto). E. of the Delta: 1. Pelūsium (surrounded by swamps, and called, from its situation, the Key of Egypt); E. of this, Casius Mons, with a temple of Jupiter; here also was the grave of Pompey; 2. Heliŏpŏlis, or On, O.T. (with a celebrated temple, the chief seat of the worship of the Sun); 3. Bubastis (where the great annual festival to the goddess Bubastis, or the Moon, was held).

HEPTANOMIS.— *Cities.* — On the W. side of the Nile: 1. Memphis or Moph, the Capital (near which were the celebrated Pyramids): of its splendid buildings the chief were, the Palace of the Pharaohs and the temples of Apis and Serapis; 2. Crocŏdīlŏpŏlis or Arsĭnŏë

GEOGRAPHY.

(the chief seat of the worship of the Crocodile): near this, the famous Labyrinthus, containing 3000 apartments, in which the kings and sacred crocodiles were buried; 3. Oxyrhyncus, *Behneseh*, so called from the fish of that name there worshipped.

ÆGYPTUS SUPERIOR vel THEBAIS. — *Cities.* — On the W. side of the Nile: 1. Ptolemāis, *Menshieh* (an important city under the Ptolemies); 2. Abȳdos, with a Memnonium, (i. e. a building erected by, or in honour of Memnon), and a temple of Osīris; 3. Thebæ vel Diospŏlis, on both sides of the Nile, Capital of Thebāis, and the most ancient residence of the Egyptian kings: this city, called the hundred-gated. (ἑκατόμπυλοι), possessed many magnificent buildings, the ruins of which now enclose a space two miles in length; 4. Elephantīne, and 5. Philæ, on two small islands, with many architectural remains. On the E. side of the Nile: 1. Syēne, *Assouan*, the S. frontier city of Egypt; 2. Coptos, *Koft*, (the central point of commerce between India and Arabia, by way of Berenice, on the Arabian Gulf).

At the N. of the Red Sea: Cleopatris vel Arsĭnŏē, *Suez.*

South of Egypt: Æthiopia, *Nubia, Senaar, Kordofan,* and *Abyssinia.*

Rivers. — Astăpus and Astabōras, flowing into the Nile.

City. — Mĕrŏē (the Capital of the powerful kingdom of Meroe), with a famous oracle of Ammon.

NORTHERN COASTS OF AFRICA.

DIVISIONS. — I. Libya, *Barca*, with the provinces; 1. Marmarĭca; 2. Cyrenaĭca. II. Tripolitana vel Regio Syrtica, *Tripoli.* III. Africa Propria, *Tunis*, with Zeugitāna and Byzacium vel Emporia. IV. Numidia,

Algiers. V. Mauritania, *Morocco* and *Fez*, divided into Mauritania Cæsariensis, E., and Mauritania Tingitāna, W.

LIBYA, *Barca.* — *Towns.* — In Marmarica. — On the coast: Parætonium, *El-Bareton;* S. of this, Oāsis of Ammon, famous for its temple, visited by Alexander; W. of Parætonium, Catabathmos, generally considered the boundary between Egypt and Cyrenaïca. In Cyrenaïca: Cyrēnē, the chief city (founded by Battus, B.C. 631), the birth-place of Aristippus, the philosopher, and Callimachus, the poet; S.W. of Cyrēne, Barce, *Barca,* chief town of the Barcitæ. On the coast: 1. Ptolemais; 2. Berenīce, the fabled site of the Gardens of the Hesperides.

TRIPOLITANI, *Tripoli.*—*Towns.*—On the coast: 1. Leptis Magna vel Neapolis; 2. Oea, *Tripoli;* 3. Sabrăta (these three cities formed the African Tripolis).

Tribe. — On the coast: Lotophagi or Eaters of the Lotus, the taste of which was so delicious, that those who eat of the fruit lost all desire to return to their native country.

AFRICA PROPRIA, *Tunis,* divided into Byzacium and Zeugītana. — *Towns.* — In Byzacium. — On the coast: 1. Tacăpe, *Cabes;* 2. Thapsus, *Demas* (battle, B.C. 46, Cæsar defeated the Pompeian army); 3. Leptis Minor, *Lamta;* 4. Hadrumētum (the Capital of Byzacium under the Romans). Inland: Tritōnis Palus, *El Sibkah* (in which Minerva is said to have been born, and hence called "Tritonia"). In Zeugitana. — On the coast: 1. Tunes, *Tunis;* 2. Carthāgo, the Capital of Africa, situated at the head of a bay, formed by two promontories, Hermæum Prom., *C. Bon,* and Apollinis Prom., *C. Farina.* The Tyrian colony of Carthage was said to have been founded by Dido, about B.C. 853 — its citadel was termed Byrsa (Βύρσα, "a hide"), in reference to the manner in which the portion of land for building the first city was

GEOGRAPHY.

obtained by Dido (destroyed, B.C. 146, by Scipio Africanus the Younger); 2. U t i c a, near the mouth of the Bagrădas, the second city in Africa, and even more ancient than Carthage (the birth-place of Cato, whence he received the surname of Uticensis). Inland: Z a m a (battle, B.C. 202, Hannibal defeated by Scipio, and the Second Punic war ended).

NUMIDIA, E. part of *Algiers.*— *Town.*— C i r t a, the Capital, the city of Syphax and Masinissa.
Tribe.— Massyli.

MAURITANIA, *Morocco, Fez,* and part of *Algiers.*— *Towns.* — On the coast: 1. C a r t e n n a, *Tennez;* 2. S ī ga; 3. T i n- g i s, *Tangier;* 4. S a l a, *Sallee.* S. of Mauritania: A t l a s M o n s, *Mt. Atlas. Tribes.*— S. of Atlas Mons, Numidia and Africa Propria, G æ t u l i, E. of which G a r a m a n t e s, dwelling in the region Phazania, *Fezzan,* Cap. Garăma, *Mourzouk.*

ISLANDS. — In the Atlantic: I n s u l æ P u r p u r ā r ī æ, pro- bably the *Madeira,* S. of which I n s u l æ F o r t u n a t æ, Canary islands, in which the ancients supposed the Elysian fields to be situated; H e s p e r i d u m I n s u l æ, *Cape Verde Islands,* or the *Bissagos* group.

MYTHOLOGY.

THE TWELVE OLYMPIAN OR NATIONAL DEITIES OF THE GREEKS AND ROMANS.

JUPITER (Ζεύς), son of Saturn and Ops, king of gods and men, and the most powerful of all the deities. He was educated in a cave on Mount Ida. When a year old he made war against the Titans, in the cause of his father Saturn, and liberated him. He is usually represented as sitting on an ivory or golden throne, holding in his hand thunderbolts. He bore a shield or goat-skin called Ægis.

NEPTUNE (Ποσειδῶν), son of Saturn and Ops, and chief deity of the sea; he was on this account entitled to more power than any other god except Jupiter. He is represented as carrying the trident, or three-pronged spear, attended by dolphins. Amphitrīte was his queen.

VULCAN (Ἥφαιστος), son of Juno; the god of fire, and patron of all workers in iron and metals: his palace, which was in Olympus, contained his workshop, in which he made many ingenious and marvellous works, both for gods and men. His abode is said by some to have been in a volcanic island. The Cyclops were his workmen.

MARS (Ἄρης), the god of war; son of Jupiter and Juno. He presided over gladiators, and was the patron of manly and warlike exercises. He is generally represented as riding in a chariot, drawn by furious horses, called *Flight* and *Terror*. In the Trojan war he is said to have taken the part of the Trojans In Rome he received the most unbounded honours.

MYTHOLOGY.

MERCURIUS ('Ερμῆς), son of Jupiter and Maia; messenger of the gods, and deity of eloquence, commerce, and the a ts. He conducted the souls of the dead into the lower world, and is usually represented with a winged hat and sandals, bearing the *caduceus* in his hand. Hermēs was born on Mount Cyllēne, in Arcadia.

APOLLO, son of Jupiter and Latona; god of music, medicine, augury, painting, poetry, and all the fine arts. He was born, with his sister Diana, near Mount Cynthus, in Delos, an island in the Ægean Sea. When he grew up he slew the serpent Python, which infested the country near Delphi, and established the famous oracle. He received the surname of Phœbus from his connexion with the Sun (Φοῖβος, the bright).

JUNO ("Ηρα or "Ηρη), the daughter of Saturn and Ops, sister and wife of Jupiter, and queen of all the gods. She was born at Argos (some say Samos), and is noted for her jealousy and severity to the illegitimate children of Jupiter.

MINERVA or ATHENA ('Αθήνη or 'Αθηνᾶ, Πάλλας), daughter of Jupiter, said to have sprung from his forehead completely armed. She was goddess of wisdom, war, and the liberal arts, the guardian and aider of heroes, and presiding goddess of Athens. She is always represented with a helmet, breast-plate (or Ægis), and shield; on the latter was the Gorgon's head. Her favourite bird was the owl, which was sacred to her.

VESTA ('Εστία), the goddess of the hearth, and also of fire. Her worship was introduced into Italy by Æneas. The fire on the altar in her temple was never allowed to go out; but, when such was the case, it was kindled again by the rays of the sun. The priestesses dedicated to her service were called *Vestals*.

CERES (Δημήτηρ), daughter of Saturn and Rhea (or Ops); goddess of corn and plenty, the same as Isis of the Egyptians. She was mother of Proserpine, and is represented holding a sceptre or torch, and a garland of ears of corn round her head.

VENUS ('Αφροδίτη), daughter of Jupiter and Dione and wife of Vulcan, the goddess of love and beauty, queen of laughter, and mistress of the graces and pleasures. Venus is supposed to have sprung from the foam of the sea near the island of Cyprus or Cythera. In the contest for the golden apple of beauty, Paris awarded it to Venus, in preference to Pallas and Juno. Her favourite birds were swans and doves, her sacred flowers the rose and myrtle.

DIANA ('Αρτεμις), daughter of Jupiter and Latona, and sister of Apollo; the goddess of woods and hunting. On earth she was called Diana, in heaven Luna, in the lower world Proserpina or Hĕcăte.

Note. — The deities of the Romans were adapted to those of the Greeks, with which they do not entirely correspond.

MINOR DEITIES.

ÆOLUS, a king of the Æolian Islands. He is fabled to be the god of the winds, from his foretelling the changes of the winds and weather.

ÆSCULAPIUS ('Ασκληπιος), the god of medicine, instructed in this science by Chīron. He was worshipped throughout Greece; and his temples, which were built in healthy places, on hills, or near wells, were not only places of worship, but frequented by sick persons.

AMMON, a surname of Jupiter, worshipped in Libya, and afterwards in Egypt.

AMPHITRITE, a NEREID or OCEANID, wife of Neptune, and goddess of the sea.

APIS, the bull of Memphis, worshipped by the Egyptians. He was allowed to live but about twenty-five years, and was then slain and secretly buried; but if he died a natural death, he was buried publicly, with great solemnity.

ASTRÆA, daughter of Zeus and Thĕmis; goddess of justice She lived on earth during the golden age; but the wickedness of mankind drove her to heaven during the brazen and iron ages. She was placed among the constellations, under the name of Virgo, and is represented holding a pair of scales in one hand, and a sword in the other.

AURORA (*Eōs*, Ἐως), the goddess of the morning, daughter of Hyperion, and wife of Tithonus son of Laomedon. She is represented as setting out before Helios her brother, drawn in a chariot by four white steeds, and dispelling darkness and sleep.

BACCHUS (*Dionȳsus*, Διόνυσος), the god of wine, son of Jupiter and Sĕmĕle the daughter of Cadmus of Thebes. He is usually represented as an effeminate youth, crowned with ivy and vine leaves.

BELLONA, the Roman goddess of war, and companion of Mars. She is usually described as his wife, and represented armed with a scourge, to animate the combatants.

CUPIDO or AMOR (Ἔρως), the god of love; the son of Venus and Zeus (some relate of Mars and Mercury). He is usually represented as carrying a bow and arrows, which he darts into the bosoms of gods and men.

FAUNI, rural deities, represented as half men and half goats.

FLORA, the goddess of flowers among the Romans.

FORTUNA (Τύχη), daughter of Oceanus; the goddess of fortune. From her were derived riches and poverty, pleasures and misfortunes. The Romans paid great attention to this goddess, and had eight temples dedicated to her at Rome.

FURIÆ or DIRÆ, called by the Greeks Erīnyes (Ἐρινύες) or Eumĕnĭdes (Εὐμενίδες), three goddesses sprung from Gē and the blood of Urānus, namely, *Tisiphŏne, Alecto*, and *Megœra*. They haunted the impious with remorse for their crimes.

GE or GÆA (Γῆ or Γαῖα), also called by the Romans TELLUS and TERRA, was the personification of the earth, and as such was worshipped by the ancients as a deity.

GENIUS, the guardian or protecting spirit of each man's life. Such spirits were called by the Greeks δαίμονες, by the Romans *Genii*, and were regarded as the ministers of Zeus, and guardians of men and justice. Hesiod numbers the Dæmones at 30,000.

GRATIÆ, the three goddesses presiding over all elegant arts and social enjoyments. They are generally represented dancing. Their names were *Aglaia* (splendour), *Euphrŏsÿne* (joy), *Thalīa* (pleasure).

HADES or PLUTO ('Αἰδης), god of the (*unseen* or) nether world. He is also known as *Orcus, Tartarus*, and *Dis*. The word Hades is also frequently used to designate the infernal regions.

HEBE vel JUVENTAS, daughter of Jupiter and Juno; the goddess of youth. She was for some time cup-bearer to the gods, to which office Ganymēde succeeded; she was also employed by Juno in preparing her chariot, &c. She was supposed to have the power of making aged persons young again.

HECATE, a Titan goddess, whose power extended over heaven, earth, and sea. Also a name for Diana or Proserpĭna.

HELIOS, called SOL by the Romans, god of the sun; brother of Aurora.

HORÆ, daughters of Zeus and Thĕmis. Originally the goddesses of the seasons, but in later times of order and justice. They were three in number, *Eunŏmia* (good order), *Dikĕ* (justice), *Irēne* (peace).

HYGIEA or HYGEA, the goddess of health; daughter of Æsculapius. She is represented as a virgin, draped in a long robe, and feeding a serpent from a cup.

HYMEN vel HYMENÆUS, the god of marriage; described by some as the son of Bacchus and Venus, by others as the son of Apollo and one of the Muses.

IRIS, the goddess of the rainbow, and the messenger of the deities, particularly of Juno.

ISIS, a celebrated deity of the Egyptians, described as the wife of Osīris; goddess of the earth, and deity of the moon; inventor of the cultivation of wheat and barley.

JANUS, a Roman deity; god of the temple of war. He is represented with two faces, sometimes with four heads. Numa dedicated a temple to Janus, open in times of war, and closed in times of peace.

MYTHOLOGY.

LARES, inferior gods at Rome, who presided over houses and families, and were divided into *Lares publici* and *Lares domestici;* all the latter were headed by the *Lar familiaris*, regarded as the founder of the family. Their images stood on the hearth, and offerings were made to them daily.

LUNA or SELENE, daughter of Hypĕrīon; the goddess of the moon, identified afterwards with Diana.

MANES, the general name for the souls of the departed. They were regarded as gods, and received divine honours.

MOMUS, the god of pleasantry, wit, and satire; driven from heaven by the gods for turning all their actions into ridicule.

MORPHEUS, son of the deity Somnus, and god of dreams.

MUSÆ, goddesses who presided over poetry, &c. They were the daughters of Jupiter and Mnēmŏsȳne (Memory), and nine in number: 1. *Clio*, the muse of History; 2. *Euterpe*, of Lyric Poetry; 3. *Thălia*, of Comedy; 4. *Melpŏmĕne*, of Tragedy; 5. *Terpsichŏre*, of Choral Dance; 6. *Erāto*, of Amatory Poetry; 7. *Pŏlyhymnia*, of Rhetoric and Eloquence; 8. *Urănia*, of Astronomy; 9. *Callĭŏpe*, Epic Poetry. At the Olympian banquets they sang to Apollo's lyre. Their favourite haunts were the hills Pindus, Helicon, and Parnassus.

NEMESIS, daughter of Nox, goddess of vengeance, and always prepared to punish the wicked and reward the good.

NEREUS, a deity of the sea, and father of the fifty Nerĕīdes. He is represented as an old man, and described as the wise old man of the sea, at the bottom of which he dwelt.

NYMPHÆ, a numerous class of female deities, generally divided into two classes, viz. *land* and *water nymphs*. The chief land nymphs were: 1st, Orēădes, of the mountains and grottoes; 2d, Năpææ, of the forests, glens, and groves; 3d, Drȳădes and Hamadryades, of the woods and trees. The chief water nymphs were: 1st, Oceănĭdes, or ocean nymphs, three thousand in number; 2d, Nerĕīdes, or sea nymphs, fifty in number (among them we find Amphitrīte, Thĕtis, and Galatea); 3d, Näiădes, a general name for those nymphs presiding over either rivers, lakes, brooks, or springs; 4th, Potamēīdes, or river nymphs.

OCEANUS, the god of water; son of Urănus and Gē; represented as an old man, sitting on the waves of the sea.

OSIRIS, a great Egyptian divinity, husband of Isis, and god of the Nile. He taught the use of the plough, and is sometimes represented as the deity of the sun.

PALES, the divinity of sheep-folds and pastures among the Romans.

PAN, the god of shepherds; son of Hermēs. He was usually represented as a monster with two small horns on his head, ruddy complexion, flat nose, and with the legs, tail, and feet of a goat. He resided chiefly in Arcadia, and is said to have invented the pipe with seven reeds, called Sȳrinx, from a nymph of that name whom he loved.

PAX, the Roman goddess of peace; daughter of Zeus and Thĕmis.

PENATES, the household gods of the Romans, called *Penates* from being placed in the innermost part (*in penitissima parte*) of the house; they were generally made of wax, ivory, silver, or clay.

PHŒBE, a name given to Diana as goddess of the moon (Luna); Apollo, her brother, being surnamed Phœbus, god of the sun.

PHŒBUS, expressive of brightness, a surname given to Apollo as god of the sun.

PLUTO, the son of Saturn and Rhea; god of the infernal regions. He is described as gloomy and inexorable; on which account, as none of the goddesses would marry him, he bore off Proserpine by force. He is also known as Orcus, Hades, Dis, &c.

PLUTUS, son of Ceres and Iasion; the god of wealth. Jupiter is said to have deprived him of sight, that he might not bestow his gifts on the righteous alone.

POMONA, the goddess of fruits among the Romans.

PRIAPUS, a deity who presided over gardens, and was worshipped as a protector of flocks, goats, bees, and fishing.

PROSERPINA vel PERSEPHONE, daughter of Jupiter and Ceres, and wife of Pluto as queen of the lower world. She presided over the death of mankind.

MYTHOLOGY.

PROTEUS, a sea deity (the prophetic old man of the sea), remarkable for his custom of assuming different forms when consulted. He is described as a subject of Neptune, whose flocks (the seals) he tended.

PARCÆ vel MOIRÆ, the Fates, powerful goddesses, who presided over the life and death of mankind. They were three in number, viz.: *Clotho*, or the *spinning* fate, who presided at the birth; *Lachesis*, who spun out all the events of each man's life, and assigned his *lot* or fate; *Atrŏpos*, the *inflexible* fate that cannot be avoided, who cut the thread of life.

SATURNUS (Κρόνος), a son of Cœlus and Uranus, and the father of Jupiter. As the god of time he is represented as an old man, holding a scythe in his right hand.

SILENUS, a rural deity; an attendant on Bacchus. Usually represented in a state of intoxication, and never seen without his wine-bag.

SILVANUS, a Roman deity, who presided over the woods and forests.

THEMIS, daughter of Uranus and Ge; the mother of Astræa, Irene, the Parcæ, &c., &c. She is the personification of Law and Equity.

THETIS, one of the sea deities or Nereides (daughters of Nereus), and the mother of Achilles.

URANUS, CŒLUS, or HEAVEN, a Titan; the most ancient of all the gods; father of Saturn, Oceanus, &c.

VERTUMNUS, the Roman deity who presided over plants and flowers.

HEROES, MYTHICAL PERSONS, &c.

ACHERON, a river of the lower world, over which the dead were first conveyed: the word is sometimes used to designate the whole of the infernal regions.

ADMETUS, son of Pheres and Periclymene, king of Pheræ, in Thessaly, husband of Alcestis, and one of the Argonauts.

ADONIS, a beautiful youth, the favourite of Venus; at his death she transformed him into the flower called Anemone.

ÆACUS, son of Zeus and Ægina: he was so famed throughout Greece for his justice and piety, that he was called upon to settle the disputes not only of men, but sometimes of the gods; on his death he became one of the three judges in Hades.

ÆGÆON (vide Briareus).

ALCESTIS, daughter of Pelias, and wife of Admetus, who having on the day of his marriage neglected to sacrifice to Artemis, Apollo reconciled the offended goddess, and induced the Fates to deliver Admetus from death, if his father, mother, or wife, would die for him; Alcestis died in his stead, but was brought back from the lower world by Hercules.

AMAZONES, a nation of female warriors, said to have come from the Caucasus, and settled near the river Thermōdon, in Pontus; Hippŏlўte was their queen.

ARIADNE, daughter of Minos and Creta; she fell in love with Theseus, who married her, but afterwards forsook her.

ATLAS, one of the Titans, who is generally represented as supporting the world on his shoulders; which task was allotted him in consequence of his having, with the other Titans, made war upon Zeus (vide Titānes).

BELLEROPHON, son of Glaucus a Corinthian king. To be purified from the murder of his brother Bellerus, he fled to Prœtus, king of Argos, by whom he was sent to Iobātes, king of Lycia, his father-in-law, who ordered him to slay the monster Chimæra, thinking he would perish in the contest; but Bellĕrŏphon, having obtained the aid of Pegăsus, the winged horse, conquered the Chimæra: he was also sent against the Amazons, and encountered the bravest of the Lycians, always returning victorious. Iobātes, seeing it was hopeless to kill the hero, made him his successor, and gave him his daughter in marriage. Some relate that Bellĕrŏphon attempted to fly to heaven on Pegăsus, but Zeus sent a gad-fly to sting the horse, which threw off the

MYTHOLOGY. 77

rider, who became lame or blind, and wandered about the earth till the day of his death.

BRIAREUS vel ÆGEON, a famous giant, who had 100 hands and fifty heads, called by men Ægæon, and only by the gods Briareus. He is said to have conquered the Titans, when they made war on the gods.

CALYPSO, one of the ocean nymphs who dwelt in the mythical island of Ogȳgĭa, on which Ulysses was shipwrecked.

CASTOR, son of Jupiter and brother of Pollux, distinguished for his skill and management of horses. Castor and his brother enjoyed immortality, and were called the *Dioscŭri*.

CENTAURI, a race inhabiting Mount Pelion, in Thessaly, represented as half men and half horses; Chiron was the most celebrated of the Centaurs (vide Pīrĭthŏus).

CERBERUS, the dog of Pluto: he guarded the entrance to Hades, and is said by some to have had fifty heads, by others only three; his den was near the spot where Charon landed the dead.

CHARON, a son of Erĕbus (darkness): he conducted the souls of the departed in a boat over the rivers Achĕron and Styx to the lower regions, for an obolus (about 1½d.); as all the dead were obliged to pay, a small coin was usually placed in the mouth of the deceased.

CHIRON, the most celebrated of the Centaurs: he lived on Mt. Pelion, and was famed for his knowledge of hunting, medicine, music, and prophecy; he instructed the chief heroes of his age, namely, Hercules, Jason, Achilles, Peleus, &c., and was wounded accidentally in the knee by a poisoned arrow shot by Hercules in his contest with the Centaurs. After his death, Chiron was placed among the constellations by Zeus.

CIRCE, a mythical sorceress, daughter of Sol and Perseus, celebrated for her knowledge of magic and venomous herbs.

COCYTUS, a river in Epirus, and tributary of the Acheron; it was supposed to be connected with the lower world, and hence was described as one of the five rivers of hell.

7 *

CYCLOPES, a race of men of gigantic stature; they had but one *circular* eye in the centre of their forehead, whence the name Κύκλωπες; they were three in number according to Hesiod, and called *Arges, Brontes,* and *Steropes;* but this number was afterwards increased.

DÆDALUS, the most ingenious artist of his time: he invented sails for ships, and made wings with wax and feathers for himself and son Icarus; with these they took flight from Crete: but the heat of the sun melted the wax on the wings of Icarus, and he fell into the part of the ocean called after him the Icarian Sea.

DAPHNE, daughter of the river-god Penēus in Thessaly or Ladon in Arcadia: she was much beloved by Apollo, and fearful of being caught by him, was changed into a laurel tree, which thence became the favourite tree of Apollo.

DEUCALION, son of Prometheus, and king of Phthia in Thessaly, saved with his wife Pyrrha, on account of their piety, when Zeus destroyed by a flood the race of men. On the waters subsiding, Deucalion and Pyrrha offered a sacrifice, and consulted the oracle of Themis how the human race might be restored; the oracle ordered them to cast behind them the bones of their mother, which they interpreting to be the Earth, threw stones behind their backs, when those thrown by Deucalion turned into men, and those by Pyrrha into women.

ELYSIUM, a place in the lower world, the abode of the virtuous after death: the Elysian regions are placed by some in the middle region of the air or ocean; by others in the moon and sun; and by others in the centre of the earth, near *Tartărus.*

ENDYMION, a youth celebrated for his beauty and perpetual sleep.

EREBUS (signifying darkness), a deity of hell; the word is applied to the gloomy regions, the abode of the wicked as well as of the good, and is distinguished both from Tartărus and Elysĭum.

EUROPA, daughter of Agenor, king of Phœnicia: her beauty captivated Zeus, who, taking the form of a bull, mingled with the herd of Agenor; when Europa, encouraged by the tameness of the animal, mounted his back, whereupon Zeus rushed into the sea and swam with her in safety to Crete, where she became the mother of Minos, Rhadamar. thus, and Sarpēdon.

GIGANTES, the giants, sons of heaven and earth, a savage race, destroyed on account of their insolence to the gods.

GORGONES, three celebrated sisters, daughters of Phorcys the sea deity; their names were *Stheno, Eurўāle*, and *Medūsa*; they were frightful creatures, and instead of hair their heads were covered with serpents; they had wings, brazen claws, and enormous teeth. Perseus slew Medūsa, whose head was placed in the centre of Minerva's shield, and had the power of turning all that looked at it into stone.

HARPYIÆ, winged monsters, with the face of a woman and body of a vulture; they were three in number, *Aello, Celæno*, and *Ocўpete*.

HERACLYDÆ, a name given to the descendants of Hercules, who, with the Dorians, conquered the Peloponnesus (B. C. 1104).

HERCULES, the most celebrated hero of antiquity: he was the son of Jupiter and Alcmēna, and born at Thebes. Juno early plotted his destruction, and her cruelty rendered him subject to the will of Eurystheus, king of Mycenæ, who imposed on him twelve labours (vide infra). His first exploit previous to entering the service of Eurystheus, was killing the enormous lion which destroyed the flocks of Amphitryon and of Thespius, king of Thespiæ: the gods, charmed with the bravery of Hercules, presented him with a complete suit of armour; Jupiter gave a shield, Apollo a bow and arrows, Mercury a sword, Vulcan a golden cuirass and a club of brass, and Minerva a coat of mail.

HESPERIDES, the celebrated guardians of the golden apples, which Ge gave to Juno on the day of her marriage with Jupiter: they were called the daughters of Atlas and Hesperis, whence their name; they resided near Mount Atlas, in Africa.

HIPPOLYTE, daughter of Mars, queen of the Amazones; she wore a girdle given her by her father, which was taken from her by Hercules (vide 9th labour).

HYPERION, a Titan, son of Urănus (heaven) and Gē (earth), (father of Hēlĭos) the sun.

HYADES (i. e. the rainy), a name given to seven nymphs, who formed, with the Plēĭādes, the constellation known by that name.

IAPETUS, one of the Titans; being the father of Prometheus, he was regarded by the Greeks as the father of all mankind.

IO, the daughter of Inachus, king of Argos. Hera being jealous of her, Zeus changed her into a white heifer: Hera then sent the hundred-eyed *Argus* to watch her; but he being slain by Hermes, the goddess persecuted her with a gad-fly; she swam across the Thracian Bosporus (hence its name *Ox-ford*), and, after wandering over the earth, gave birth to Epaphus, on the banks of the Nile.

IXION, king of the Lapithæ, and father of Pirithous. He treacherously murdered his father-in-law, Deioneus, and having proved ungrateful to Zeus, who had purified him, the god condemned him to be tied to a wheel which perpetually revolved in Hades.

JASON, the celebrated leader of the Argonautæ, in the expedition to Colchis; he was the son of Æson and Alcĭmēde, and brought up by the Centaur Chiron (vide Argonautic Expedition).

LAPITHÆ, a savage race inhabiting the mountains of Thessaly; Pirīthoüs was their king (vide Pirithous).

LATONA (Λητώ), a Titaness, the mother of Apollo and Diana.

LEDA, daughter of Thestius, and wife of Tyndarus, king of Sparta; she was the mother of Helena by Zeus, who visited her in the form of a swan.

LETHE, a river in the lower world, whose waters, if the souls of the dead drank, had the power of making them forget all they had done before (derivation λήθη, oblivion).

MAIA, daughter of Atlas, and one of the Pleiades, the most luminous of the seven sisters.

MEDEA, daughter of Æëtes, king of Colchis, celebrated for her skill in music; she fell in love with Jason, and assisted him in obtaining the golden fleece (vide Argonautic Expedition).

MINOS, son of Zeus and Europa, brother of Rhadamantlus and the king and legislator of Crete. On his death, Minos became one of the judges of the lower world.

NARCISSUS, a beautiful youth, changed into the flower which bears his name.

NIOBE, daughter of Tantalus, sister of Pelops, and wife of Amphīon: being the mother of seven sons and daughters, she considered herself superior to Latona, who had borne only two; for this conduct, her children were slain by Apollo and Diana, she herself being turned into stone.

ORION, a celebrated giant, sprung from Jupiter, Neptune, and Mercury; after his death, Orion was placed among the constellations.

ORPHEUS, one of the Argonauts, supposed to be a son of Apollo, and regarded by the Greeks as the most celebrated of the early poets. His skill on the lyre was such that he charmed even Cerberus and the inhabitants of Hades, when he went thither to recover his wife Eurydice, whom he lost by looking back upon before they had regained the earth.

PANDORA (πανδώρα), a woman so named from having received every necessary gift:- from Venus, beauty; from Mercury, eloquence; and from Minerva, splendid ornaments. Pandōra was the first woman on earth, and made by Vulcan from clay, by order of Jupiter, who might, by her charms, bring woes upon the earth, because Prometheus had stolen fire from heaven. She was married to Epīmētheus, brother of Prometheus: in his house was a jar or box, which he had been forbidden to open; but Pandōra's curiosity could not resist the temptation, and as soon as it was opened all the evils incident to man escaped, Hope alone being left. Others relate that it was a jar, not a box, which Pandōra brought from heaven.

PEGASUS, a celebrated winged horse (sprung from the blood of Medūsa, one of the Gorgons, when Perseus cut off her head): he is described as the thunder-bearer of Jupiter; but by later writers as the horse of Aurora.

PERSEUS, a famous hero, son of Jupiter and Danaë, and husband of Andromeda; he is said to have founded Mycenæ (vide Gorgŏnes).

PHAETHON (i. e. the shining), a surname of Sol, commonly known as a son of Sol by one of the Oceănĭdes: he was killed by Zeus with lightning, for his attempt to drive the chariot of the sun across the heavens.

PHLEGETHON, a river of hell, in which fire flowed instead of water.

PIERIDES, a name given to the Muses, derived from Pieria, in Thessaly, where they were first worshipped.

PIRITHOUS, a hero worshipped at Athens, and king of the Lapĭthæ, in Thessaly: at his marriage with Hippŏdămĭa the Centaur Eurўtion carried her off; which occasioned the war between the Lapĭthæ and Centaurs, in which the latter were defeated.

PLEIADES, a name given to the seven daughters of Atlas— *Electra, Maia, Tāÿgĕte, Alcÿŏne, Celœno, Sterŏpe, Merŏpe.*

POLLUX, son of Jupiter and Leda, and brother of Castor, famed for his skill in boxing (vide Castor).

POLYPHEMUS, son of Neptune, a celebrated Cyclops, who fed on human flesh, and kept his flocks on the coast of Sicily.

PROMETHEUS (the Forethinker), the son of Iapetus, one of the Titans. Jupiter, to punish him and the rest of mankind, deprived the earth of fire; but Prometheus stole it from heaven, for which Zeus chained him on Mount Caucasus, where an eagle preyed on his liver for ages: it was ultimately slain by Hercules.

PSYCHE (Ψυχή), signifying "the soul," a nymph whom Cupid married: Venus for a time imposed on her the most unpleasant labours, which well-nigh killed her: but Jupiter, at Cupid's request, conferred on her immortality.

PYTHON, a celebrated serpent, lived in the caves of Mount Parnassus, and was slain by Apollo, who, in commemoration of his victory, founded the Pythian games.

RHADAMANTHUS, son of Zeus and Europa, and brother of Minos, king of Crete, from whom he fled to Bœotia, and married Alcmene. From his justice throughout life, he became after death one of the judges of hell.

RHEA, OPS or CYBELE, daughter of Cœlus and Terra, wife of Saturn, and mother of Jupiter and the gods.

SATYRI, the name of a class of demigods, attendants on Bacchus, represented with the legs and feet of a goat, short horns, bristly hair, and pointed ears; the elder Satyrs were called Sileni.

SIRENES, sea nymphs, who had the power of charming by their songs all who heard them: they are usually stated to have been three in number, the daughters of Phorcys, a sea deity. Ulysses, when sailing near their abode, stopped the ears of his companions with wax, and tied himself to the mast, to avoid being charmed by their songs, and thus delayed.

SPHYNX, a monster who had the head and breasts of a woman, body of a dog, tail of a serpent, wings of a bird, paws of a lion, and a human voice.

STYX, one of the rivers of hell, round which it was said to flow nine times: it was held in such veneration by the gods, that they took oaths by it; and Zeus caused those who swore falsely to drink of it, which had the effect of stupefying them for a year.

TARTARUS, one of the regions of Hades or hell, where the most impious of men were punished. The principal criminals were, 1. Tityus, slain by Apollo and Diana for his conduct to their mother, Latona; in Tartarus his body covered nine acres of land, and a vulture preyed, without ceasing, on his liver. 2. Ixion, fixed by Zeus on a revolving wheel for having aspired to the love of Juno. 3. Tantalus, who, for having, at an entertainment given by him to the gods, served up the flesh of his son Pelops, was punished with insatiable thirst; he is represented as placed up to the chin in a pool of water, which flowed away whenever he attempted to taste it. 4. Sīsȳphus, a son of Æolus, and king of Corinth; he is said to have greatly promoted navigation and commerce; but his wickedness was great, and as a punishment for his crimes, he was condemned in hell to roll to the top of a hill a large stone, which no sooner reached the summit than it rolled down again into the plain. 5. The Danaïdes, forty-nine maidens, who, for stabbing their husbands, the sons of Ægyptus, on their wedding-night, were sentenced to fill a perforated tub with water. Hypermnestra, the fiftieth, spared the life of her husband, Lynceus.

TITANES, children of Uranus and Ge: they were twelve in number, six sons and six daughters, viz. Oceanus, Ceus, Crius, Hyperion, Iapetus, Cronus: Thea, Rhea, Themis, Mnemosyne, Phœbe, Tethys. Zeus and his brothers rebelled and waged war against Saturn and the Titans: this contest was carried on for ten years, Saturn's party fighting from Mount Othrys, Jupiter's from Mount Olympus; at length Jupiter released the Hecaton-Cheires (the hundred-handed), the Titans were defeated and confined in Tartarus. The name Titānes is also given to the descendants of the Titans.

TRITON, a son of Neptune and Amphitrīte: he is represented riding over the sea on horses or sea-monsters, holding a trumpet made out of a shell (concha).

TYPHON, a monstrous giant, described as having a hundred heads, and vomiting flame. He was no sooner born, than he made war against the gods, who were so terrified that they assumed different shapes, Jupiter a ram, &c.; eventually, Typhon was crushed by a thunderbolt from Jupiter, and placed under Mount Ætna

EARLY GRECIAN LEGENDS.

THE ARGONAUTIC EXPEDITION.

ATHAMAS, a king of Bœotia, married Něphěle, by whom he had two children, Phrixus and Helle. On the death of his wife, Athamas married Ino, whose jealousy of her step-children induced her to destroy them; they, however, contrived to escape, and attempted to cross the sea to Colchis, on the back of a golden-fleeced ram, given by Hermes. Helle, being unable to keep her seat, was drowned in the strait called from her the Hellespont. Phrixus, having reached Colchis in safety, offered up the ram to Zeus, and presented the fleece to King Æētes, who had received him kindly; the fleece was nailed to an oak in the sacred grove of Mars, and guarded by a dragon.

Jason, son of Æson, king of Iolcos, in Thessaly, undertook to recover this fleece. He gave orders to Argus, a son of Phrixus (who was assisted by Minerva), to build a vessel of fifty oars; the ship was named "Argo," from the builder, and those who went on the expedition "Argonautæ" (i. e. "sailors of the Argo"). Jason was accompanied by the most renowned heroes of the time, to the number of fifty; among whom were Hercules, Theseus, Pīrithous, Castor and Pollux, Telămon, Peleus, Admētus, Oileus, Neleus, Laertes, Menœtius, Orpheus the minstrel, Mopsus the seer, Æsculapius the physician, Tiphys the pilot. After various adventures, the Argo entered the river Phasis, in Colchis, the heroes landed, and Jason immediately informed the king of his mission; the monarch consented to his taking the fleece, provided he performed the necessary conditions, viz., ploughing a piece of land with the brazen-footed bulls of Vulcan, sowing it with the teeth of the dragon slain by Cadmus, and destroying the armed crop which would spring up. Medēa, the king's daughter, fell in love with Jason, and with her assistance he obtained the golden fleece, and left the country, accompanied by Medea. Æētes, finding that Jason had departed, and taken his daughter, got on shipboard, and pursued; but, to detain him, Medea murdered her brother Absyrtus, and cut him in pieces, so that, while her father was collecting the scattered limbs, the Argo escaped, and eventually arrived in safety at Iolcos.

EARLY LEGENDS RELATING TO THEBES.

Thebes, the Capital of Bœotia, is said to have been founded (c. B.C. 1500) by CADMUS, son of Agenor, king of Phœnicia. According to the legend, Cadmus, failing to find his sister Europa, who had been carried off by Zeus, settled in Thrace, and being ordered by the Delphic Oracle to build a town where a cow, which he was to follow, should sink down with fatigue, he founded Cadmea, the citadel of Thebes. He also there killed a dragon which guarded a well of Ares, and, by the instruction of Athena, sowed its teeth, from which armed men, called Sparti (i. e. *sown*), sprung up and slew each other, except five, who became the ancestors of the Thebans.

Cadmus was succeeded by his son Polydōrus, who was in turn succeeded by his son Labdăcus. He was the father of Laīus, the next king, who had a son, Œdipus, by Jo-casta, the daughter of Menœceus and sister of Creon.

STORY OF ŒDIPUS, AND OF THE WAR OF THE SEVEN AGAINST THEBES.

An Oracle having foretold that Laīus should be slain by his son, Œdipus was exposed at his birth on Mt. Cithærcn, but was found by a shepherd, who (from his feet being pierced through) gave him the name of Οἰδίπους (i. e. *swollen-footed*), and brought him to his master, Polybus, king of Corinth, and husband of Merope or Periboea, and by whom Œdipus was brought up. On attaining manhood, his birthright being called in question, Œdipus consulted the Delphic Oracle, which replied that he was destined to slay his father and marry his mother. Soon afterwards, near Daulis, he met his father in a chariot, and, refusing to make way for him, was struck by Laius, whom he killed, together with the slight escort which attended the chariot. Purposely avoiding Corinth, he arrived at Thebes, where he foiled the Sphynx, a monster who used to murder all those who were unable to solve the riddles which she put to them. Œdipus having explained the riddle of the being with *four, two,* and *three feet,* to mean *man crawling in infancy, walking in manhood,* and *leaning on a staff in old age,* the monster was so enraged at the solution, that she threw herself down from the rock on which she was seated. The Thebans, according to their promise, rewarded Œdipus with the hand of their queen, Jocasta, by whom he became the father as well as brother of Eteŏcles, Polynīces, Antĭgŏne, and Ismēne. In consequence of his marriage a plague was sent, and Creon brought back word from Delphi that the murderer of Laius must be banished. Tiresias, the blind seer, forced by Œdipus, revealed to him his crimes; whereupon Jocasta hung herself, and Œdipus put out his own eyes, was expelled by his sons, and wandered an outcast, under the guidance of his daughter Antigone, to Colonos, in Attica, where he died. Eteocles having violated the agreement with Polynīces to reign in turns, the latter fled to Adrastus, king of Argos, married his daughter Argīa, and persuaded her father to assist him against Eteocles. Polynices, accompanied by Adrastus, Tydeus, Amphiaraus, Capănus, Hippomĕdon, and Parthenopæus, advanced against Thebes, and each assailed one of its seven gates; but were all slain except Adrastus; Eteocles and Polynīces falling by each other's hands. Antigone performed the rites of burial over

Polynīces, in defiance of the orders of Creon (who was regent for Laŏdămas, son of Eteocles), and was buried alive by her uncle's command; whereupon Hæmon, her lover, son of Creon, slew himself in despair. Ten years after the war of the "*Seven against Thebes,*" the descendants ('Επίγονοι) of the heroes stormed Thebes, and razed it to the ground.

EARLY KINGS OF TROY.

1. TEUCER (c. b.c. 1400?), hence the Trojans were called Teucri. His daughter Batea married—2. DARDANUS, who came from Arcadia and Samothrace, and built Dardania, hence the name Dardanelles. 3. ERICTHONIUS, his son, was the wealthiest of mortals, and was succeeded by his son —4. TROS, hence Troja, *Troy;* he was the father, by Callirhoë, of—5. ILUS, after whom Troy was called Ilium. The brothers of Ilus were Assaracus (grandfather of Æneas) and Ganȳmēdes, who was carried off by Zeus to be his cup-bearer, in place of Hebe. Tros was compensated for his loss by a present of horses. Zeus also gave Ilus the Palladium, or image of Pallas, with the promise that, as long as it remained in Troy, the city should be safe. 6. LAOMEDON, son of Ilus, and husband of Strymo. Jupiter condemned Neptune and Apollo to serve him for a year; the former built the walls of his city, the latter became his shepherd. Upon his insolently refusing them their wages, Neptune sent a sea-monster to ravage the country. Hesiŏne, the daughter of Laomedon, was chosen by lot as a sacrifice to appease this scourge; but Hercules came to her assistance, and offered to save her if the king would give him the horses of Zeus. After Hercules had slain the monster, Laomedon refused to fulfil the conditions he had agreed to; the hero therefore slew him and all his sons, except Priam, whom Hesiŏne ransomed with her veil. 7. PRIAM (i. e. *ransomed,* πρίαμαι), originally called Podarces, married Hecuba, by whom he had Hector, Paris, Hĕlĕnus, Deiphŏbus,

Polydōrus, Trōĭlus, also Creusa, Laŏdĭce, Polyxĕna, Cassandra, and other children. At the taking of Troy, he was slain by Pyrrhus at the altar of Zeus, before which his son Pŏlītes had just fallen by the same hand.

LEGEND OF THE TROJAN WAR.
B. C. 1194 — B. C. 1184.

To the marriage of Peleus, king of the Myrmidons, in Thessaly, and Thetis, parents of Achilles, all the deities were invited, except the Goddess of Discord ('Ερις), who, in revenge, threw among the guests a golden apple, inscribed "*To the fairest.*" Juno, Venus, and Minerva each claiming it, Jupiter referred the decision to Paris, also called Alexander, a son of Priam, and at that time a shepherd on Mt. Gargarus (a part of Mt. Ida), on which he had been exposed at his birth, owing to his mother Hecuba having dreamed that she had brought forth a firebrand, which should devastate Troy. Paris, at the risk of drawing down on himself and on his country the resentment of the two other goddesses, awarded the apple to Venus, who had promised him the most beautiful woman for his wife. This was Helen, daughter of Jupiter and Leda, and wife of Menelaus, king of Sparta, whence Paris carried her off, together with the treasures of her husband. Upon the commission of this outrage, the various Grecian chieftains, who had been suitors of Helen, collected at Aulis, in Bœotia, an army of about 100,000 men, and a fleet of 1186 ships, and placed them under the command of Agamemnon, king of Mycenæ, brother to Menelaus, and the most powerful of the Greeks. Before, however, the expedition started, Menelaus and Ulysses attempted a fruitless negotiation at Troy. Agamemnon having, at Aulis, killed a stag sacred to Diana, a pestilence was sent on his followers, and a calm detained their vessels. Calchas (the son of Thestor) the Grecian soothsayer, ordered him to appease the anger of the goddess by sacrificing his

8 *

daughter Iphigenīa. Diana, however, substituted a stag as a victim, and carried off Iphigenīa to be her priestess at Tauris, where she subsequently delivered her brother Orestes, when he was on the point of being sacrificed to Diana.

The Greeks, on their arrival at Troy, drew their ships on shore, and surrounded them with a fortification; but being unable to take the city, they blockaded it, and ravaged the neighbouring country. Among the spoils of Chrysa (one of the captured cities) was Chrysēis, who fell to the lot of Agamemnon. On his refusing to release her, Chryses, her father, obtained from Apollo, whose priest he was, the infliction of a pestilence on the Greeks. Calchas having declared the cause of the plague, Chrysēis was released, and Agamemnon consoled himself by taking away Brisēis from Achilles, into whose hands she had fallen at the capture of Lyrnessus. Achilles, being deeply enraged, refused to take any further part in the war; at last, finding that the Greeks, from being deprived of his aid, were worsted, and even their ships assailed with fire, he permitted his friend Patroclus to put on his armour, and lead his Myrmidons to the fight. Patroclus was slain by Hector; and Achilles, in consequence, roused by grief and resentment, and being furnished by his mother with fresh armour, forged by Vulcan, rescued his friend's dead body, and burnt it. He then pursued Hector thrice round the walls of Troy, slew him, tied him to his chariot, and dragged him to the ships.

The aged Priam ransomed in person his son's corpse, and buried it: with this event, the subject of the Iliad of Homer closes. The same poem also relates several single combats between the various heroes, in which the gods and goddesses often take part; Juno, Minerva, Neptune, Mercury, and Vulcan, espousing the side of the Greeks, while Mars. Phœbus, Diana, Venus, and Latona, aid the Trojans. Homer also gives an account of the slaughter, by Ulysses and Diomēdes, of Rhesus, king of Thrace, and the carrying off his snow-white horses before they drank of the Xanthus, and fed on the Trojan plains; which had they done, Troy, according to a prediction of an oracle, could not have been taken.

Helenus (son of Priam), who had deserted from the Trojans, having foretold that the presence of Pyrrhus or Neoptŏlĕmus (son of Achilles and Deidamia) and Philoctētes was necessary for the success of the Greeks, the former was brought by Ulysses from the court of his grand father, Lycomēdes, king of Scyros; and afterwards either he or Diomedes aided Ulysses in bringing Philoctētes, who had been bitten by a serpent nine years previously, and left behind at Lemnos by the Greeks, on their way to Troy. Philoctētes, being cured on his arrival, employed against the Trojans the arrows Hercules had given him, and mortally wounded Paris. The carrying off the Palladium from Troy is ascribed to Diomedes and Ulysses; and the latter hero has also the credit of contriving the huge wooden horse (constructed by Epēus, with the aid of Minerva), which Sinon, a pretended deserter, persuaded the Trojans had been left by the Greeks, on their departure for the Peloponnesus, as an atonement for carrying off the Palladium, and made of a large size, in order that it might not be drawn into the city. Notwithstanding the opposition of Laŏcŏon (who, with his two sons, was killed by serpents sent by Pallas), the infatuated Trojans drag the horse within their walls, and Sinon by night releases the Greeks who had been concealed in it. Meanwhile the Grecian army, which had retired only to Tenedos, arrives, and the ill-fated city is sacked and burnt. Æneas, however, escapes, with his father, son, and household gods (his wife, Creusa, being parted from him in the confusion); and, after many adventures, he reaches Italy, and founds Lavinium.

GRECIAN HEROES, &c., CONNECTED WITH THE TROJAN WAR.

ACHILLES, son of Peleus and Thetis; leader of the Myrmidons from Phthiotis, in Thessaly. His mother gave him the choice between a long but inglorious life, and one of renown and short duration; the latter of which he chose Thetis, knowing his fate, concealed him, when a child, among the daughters of Lycomedes, king of Scyros; but Ulysses discovered his place of concealment. He was reluctantly led to the Trojan war, of which he was the chief hero, and, after exhibiting deeds of great prowess, he was slain in battle, at the Scæan Gate, before the capture of Troy; but some say he was shot by Paris in the heel, the only part of his body which was vulnerable, Thetis having held him there when she dipped him in the Styx.

AGAMEMNON, son of Atreus and grandson of Pelops, and commander-in-chief in the Trojan war. On his return to Mycenæ, he was slain by his wife, Clytemnestra, daughter of Tyndarus, who had married Ægisthus in her husband's absence. Orestes, aided by his friend Pylădes, avenged his father's death.

AJAX, son of Oīleus, king of the Locrians. On his return from the war, he was drowned by Neptune, for setting at nought the god's assistance during a shipwreck, in which his companions perished. Virgil relates that he was dashed on a rock by Minerva, in whose temple he had insulted Cassandra, at the capture of Troy.

AJAX, son of Tĕlămon, king of Salamis, and inferior only to Achilles in bravery. Ulysses having defeated him in the contest for the armour of Achilles, he became mad, and slaughtered a flock of sheep, imagining them to be the Greeks; on discovering his mistake, he committed suicide. By Tecmessa he had a son, Eurȳsăces, named after his father's *broad shield*.

ANTILOCHUS, son of Nestor; slain at Troy by Memnon, after many deeds of bravery.

AUTOMEDON, charioteer and companion of Achilles, and afterwards of Pyrrhus.

CALCHAS, the soothsayer who foretold the length of the Trojan war, and died of grief because Mopsus excelled him in his art.

DIOMEDES or TYDIDES, son of Tydeus and Deipȳle; king of Argos. On his return from the war, finding his wife,

Ægiălea, married to Hippolȳtus, he went to Ætolia. As he was returning, a storm cast him on the coast of Daunia, in Apulia, where he is said to have founded several towns, Arpi, Beneventum, Brundusium, Venusia, &c

HELENA, daughter of Zeus and Leda. On the death of Paris, she married his brother, Dēïphŏbus, but afterwards became reconciled to her former husband, Menelaus.

IDOMENEUS, son of the Cretan Deucalion, king of Crete; one of the bravest warriors on the side of the Greeks. It is said that he sacrificed his son (who first met him on his return) to Neptune, owing to a rash vow he had made in a storm.

LAODICE or ELECTRA. After the murder of her father, Agamemnon, she sent her brother, Orestes, to King Strophius, in Phocis, where he became intimate with Pylădes, whom Electra married, after she had incited Orestes to avenge his father's death.

MACHAON, son of Æsculapius, and surgeon of the Greeks.

MENELAUS, son of Atreus, and husband of Helen, by whom he had Hermĭŏne, wife of Neoptŏlĕmus.

MERIONES, a brave warrior, who came with Idomeneus from Crete.

NEOPTOLEMUS or PYRRHUS, son of Achilles; called Neoptŏlemus (νέος, π(τ)όλεμος), because he came *late* to the Trojan *war*, and Pyrrhus (πυῤῥός), from the *bright* *id* colour of his hair. He was slain at Delphi.

NESTOR, son of Neleus, king of Pylos, in Elis, and the most venerable of the Greeks, by whom he was greatly respected for his wisdom, oratory, and skill in war.

PATROCLUS, the intimate friend of Achilles. He was son of Menœtius, the brother of Æacus, who was grandfather to Achilles.

PHILOCTETES, the best archer in the Trojan war. He was the friend of Hercules, who gave him his poisoned arrows, as a reward for setting fire to the pile on Mt. Œta, on which Hercules burnt himself.

PHŒNIX, son of Amyntor. He fled to Peleus, king of

Thessaly, who made him ruler of the Dolopes, and tutor of Achilles, whom he accompanied to the Trojan war.

PYRRHUS. See Neoptolemus.

STHENELUS, son of Capaneus, and friend of Diomedes.

TALTHYBIUS, herald of Agamemnon.

TEUCER, son of Telamon, king of Salamis, who refused to receive him on his return from Troy, because he had not avenged his half-brother Ajax's death. Teucer sailed to Cyprus, and there founded a second Salamis.

ULYSSES ('Οδυσσεύς), son of Anticlēa and Laertes, king of Ithaca. To avoid going to the Trojan war, he feigned madness, by yoking an ox and an ass together, and ploughing the sea-shore, which he sowed with salt. Palamēdes detected him, by placing his infant son, Telemachus, before the plough, which the father stopped. After he left Troy, he underwent a variety of adventures, which are related in Homer's "Odyssey." He blinded the Cyclops Polyphemus, who had devoured six of his companions. After encountering various dangers from the Sirens (vide Mythol.), from shipwreck, and at the islands of Æolus, Æea (inhabited by the sorceress Circe, who changed his associates into swine), Sicily, Ogȳgīa (where he was detained by Calypso, vide Mythol.), and Scheria, he reached Ithaca. In the meantime, the hand of his wife, Penelope, had been sought by numerous suitors, whom she had declined answering till she should have finished a web or robe for Laertes; this she contrived to delay, by undoing by night her day's work. At last Ulysses, after an absence of twenty years, arrived in the disguise of a beggar; and, after vanquishing the suitors in drawing the bow of Eurytus, he slew them, by the aid of Telemachus and Minerva, and was recognized by his wife and aged father.

TROJAN HEROES, &c.

ACESTES, son of the Sicilian river-god Crimīsus, and the Trojan Egesta or Segesta. He aided Priam in the Trojan war, and afterwards, together with Elymus (son of Anchises), hospitably received Æneas, who built the towns of Ægesta and Elyme, in Sicily.

ÆNEAS, son of Anchises and Venus, and one of the bravest of the Trojans. By his wife, Creusa (who was parted from him in the confusion at the taking of Troy), he had a son, Ascanius or Iulus. After escaping from Troy, he wandered over the Ægean and Ionian Seas to Sicily, and Latium, in Italy, where he married Lavinia, daughter of the king Latinus, and built Lavinium. Latinus and Turnus, king of the Rutuli, having fallen in battle, Æneas succeeded to their power, but was slain by Mezentius, king of the Rutuli. Virgil, by an anachronism, represents Æneas as visiting Dido, queen of Carthage, who fell in love with him, and burnt herself alive on his leaving her.

ALEXANDER. See Paris, page 89.

ANCHISES, father of Æneas by Venus. Having accompanied his son after the fall of Troy, he died in Sicily, and was buried on Mt. Eryx.

ANDROMACHE, daughter of Eëtion (king of Thebes, in Cilicia), and wife of Hector, by whom she had Scamandrius or Astyanax. At the capture of Troy, her son was thrown from the walls, and she became the prize of Pyrrhus, but afterwards married Helĕnus, king of Chaonia, in Epirus.

ANTENOR, one of the wisest of the Trojans. He advised the surrender of Helen before the war began. After it was over, he is said to have founded Patavium (*Padua*), in Italy.

CASSANDRA, daughter of Priam; loved by Apollo, who gave her the gift of prophecy; but, on her offending the god, he caused her prophecies to be discredited. At the taking of Troy, she was insulted by Ajax, son of Oïleus, in the temple of Minerva. She afterwards became the prize of Agamemnon, and was murdered, at Mycenæ, by Clytemnestra.

CORŒBUS, a Phrygian; son of Mygdon. He fought at Troy with the hope of marrying Cassandra, but was killed by Penĕlĕus or by Pyrrhus.

DEIPHOBUS, son of Priam, and, next to Hector, the bravest among the Trojans. On the death of Paris, he married Helen, and was slain by Menelaus at the capture of Troy.

GLAUCUS, grandson of Bellerophon, a Lycian ally of the Trojans, slain by Ajax.

HECTOR, eldest son of Priam, the bravest of the Trojans, and husband of Andromăche. He slew Patroclus, and he himself fell by the hand of Achilles.

HECUBA, daughter of Dymas, or of Cisseus, king of Thrace, and wife of Priam. After the fall of Troy, she was taken by the Greeks to the Thracian Chersonesus, where, according to Euripides, her daughter, Polyxĕna, who had been beloved by Achilles, was taken from her by Ulysses, and sacrificed by Pyrrhus. On the same day, Hecuba also beheld the murdered corpse of her son, Polydōrus, cast on the shore. He had been entrusted to the care of Polymnestor, king of the Chersonese, by whom he was murdered, for the sake of the riches he had brought with him. Hecuba, in revenge, enticed Polymnestor to come to her, under pretence of revealing some Trojan treasure, when she blinded him and slew his sons.

HELENUS, son of Priam, gifted with prophecy; he fell to the lot of Pyrrhus, after whose death he married Andromache. When Æneas came to Epirus, Helenus foretold his destinies.

MEMNON, son of Tithonus and Aurora, an Ethiopian prince, who came to the assistance of his paternal uncle, Priam, and was slain by Achilles.

PANDARUS, a Lycian archer; slain by Sthenelus or Diomedes.

PARIS or ALEXANDER, son of Priam, vide page 89.

PRIAM, vide page 88.

SARPEDON, son of Zeus and Laodamīa, a Lycian prince; renowned for his valour. He was slain by Patroclus. Apollo, by order of Zeus, cleansed Sarpedon's body from blood and dust, covered it with ambrosia, and entrusted it to Death and Sleep to carry into Lycia to be buried.

TROILUS, son of Priam and Hecuba, or of Apollo; slain by Achilles.

Note. — After their death, many of the Grecian and Trojan warriors were worshipped as heroes and had various temples erected to them.

GREEK ANTIQUITIES.

THE INHABITANTS OF ATTICA were divided into *three classes:* I. Πολῖται, or freemen; II. Μέτοικοι, or foreigners settled in the country; III. Δοῦλοι, or slaves.

THE INHABITANTS OF SPARTA were divided into *two classes:* I. Σπαρτιᾶται and Περίοικοι, town and provincial freemen; II. Εἵλωτες, slaves.

MAGISTRATES.

The form of government at Athens was, as in many states, frequently changed: it began with Monarchy, and, having passed through a Dynasty (in which the power was confined to one family) and Aristocracy, ended in Democracy. Theseus may be called the first king, and Codrus the last, after whom (B.C. 1045) the Athenians elected the

ARCHONS,

who were the chief magistrates at Athens, nine in number; their power was originally for life, but was afterwards limited to ten years, and latterly to one. The names and offices of these magistrates were distinct: the President was styled ὁ Ἄρχων or ἐπώνυμος, from the year being called after, and registered in, his name; the second was called βασιλεύς; the third, πολέμαρχος, or commander-in-chief; and the remaining six, θεσμοθέται, or legislators.

The functions of the Ἄρχων were: 1. To provide for the celebration of the feasts, as the Dionysia, &c.; 2. To settle disputes arising between neighbours and citizens, and to determine all causes between married people; 3. To take care of orphans, provide them tutors, and superintend their estates.

The duties of the Βασιλεύς were: 1. To superintend the festivals, and especially the Eleusinia; 2. To settle all disputes respecting the priesthood, and judge those accused of impiety.

The duties of the Πολέμαρχος were: 1. To celebrate rites in honour of Mars and Diana; 2. To have under his care all foreigners and strangers, and settle actions brought against them; 3. To superintend the wars, over which he had the chief command, and thence received his name.

The functions of the Θεσμοθέται were connected with the administration of justice, such as, 1. Receiving indictments, bringing cases to trial, and appointing the day of sitting; 2. Annually revising the code of laws; 3. Drawing up agreements with foreign states, &c.; 4. Examining the magistrates, and taking the votes in the assemblies.

THE ARCHONS were elected by lot, and, before they were admitted to office, passed an examination as to their family, age, past conduct, &c., and took oath that they would observe the laws, administer justice, and accept of no presents.

Inferior Magistrates.—1. Οἱ ἕνδεκα, *the eleven*, elected one from each of the ten tribes; and, to complete the number, there was added a Γραμματεύς, or registrar. 2. Φύλαρχοι, who presided over the tribes. 3. Δήμαρχοι, the chief magistrates of the Δῆμοι, or boroughs in Attica. 4. Ληξίαρχοι, six in number, assisted by thirty inferiors; they fined those absent from the Assembly, took the votes of those present, and kept the public registers. 5. Νομοθέται, 1000 in number; they inspected old laws, and, if found useless, caused them to be abolished by an act of the people.

THE EPHORI.

The Ἔφοροι, or "overseers," were the chief magistrates at Sparta: they were five in number, and elected annually, from and by the people, without any qualification of age or property. Though at first only judicial officers, in time their authority became so great, that even the two hereditary kings of Sparta, as well as the magistrates, were prosecuted or suspended at their discretion. They had the superintendence of the public morals, convened the public assembly, levied troops, &c., &c., and had great influence in the most important matters. Every month they exchanged an oath with the kings, promising to defend the royal authority, provided it did not violate the laws. The tribunal of the Ephori was the ἀρχεῖον or ἐφορεῖον, a Council Hall in the Forum.

ASSEMBLIES.

Ἐκκλησία, THE GENERAL ASSEMBLY of the citizens at Athens, in which they met to discuss matters of public interest. This assembly had the power of making laws, electing magistrates, proclaiming war, &c.; the place of meeting was either the Agora (ἀγορά) or Pnyx (πνύξ), in later times, the theatre of Bacchus. The magistrates who presided in the Assembly were: 1. Prytanes (πρυτάνεις), who summoned the people, and announced the subject for decision; 2. Proëdri (πρόεδροι), who occupied the front seats; 3. ἐπιστάτης, or President, chosen by lot from the Proëdri. The usual manner of giving votes was by holding up the hand, called χειροτονία, and as soon as the voting was ended, the Proëdri examined the suffrages, and pronounced the decree, ψήφισμα, so called from the ψῆφοι, pebbles, which, together with beans (κύαμοι), were sometimes used in voting.

Ἡ βουλὴ ἡ τῶν πεντακοσίων, THE SENATE OF THE FIVE HUNDRED. The institution of this body is attributed to Solon, in whose time the Council consisted of only 400 members; but, on the tribes being remodelled by Cleisthenes, B.C. 510, the Council was increased to 500, and the members were divided into ten sections of fifty each, and were called Prytanes (πρυτάνεις): they presided in the Council, as well as the Assembly, during thirty-five or thirty-six days, so as to complete the lunar year of 354 days. Each tribe presided in turn, and the period of office was called a Prytany (πρυτανεία). The members of the Council remained in office for a year, at the end of which they were obliged to give an account of their conduct (εὐθύνη); and previous to entering office, they submitted to the δοκιμασία, or scrutiny into their private character.

Γερουσία was the name given to the Council of Elders, γέροντες, or Senate at Sparta; it was composed of the two Kings and twenty-eight citizens, who had reached at least their sixtieth year. They were elected by the people, and were irresponsible. The functions of this Council were: 1. To propose measures to be laid before the Popular Assembly; 2. To discharge the highest offices of government; 3. To sit as the supreme criminal tribunal; and, 4. To watch over the public morals.

JUDGES AND COURTS OF JUSTICE.

THE COURT OF AREOPAGUS.—This was the most ancient and venerable seat of justice in Athens; it derived its name from ὁ Ἄρειος πάγος (the hill of Mars), because, it is said, Mars was the first criminal tried. The court was composed of ex-archons who had discharged their office unblamably, and of the most distinguished citizens: the number of judges varied at different times. They were termed ἀρειοπαγῖται, and took cognizance of all crimes, vices, and abuses, such as robbery, murder, poisoning, arson, &c.; they overlooked religious matters, and punished severely for impiety and contempt of holy mysteries. So great was their power, that they sometimes even annulled the decrees of the Popular Assembly.

THE HELIASTS, so named from their court, ἡλιαία, were a body of Judges chosen by lot, and varied in number; sometimes the ἡλιασταί were 6000 in number. They took cognizance of affairs of the greatest importance, but were not permitted to pass sentence until they had taken oath to decide according to the decrees of the people.

THE DIÆTETÆ. THE FORTY.—The διαιτηταί were inferior judges who settled private disputes, subject to an appeal before the Heliasts. They were chosen yearly from the φυλαι, or tribes, and were required to be fifty or sixty years of age The Forty, οἱ τεσσαράκοντα, were also inferior judges, who annually took a circuit through the Dēmi, and decided causes where the matter in dispute did not exceed 10 drachmæ.

COURT OF THE EPHETÆ.—The ἐφέται were judges, fifty-one in number, selected from noble families, and required to be more than fifty years of age. Their jurisdiction extended to cases of justifiable and unintentional murder; when judging of the former, they sat at the Delphinium— when of the latter, at the Palladium.

AMPHICTYONES were members of the ἀμφικτυονία, which was a confederation formed for mutual security, and for the protection of a temple at which the members assembled to transact business and celebrate their festivals. The most celebrated was the Delphic Amphictyonia, originally composed of twelve tribes, whose deputies met annually at Delphi in the spring, and at Thermopylæ in the autumn. The Council itself was called Pylæa, πυλαία.

PUNISHMENTS.

OSTRACISM (ὀστρακισμός) was a political plan for removing from the country for ten years those who had either power or popularity enough to attempt any thing against the State. The word is derived from ὄστρακον, a tile, as it was on this each individual wrote the name of the person he wished to be ostracised. The assembly was held in the Agora, where each voter deposited his tile; but no decision was valid unless the number of votes exceeded 6000. If this number were obtained, the ostracised was obliged to leave the city within ten days; but in his absence no injury was done to the house or property of the banished, nor was any disgrace attached to ostracism. As by the votes of the tribes a man was ostracised, so was it in their power to recall him before ten years had elapsed, if they chose.

'Ατιμία was a public disgrace, by which the person on whom it was inflicted was deprived, either partially or totally, of his political privileges.

Δουλεία (servitude), by which a criminal was reduced to the condition of a slave.

Στίγματα, marks impressed with a hot iron on the foreheads or hands of slaves who had fled from their masters, or of criminals convicted of grievous offences.

Στήλη, a pillar, on which was engraven the crimes of an offender.

Δεσμός, the punishment of imprisonment or chains. The instruments used were: 1. κύφων, the collar; 2. χοίνιξ, the stocks; 3. σανίς, a piece of wood to which criminals were fastened; 4. τροχός, a wheel to which slaves were bound, and beaten with stripes.

Φυγή, banishment. Persons condemned to this punishment lost their estates, and had no hope of returning to their country, unless recalled by those who banished them.

Θάνατος, capital punishment. This was performed in various ways: 1. By the sword (ξίφος); 2. By a rope (βρόχος); 3. By poison (φάρμακον); 4. By stoning (λιθοβολία); 5. By fire (πῦρ), 6. By the cross (σταυρός), &c., &c.

TEMPLES, PRIESTS, AND SACRIFICES.

The objects employed in the worship of the gods were either temples (ναός, δόμος), consecrated groves or enclosures (τέμενος), or altars (βωμός). The temples were generally built in an oblong or round form, and adorned with columns. The larger temples were divided into *three parts:* 1. πρόναος or πρόδομος, the vestibule; 2. ναός, σηκός, or ἄδυτον, the temple or habitation of the deity whose statue it contained; 3. ὀπισθόδομος or θησαυρός, the chamber in which the treasures of the temple were kept.

The priests, set apart for the service of certain gods or temples, were called ἱερεῖς, ἀρητῆρες, θυοσκόοι: divines and wizards, μάντιες or θεοπρόποι. They foretold events from signs (τέρατα, σήματα), such as thunder and lightning; from the song and flight of birds, especially of prey (οἰωνοπόλοι, οἰωνισταί, δεξιὸς ὄρνις); or from dreams, ὀνειροπόλοι.

The sacrifices were of *three kinds*. I. Occasionally human. II. Animal, called ἱερεῖον, *victima, hostia*. The victim was in early times burnt whole, and termed holocaust; but in Homer's time the thighs (μηροί, μῆρα) were inclosed in fat and consumed, from which omens were often taken. As the gods were supposed to delight in a number of victims, a hundred bulls (ἑκατόμβη) were often sacrificed. The word hecatomb is also used to signify any large sacrifice. The animals sacrificed were usually oxen, sheep, and goats, without blemish (τέλειος). Previous to being slain, the head of the victim was strewed with barley and salt (οὐλοχύται, *mola salsa*), adorned with garlands, and a tuft of hair was cut off from the forehead as a beginning (ἀπαρχή, *primitiæ*) of the sacrifices; the animal was then killed by drawing back the head (ἀναρρύω) and cutting the throat. III. Unbloody sacrifices. These were: 1. Libations (λοιβαί, σπονδαί, or χοαί) of wine, milk, and honey, &c.; 2. Cakes (πέλανοι), dishes of fruit (κέρνα), &c., &c.

ORACLES.

The word *oraculum* was used by the ancients to describe the revelations of the deities to men. The responses were sometimes given in verse, or written on tablets; and their meaning was always ambiguous and obscure. The most celebrated oracles were: I. ORACLE OF ZEUS, at DODONA, the most ancient in Greece, founded by Pelasgians. The oracle was given from lofty oaks, which were said to have human voices and the spirit of divination, and were hence called the "prophesying or speaking oaks." With regard to this fable, the fact appears to be, that those who gave the oracles were men, and when consulted mounted an oak, and there gave the replies. The decisions of the oracle were afterwards given by two or three old women (called πελειαδες). As this word also signifies *doves*, the fable originated respecting the oracles being delivered by doves. The usual form in which the oracles were given at Dodona was in hexameter verse. II. ORACLE OF APOLLO, at DELPHI. This oracle, the most celebrated of antiquity, was situated on Mt. Parnassus, in Phocis, supposed by the ancients to be the centre of the world. The oracle was at first called Pytho; the priestess was named Pythia. In the innermost sanctuary the statue of Apollo was placed, and on an altar before it burnt an eternal fire; in the centre of the temple was a small opening in the ground, from which the most intoxicating vapours arose; over this chasm the Pythia took her seat on a high tripod when the oracle was to be consulted, and the suffocating fumes caused her to utter sounds which were taken down by the Prophetes, and were believed to contain the revelations of Apollo. The Pythia was always a native of Delphi, not allowed to marry; and bound, after once entering, never to leave the service of the god. The times for consultation, as well as the number of priestesses, were from time to time changed, to meet the wants of those who flocked to the oracle. Valuable presents were required to be made, and hence this temple exceeded all others in splendour, riches, and magnificence. It must, however, be borne in mind, that many of these valuables were only deposited in the temple for the sake of safety.

The replies were always returned in the Greek tongue, and usually in hexameter verse, in the Ionic dialect. They had at all times a leaning in favour of Doric Greeks.

The chief of the remaining oracles were—I. Of Zeus: 1. The oracle at Olympia, in Elis; 2. Zeus Ammon, in Libya, N. W. of Egypt. II. Of Apollo: 1. At Abæ, in Phocis; 2. At Delos, in the Ægean Sea; 3. Of the Branchidæ, at Didỹma, in the territory of Miletus; 4. At Claros, near Colophon, in Ionia. III. Of Heroes: 1. Oracle of Trophonius, at Lebadēa, in Bœotia; 2. Of Amphiaraus, near Thebes, and at Oropus, between Bœotia and Attica.

FESTIVALS.

Festivals were instituted — 1. In honour of the gods, for benefits received from them; 2. In order to procure some favour; 3. In memory of deceased friends, who had done good service for their country; 4. As a season of rest to labourers, that, as a recompense, some days of ease and refreshment might be obtained. The chief festivals among the Greeks were:—

'Αδώνια, in honour of Venus and Adonis. The solemnity lasted two days; the first was given up to mourning and lamentation, the second to mirth and joy.

'Ανθεστήρια, the chief of the Dionysian festivals, celebrated, in honour of Bacchus, for three days; the first called Πιθοιγία, second, Χόες, third, Χύτροι.

'Απατούρια, celebrated at Athens, and lasted three days. The first called Δόρπεια, because each tribe assembled at an entertainment; second, 'Ανάρρυσις, because victims were offered to Jupiter; third, Κουρεώτις, because the young children born that year were then taken to have their names enrolled in the public register.

Δαφνηφόρια, celebrated every ninth year by the Bœotians, in honour of Apollo; when an olive bough, adorned with garlands, was carried in procession; on the top of the bough was a globe, the emblem of the sun or Apollo.

Διονύσια, four festivals celebrated in honour of Dionȳsus or Bacchus, and observed at Athens with great splendour. The wildest mirth abounded at the various Dionysiac festivals; some wore the dress of satyrs, others comic dresses, others, dancing ridiculously, personated madmen, and shouted Εὐοῖ Βάκχε, ὦ Ἴακχε, Ἰὼ Βάκχε. Choruses were sung at these festivals, called Dithyrambs, and theatrical representations were also given.

'Ελευσίνια, the most celebrated and mysterious solemnity in Greece (sometimes called, by way of eminence, Μυστήρια), was observed every fourth year at Eleusis, in Attica. The mysteries were divided into μικρά, in honour of Proserpine, and μεγάλα, in honour of Ceres; they lasted nine days: on the first day the worshippers first met together; second day, they purified themselves by washing in the sea; third day, they sacrificed; fourth day, they made a solemn procession, in which the καλάθιον, or holy basket of Ceres, was carried; fifth, the women ran about with torches; sixth, the statue of Ἴακχος, crowned with myrtle and bearing a torch, was carried from Ceramicus to Eleusis in procession; seventh, there were sports; eighth, the lesser mysteries were repeated, and those were initiated who did not enjoy that privilege; on the ninth, and last day, two earthen vessels filled with wine were thrown down, and the wine spilt was offered as a libation.

Θεσμοφόρια ("the lawgiver"), in honour of Ceres; celebrated by the Athenians with great pomp and devotion; the worshippers were free-born women, assisted by a priest and by certain virgins, kept at the public charge. The women were dressed in white for four or five days before the festival, and on the 11th of the month Pyanepsion, they carried the books of the law to Eleusis, where the festival commenced, and lasted three days.

Παναθήναια, an Athenian festival in honour of Minerva, the protectress of Athens; it was instituted by Erichthonius, who called it Ἀθήναια; but afterwards revised by Theseus, who, having united all the Athenians into *one* body, called the festival Παναθήναια. There were two solemnities called Παναθήναια; μεγάλα, the greater, celebrated once in five years, and μικρά, the lesser, celebrated once every year. The chief difference between the two festivals was, that at the greater one, which was attended with more solemnity, the Peplus, or garment of Minerva, was carried in procession to her temple on the Acropolis. The solemnities, games, and amusements of the Panathenæa were: rich sacrifices, foot, horse, and chariot-races, gymnastic and musical contests, and the *lampadephoria*, or race with torches; at these festivals the works of Homer and other Epic poets were recited, philosophers disputed, and the people indulged in a variety of amusements; the chief solemnity, however, was the procession in which the greater part of the Attic population took part.

These festivals were at first celebrated for one day, but were afterwards prolonged for several. The prizes awarded were vases, containing oil from the sacred olive-tree of Athena, on the Acropolis.

PUBLIC GAMES.

These were instituted in honour of the Gods or of deified heroes, and the victors, especially in the Olympian games, received the highest honours. On their return home they rode in a triumphal chariot into the city, a portion of the wall being thrown down to give them admittance; they were honoured with the first places at all shows and games, were maintained at the public charge, and great honour descended to their relations.

The games were called 'Αγῶνες, and the principal exercises used in them were: I. Δρόμος, *Cursus*, running; II. Δίσκος, throwing the discus; III. Ἅλμα, *Saltus*, leaping; IV. Πυγμή, *Pugilatus*, boxing; V. Πάλη, *Lucta*, wrestling. These five exercises were called by the Greeks πένταθλον, *Pentathlon*, by the Romans, *Quinquertium*. Some, however, instead of πυγμή, place ἀκόντιον, *jaculum*, throwing the spear.

I. Δρόμος, *running;* this game was performed in a space of ground called στάδιον vel αὐλός, containing 125 paces. There were four kinds of races: 1. στάδιον; 2. δίαυλος, running twice over the stadium; 3. δόλιχος, running seven times; 4. ὁπλίτης, running armed.

II. Δίσκος, the discus, was a round quoit of stone, brass, or iron; sometimes a heavy mass called σόλος was used instead of the discus, which was thrown by the help of a thong.

III. Ἅλμα, *leaping;* this exercise was sometimes performed with empty hands, and sometimes with weights of lead or stone, called ἀλτῆρες, which were carried in their hands or upon the head and shoulders.

IV. Πυγμή, *boxing;* in this exercise balls of stone or lead were sometimes held in the hand, and the cestus was used, which was the name given to the bands of leather, sometimes loaded with iron and lead, and tied round the hands to harden the blows.

V. Πάλη, *wrestling;* this was the most ancient of the exercises, and was performed in the Xystus, a covered portico; in which two naked men anointed with oil, and sprinkled with dust, folded themselves in one another's arms, and endeavoured to throw each other to the ground. There were two kinds of wrestling; one in which the wrestlers contended on their feet, and another in which they threw themselves down, and contended rolling on the ground. [The Pancratium, παγκράτιον, was an exercise which consisted of wrestling and boxing.]

The four solemn games in Greece, called ἀγῶνες ἱεροί, were: I. The Olympic; II. Pythian; III. Isthmian; and IV. Nemean.

THE OLYMPIC GAMES.—These were celebrated in honour of Zeus Olympius, and were held at Olympia, a town in Elis, whence they received the name Olympian. Their institution is assigned to Hercules by some, but it is impossible to say with any accuracy who was the real founder. They were for some period neglected, until the time of Iphitus, who re-instituted the solemnity; but it was not till B.C. 776, when Corœbus won the foot-race, that the Olympiads were employed as a chronological era. The games were celebrated every fifth year, in the Attic month Hecatombæon, and continued five days, from the 11th to the 15th inclusive, the interval of four years between each celebration of the festival being called an **Olympiad**. The Eleans had the management of the games, and appointed the judges, who were chosen by lot from their number. Women were not allowed to be present. Those who intended to contend were obliged to swear that they were freemen, not guilty of any sacrilegious act, and had spent the proper period (ten months) in preparatory exercises. The wrestlers were chosen by lot, and the exercises, in addition to those mentioned in the last section, were horse and chariot-races, in which, as in several ot the other exercises, boys contended. There were also contests in which musicians, poets, and artists, strove for the victory.

The victors in these games were rewarded with wreaths of wild olive, and statues in the grove of Altis; and still more substantially on their return to their own cities, as mentioned before.

THE PYTHIAN GAMES were celebrated in honour of Apollo, at Delphi, anciently called Pytho, whence the name Pythian. The common tradition is, that the games were instituted by Apollo himself, after he had overcome the serpent Python. They were at first celebrated every ninth year (ἐνναετηρίς); but afterwards at the end of every fourth year (πενταετηρίς), and comprehended the space of four years, commencing with the third year of each Olympiad. The games lasted several days, and the exercises were the same as those of the Olympic games. Some say that the solemnity was at first a musical contention, and that a song (to which a dance was performed) consisting of five parts was sung, in which Apollo's contest with the dragon was represented. The rewards, when there was only a musical performance, are said to have been gold and silver; but when gymnastic exercises were introduced, garlands of laurel, palm, or parsley, were presented to the victors.

THE NEMEAN GAMES were celebrated in honour of Zeus, at Nemea, near Cleonæ, in Argolis, every third year. The institution of these games is assigned both to the Seven against Thebes, as well as to Hercules, after he had slain the Nemean lion. The various exercises were chariot and horse-racing, and the pentathlon. The reward of the victors was at first a chaplet of olive-branches, but afterwards a garland of parsley was awarded.

THE ISTHMIAN GAMES were so called from the Corinthian Isthmus, where they were celebrated. At the narrowest part of the Isthmus stood a temple (Fanum Neptuni), near which was a theatre and stadium of white marble, where the games took place. Some say they were instituted in honour of Palæmon, or Melicertes, son of Athamas, king of Thebes; others, in honour of Neptune. The games took place every third year, and the exercises were the same as those of the other sacred festivals; the rewards were chaplets of pine; at one time ivy was used.

The Isthmian games were held in great veneration, on account of the religion by which they were consecrated, as well as on account of their antiquity.

MILITARY AFFAIRS.
Divisions of the Army.

The Grecian armies consisted of free bodies of men, whom the laws of the country obliged, when arrived at a certain age, to appear in arms: at the age of eighteen, the Athenians were appointed to guard the city; at twenty, they were sent to foreign wars; at sixty, they were allowed to retire.

The army was composed of three classes of soldiers: 1. Infantry, πεζοί; 2. Charioteers, ἡνίοχοι; 3. Cavalry, ἱππεῖς.

The foot soldiers were divided into, 1. Ὁπλῖται, who wore heavy armour, and fought with broad shields and long spears; 2. Ψιλοί, light-armed men, who engaged with darts, arrows, and slings; 3. Πελτασταί, who were armed with a small shield called πέλτη.

Arms.

These were divided into *two classes:* 1. Arms for the protection of the body; and, 2. Those used to injure an enemy.

I. The defensive arms, which protected the body: 1. κράνος, κόρυς, κυνέη, or περικεφαλαία, helmet, made of brass or of the skins of animals, and surmounted by a crest (λόφος); 2. θώραξ, cuirass, made of hemp (twisted into cords, and woven close together), of brass, or of leather covered with brass; 3. κνημῖδες, greaves, for the front of the legs, made of brass or other metal; 4. ἀσπίς, a round buckler, made either of osiers twisted together, or of wood covered with leather, and bound round the edge with metal; in the centre was a projection called ὀμφαλός or μεσομφάλιον, a boss, upon which a spike was sometimes placed. The θυρεός was an oblong shield (corresponding to the Latin scutum), and the πέλτη a small shield used in the Greek army, by a body of men named from using it πελτασταί.

II. The offensive arms: 1. ἔγχος and δόρυ, the spear and lance, usually made of ash; the point, αἰχμή, was of metal; 2. ξίφος, the sword, suspended by a belt (τελαμών) from the shoulder; 3. ἀξίνη et πέλεκυς, pole-axe; 4. τόξον, the bow, said to have been invented by Apollo, who communicated his invention to the Cretans, who became first-rate archers: the arrows, which were called βέλη, ὀϊστοί, and τοξεύματα, were made of light wood and pointed with metal; 5. ἀκόντιον, the javelin, of which there were various kinds; 6. σφενδόνη, the sling, which was commonly used by the light-armed soldiers.

THE CHIEF OFFICERS OF THE ARMY were, 1. πολέμαρχος or general (vide Magistrates); 2. στρατηγοί, ten in number, one elected from each tribe: they conducted all military affairs at home and abroad; 3. ταξίαρχοι, ten in number, elected by the tribes: they had the care of marshalling the army, directing the marches and encampments, and discharging the soldiers convicted of misdemeanours; 4. ἵππαρχοι, two in number: they commanded the cavalry; 5. φύλαρχοι, ten in number, elected by the tribes, subordinate to the ἵππαρχοι: the inferior officers received their names from the number of men they commanded. Among the Lacedæmonians, the supreme command was vested in one man (usually a king of Sparta), who was attended by a body-guard of horsemen, ἱππεῖς, 300 in number.

THE DIVISIONS OF THE ARMY.—The whole body was called στρατιά; the van, μέτωπον vel πρῶτος ζυγός; the wings, κέρατα; the rear, οὐρά vel ἔσχατος ζυγός. Minor divisions: πεμπάς, a party of five soldiers; λόχος, a party of twenty-four or twenty-five, sometimes of only sixteen; τάξις vel ἑκατονταρχία, a company of 100 or 120; φάλαγξ, a body of troops in close order, whose chief weapon was a long spear. The whole army of the Spartans was divided into μόραι, regiments, and λόχοι, companies, the number of men each contained is uncertain.

NAVAL AFFAIRS.

The vessels of the Greeks may be divided into two classes:

I. Naves Onerariæ, ὁλκάδες, φορτηγοί, στρογγύλαι, πλοῖα, ships of burden, generally made of a bulky form, and chiefly propelled by sails.

II. Naves Bellicæ, τριήρεις, τετρήρεις, πεντήρεις (*triremes, quadriremes, quinqueremes*), war-galleys, propelled chiefly by oars, and distinguished from each other by the number of banks of oars. The most usual number of banks was three, four, or five, which gradually ascended in the manner of stairs. The most common ships of war in the earlier times were long vessels (*naves longæ*) called πεντηκόντοροι, with fifty rowers, twenty-five on each side.

The principal parts of the vessel were: 1. τρόπις or στείρη (*carina*), the keel; 2. πρῶρα or μέτωπον (*prora*), the prow; 3. μεσόκοιλα, or middle part of the ship; 4. πρύμνη (*puppis*), the stern; 5. πλευραί (*latera*), the sides of the ship; 6. καταστρώματα, the decks or hatches; 7. ἑδώλια (*transtra*), the benches on which the rowers sat: the upper were called θρᾶνοι (the rowers θρανῖται), the middle ζυγά (the men ζυγῖται), the lower θάλαμος (the rowers θαλαμῖται); 8. ἔμβολον (*rostrum*) or beak: this consisted of a beam pointed with brass, and was used for the purpose of sinking and disabling the enemy's vessels; 9. ἄντλος (*sentina*), the hold; 10. γράφηξ, the bulwark.

The tackling, &c., used in navigation were: 1. ἱστός (*malus*), the mast; 2. κέρατα, κεραῖαι (*antennæ*), the yards; 3. ἱστίον (*velum*), the sail; 4. τοπεῖα, the cordage, comprising σχοινία (*funes*), the cables, πόδες (*pedes*), the ropes attached to the lower corners of the square sail, and ὑπέραι, the ropes fastened to the two ends of the yards; 5. πηδάλιον (*gubernaculum*), the rudder, usually two large oars, placed on each side of the stern; 6. οἴαξ, the tiller or handle of the oar; 7. ἄγκυρα, the anchor; 8. κῶπαι or ἐρετμοί (*remi*), the oars: their blades were called πλάται (*palmulæ*), and were fastened in their holes by leather thongs, τροποί (*strophi*); 9. κοντοί (*conti*), punting poles.

The δελφίν was a mass of metal suspended from the yards, which, being thrown into an enemy's ship, by its weight either shattered or sank it.

The two principal manœuvres in commencing an engagement were the διέκπλους, or breaking the line, and περίπλους, or outflanking the enemy.

The chief naval officers were: 1. στόλαρχος, ναύαρχος, or στρατηγός, the *præfectus classis*, or admiral; 2. ἐπιστολεύς, the vice-admiral; 3. τριήραρχος, or captain of a trireme; the captains of other vessels receiving their titles from the number of ranks of rowers their vessels contained.

The common sailors were called ναῦται (*nautæ*), the rowers ἐρέται, the soldiers who served at sea ἐπιβάται (*classiarii milites*), marines; κυβερνήτης (*gubernator*), the helmsman or pilot.

On landing, the ancients used to haul their vessels on shore (ἀνέλκειν, *subducere*) by means of (ὁλκοί, *pulvini*) rollers. To launch them, was termed καθέλκειν (*deducere*).

PRIVATE LIFE OF THE GREEKS.

MEALS.

There were four daily meals taken by the early Greeks: 1. ἄριστον or ἀκράτισμα, the morning meal or breakfast; 2. δεῖπνον, or dinner; 3. δειλινόν, or afternoon meal; 4. δόρπον, supper. The Greeks of a later age partook of three meals: 1. ἀκράτισμα, 2. ἄριστον, 3. δεῖπνον: corresponding to breakfast, luncheon, and dinner. It was customary among the ancient Greeks to sit at meat; but after luxury prevailed they reclined on couches, κλίναι, that they might drink at greater ease. Two guests usually reclined on a couch, but sometimes a greater number, who were then placed according to rank.

Dress.

The Greeks in ancient times used no covering for the head, but afterwards they wore hats called πίλοι. The general name for clothing was ἐσθής. The inner garment of men, as well as of women, was χιτών, a tunic; but women of wealth wore a robe called ἔγκυκλον χιτώνιον. The exterior garments were: 1. ἱμάτιον or φάρος, a cloak (Lat *pallium*); 2. χλαῖνα, a thicker garment for cold weather; 3. φαινόλης (Lat. *pœnula*), a round garment without sleeves; 4. ἐφεστρίς, a great coat; 5. τρίβων, a threadbare coat worn by philosophers and the poor; 6. στολή, a long garment reaching to the heels; 7. χλαμύς, a military cloak. On the feet were worn: 1. ὑποδήματα, or shoes bound under with thongs; 2. κρηπῖδες, slippers. Κόθωνοι were buskins, or boots worn by tragedians.

Funerals.

The Greeks attached great importance to the burial of the dead, as they believed the souls could not enter the Elysian fields unless their bodies were buried; and it was therefore looked upon as a grave charge on the character of a man to have neglected the burial of his relations. The following customs were connected with the Greek funeral.

As soon as any one had expired: 1. the eyes were closed by the nearest relative; 2. the mouth was shut; 3. the face was covered; 4. all the members of the body were stretched out; 5. the body was washed and anointed with oil; 6. wrapped in a handsome garment, and decked with chaplets and flowers; 7. laid out (πρόθεσις) on a couch (κλίνη), with the feet towards the door; 8. a small coin (ὀβολός) was placed in the mouth, as Charon's fare for carrying the soul over the infernal river; and, 9. a small cake (μελιτοῦττα) was also placed by the side of the corpse, intended to appease the fury of Cerberus. Before the door a vessel of water (ἀρδάνιον) was placed, that those about the corpse might purify themselves by washing.

On the day after the πρόθεσις, or the third day after death, the corpse was carried out (ἐκφορά) for burial, attended by the friends and neighbours of the deceased. It was either buried (θάπτειν, κατορύττειν) or burnt (καίειν) on piles of wood, called πυραί: when these were burnt down, the remains of the fire were quenched with wine, and the relatives and friends collected the bones, which were placed, together with the ashes, in urns, either made of gold, silver, wood, stone, or clay.

The corpses not burnt were buried in coffins, usually outside the city. It was usual after a funeral to partake of a feast at the house of the nearest relation of the departed, and on the third day to offer a sacrifice to the dead, called τρίτα. Libations (χοαί) were also made for the deceased; and the relatives expressed their sorrow in various ways, either by cutting off a portion of the hair, or shaving the head, sprinkling themselves with ashes, beating their breasts, and tearing their flesh, &c., &c.

The monuments erected over the graves were either στῆλαι, pillars or stone tablets, κίονες, columns, ναίδια or ἡρῷα, small buildings in the shape of temples, and τράπεζαι, square stones; on these were inscribed the name of the deceased, and some account of his past life.

THE GREEK THEATRE (θέατρον).

The most ancient theatres were at first of wood, but afterwards built of stone, or cut in the rock. The form was semicircular, and the rows of benches for the spectators, rising one above another, were arranged in front of the stage, which was divided into the λογεῖον (*pulpitum*) in front, where the actors spoke, and the προσκήνιον (*proscenium*) behind, at the back of which was a wall, σκηνή (*scena*), usually with three doors, for the entrance of the actors; in front of the σκηνή the back-ground scenes were placed, and concealed by a curtain, αὐλαῖαι (*aulœa*), till the play commenced, when it was drawn down. The ὀρχήστρα (*orchestra*) or pit was the circular space in front of the rows of seats and the stage, and was occupied by the chorus; in the centre of this space stood the θυμέλη, or

THE GREEK THEATRE.

altar of Dionysus (*Bacchus*), on the top of which the leader of the chorus, χοραγός, sometimes stood, and behind it the prompter, ὑποβολεύς (*monitor*), and flute-player were usually placed. The ancient theatres were of vast size, capable of containing in the κοῖλον (*cavea*) many thousand spectators, who sat according to their rank, the senators, priests, &c., occupying the front seats. The buildings were open to the sky [the Romans sometimes used an awning], and, owing to their vast size, the actors wore masks, *personæ* (adapted to their characters), with mouth-pieces to aid the voice; and tragic actors wore *cothurni*, or thick-soled buskins, to elevate the figure. The ancients used in their theatres various stage machinery to give effect to the representations.

ROMAN ANTIQUITIES.

DIVISIONS OF THE INHABITANTS OF THE ROMAN EMPIRE.

THE Roman people were divided by Romulus into three tribes (*tribus*). *Ramnes* or *Ramnenses, Titienses,* and *Lucēres:* these tribes were again divided into thirty *curiæ*, each of which had its *curio*, or president, and the whole body had a *curio maximus*.

The inhabitants of Rome were at first divided into two ranks (*ordines*): I. Patricii, and II. Plebei—these were connected together as Patroni and Clientes; afterwards, the Equites, forming a kind of intermediate order, were added. The Patricii appear to have been the original citizens, and were divided into curiæ and gentes, or clans, united by religious ties or family connexion. They were entirely separated from the Plebei, no connubium or marriage being permitted between the orders, and were the only parties eligible to the senate, or the higher offices in the religious and political government of the state.

In time, however, the Plebeians increased in importance by the admission of conquered tribes into their order, so that, from the time of Servius Tullius, they took part in the *comitia* or legal assemblies, and ultimately obtained the connubium and equal rights with the Patricians. The Equites were at first only a military order, 300 in number (*celeres*), and instituted by Romulus. This number was increased by the successive kings; the Equites had a horse at the public charge (*equus publicus*) and (*æs equestre*) a sum for its support. Latterly, however, the name Equites was extended from those who had horses at the public charge to all those having horses of their own, and qualified by their property to act as judices, and thus the military character of the original order disappeared, and all free-born citizens possessing 400,000 sestertii were Equites, or of the Equestrian order. The insignia of these Knights were the *annulus aureus*, gold ring, and the *angustus clavus*, a narrow band of purple wrought in the cloth, and extending from each shoulder to the bottom of the tunica. The Equites occupied the first fourteen benches at the theatres.

When the ancient difference between Patricians and Plebeians had disappeared, then arose a new classification, Nobiles and Ignobiles; the only privilege of the Nobiles was the *jus imaginum*, an ancient custom of setting up in the *atria* or courts of their houses waxen busts or effigies of their ancestors. These Nobiles were again divided into *Optimates* or Conservatives, and *Populares* or Radicals.

When the Roman empire enlarged its territories, there arose another division, Servi, or slaves, who became such either by being taken in war, by sale, by way of punishment, or by being born in a state of servitude. They received a monthly allowance, but could not obtain property without the consent of their masters. Slaves were sold at Rome by auction, and became either the property of private indviduals or of the state.

The state of slavery was terminated by *Manumissio*, which was effected either by entering a slave's name on the Censor's books (*censu*), or by certain ceremonies with a rod (*vindicta*) before the Prætor, or by will (*testamento*).

THE SENATE (*Senatus*).

The Senate, according to tradition, was instituted by Romulus, and consisted at first of only 100 members (*senatores* or *patres*), chosen from the Patricians. This number was increased to 200 when the Sabine Tities became united to the Latin Ramnes, and another 100 were also added when the Luceres, consisting chiefly of Etruscans, were incorporated in the time of Tarq. Priscus; these new Senators were called *Patres minorum gentium*, in distinction to the old Senators, *Patres majorum gentium*. The vacancies which occurred in the Senate after the abolition of the monarchy (B.C. 509) were filled up by Plebeians of Equestrian rank, who were designated *Conscripti*, and hence the Senate was addressed as *Patres* (sc. et) *Conscripti*. The number of 300 remained until the time of Sulla, when the Senate consisted of between five and six hundred. The Senate possessed the administrative authority, in such matters as religious worship, taxation, levying of troops, negotiations with foreign states, embassies, provincial government, &c., &c.

The sittings of the Senate were either regular (*senatus legitimus*) or extraordinary (*senatus indictus*), and were held between sunrise and sunset. When the members had assembled, the presiding magistrate announced the subject (*referre ud Senatum*), and called on each member to state his opinions (*rogare sententias, sententias dicere*); this he delivered either by a single word or in a speech; then followed the voting (*discessio, pedibus ire in sententiam alicujus*). The decree, when passed (*Senatûs Consultum* vel *Decretum*), was written down and placed in the *ærarium* or treasury, under the care of the Prætor.

A certain number of Senators were required to be present to make a decree valid, and those absenting themselves without just cause were fined. For Intercessio vide Tribuni.

It was required in a candidate that he should be free-born, and possess a certain amount of property; latterly, 800,000 sestertii. The Senators were chosen (*legebantur*) by the Kings, by the Consuls, and, in later times, by the Censors; one of the qualifications necessary was, that the candidate should have fulfilled the duties of the magistracy, the first degree of which was the quæstorship. The insignia of the Senators were the *latus clavus*, a broad band of purple, extending from the neck down the centre of the tunica, and the *calceus lunatus*, a high shoe adorned with a small crescent. The Senators had also certain seats at the public shows

ASSEMBLIES (*Comitia*).

The Comitia were the legal meetings of the Roman people, at which their votes were taken on matters connected with the government of the State. The Comitia could only be held on certain days (*dies comitiales*), never on festivals; and, previous to meeting, notice was given (*promulgari*) of the subject for decision. There were three kinds of Comitia: I. *Comitia Curiata*; II. *Comitia Centuriata*; III. *Comitia Tributa*.

I. COMITIA CURIATA were held, in a part of the Forum called Comitium, first by the Kings, and afterwards by the Consuls and Prætors. Though at first they were assemblies of the whole people, and possessed power in enacting laws and confirming the authority of the Kings, on the decline of the Patrician power they lost their importance. The Comitia Calata belonged to these Comitia, which were merely meetings for the purpose of sanctioning certain proceedings, inaugurating the Flamines, &c.

II. COMITIA CENTURIATA were held, *extra Pomœrium*, in the Campus Martius, either by the Consul or Prætor. In these Comitia the Consuls, Prætors, and Censors, were elected, laws were passed, war declared, and capital offences were tried. The Comitia Centuriata were usually assembled by an edict, and summoned twenty-seven days before the period of meeting; this space of time was called *trinundinum*. All those who had the right of Roman citizens might be present, and voted according to their property. On the day of meeting, the auspices were consulted by the presiding magistrate and the augurs, and the Comitia were opened with sacrifice and prayer. After the debate, if no religious obstacle prevented, the people were called on to arrange themselves for voting. The Equites voted first, and the six classes in succession. The votes were at first vivâ voce, but were afterwards delivered in writing by means of a *tabella*. The centuries which were to vote passed over bridges into an inclosed space (*ovile*), where the *tabellæ* were supplied, and thrown by the voters into the *cistæ* or ballot-boxes, from which they were taken and counted, and the result of the voting proclaimed with a loud voice.

III. COMITIA TRIBUTA were held both *intra* and *extra Pomœrium*, under the presidency of the Tribunes of the People. At these Comitia the inferior magistrates were chosen, as well as the Ædiles Curules, and the Tribunes of the People after B.C. 471; and after B.C. 104 the members of the Colleges of Priests. Laws were passed at these Comitia called Plebiscita, which at first only bound the Plebeians; but after B.C. 306 they concerned the whole people. The Patricians seldom attended, as the votes of all were of equal force.

MAGISTRATES AND CHIEF PUBLIC OFFICERS.

N. B. — The dates affixed are those of the institution of the various offices.

ÆDILES PLEBIS, B.C. 494, two functionaries elected from the Plebei, to take charge of the public buildings, to judge in inferior cases, inspect weights and measure, and prohibit unlawful games.

ÆDILES CURULES, B.C. 365, two in number, elected at first from the Patricii. They superintended the public games, took care of the buildings, repaired the temples, theatres, baths, &c., and were appointed judges in all cases relating to the buying and selling of estates.

ÆDILES CEREALES, B.C. 45, two in number, elected from the Plebei. They inspected the public stores of corn, all commodities exposed in the markets, and punished delinquents in all cases of buying and selling. The office was instituted by Julius Cæsar. The Ædiles had various officers under them, viz., *præcones* or "criers," *scribæ* or "clerks," and *viatores* or "attendants" and "messengers."

APPARITORES, the general name given to the public officers who waited on the magistrates, such as the *Accensi, Lictores, Scribæ, Præcones, Viatores,* &c.

CENSORES, B.C. 443, two officers of high rank and authority, elected (at first from among the Patricians) for a lustrum, or space of five years; but latterly the period of office was only for eighteen months. The duties were of three kinds: I. To take an exact account of the property and estates of every person (*census*), and to divide the people into their proper classes or centuries; II. To superintend the administration of the finances of the State, and meet the expenses attendant on the erection or repairs of temples, public buildings &c.; III. To punish immorality in *any* person: the Senators they might expel from the Curia or Senate-house; the Knights they might punish by depriving them of the horse allowed them at the public charge; and the Commons they might remove from a high tribe to one less honourable, impose on them a fine, or disable them from voting in the Assemblies.

CONSULES, B.C. 509, the principal annual Roman magistrates, *two* in number. The office was established on the expulsion of Tarquinius, the last King of Rome. At the first institution, the Consuls were elected from the Patricians only; but afterwards, B.C. 366, the Plebeians obtained the right of electing one. The common age required in a candidate was forty-three years; the time of election was about the end of July or beginning of August, they were then called "*designati*" until entering on their office, the period of undertaking which varied at different times. At first their power was as great as that of the Kings, and their badges of office nearly the same, in public being always preceded by twelve lictors, with the fasces They wore the *toga prætexta*, sat on the *curule chair*, and carried an *ivory sceptre*. Their chief duties were presiding in the Senate, administering justice, levying troops, commanding armies and provinces, conducting the Circensian games, &c., &c. The first Consuls elected were L. Junius Brutus and L. Tarquinius Collatinus.

CURATORES, public officers of various kinds, viz.: *Curatores Annonæ* (of corn), *Curatores Riparum* (of the navigation of the Tiber), *Curatores Kalendarii* (of books containing the names of persons who borrowed public money), *Curatores*

Ludorum (of the public games), *Curatores Operum Publicorum* (of public works), &c., &c.

DICTATOR, B.C. 501, a magistrate with supreme authority among the Romans; he was nominated by the Consuls, the auspices being taken at midnight. The Dictator was only elected at times when great danger threatened the State. His period of office was six months, sometimes even less. So great was the power of this officer, that he might proclaim war, levy forces, and lead them to battle, or disband them, without any consultation with the Senate. He could also punish as he pleased, and there was no appeal from him, at least until later times. The insignia of the office were the *sella curulis* and *toga prætexta;* the Dictator was also preceded by twenty-four lictors, and during his tenure of office all other magistrates resigned except the Tribuni Plebis. On his election, his first act was to choose a "Magister Equitum," or *Master of the Horse*, who always attended him. T. Lartius Flavus, or Rufus, was the first Dictator, and Sp. Cassius Viscellinus the first Magister Equitum.

PRÆFECTUS URBI (office instituted by Romulus), an officer who presided in the city during the absence of the Kings or Consuls. The office was latterly merged in that of *Prætor Urbānus*.

PRÆTOR, B.C. 366, one of the chief magistrates at Rome, next to the Consuls. In B.C. 246 a Prætor was appointed, called Peregrinus, whose duty it was to administer justice in matters of dispute between *peregrini* (foreigners) or peregrini and Roman citizens. The other Prætor was then called Urbanus. Sp. Furius Camillus was the first Prætor: the number varied at different times. The duty of the Prætor was, 1. to administer justice (his tribunal was called "Prætorium"), and, 2. to act as Consul in the absence of that officer. He was entitled to the *prætexta*, the *sella curulis*, *two* lictors when at Rome, and *six* when out. The exercise of the prætorian authority was signified by the words "*do*" (when they granted licence to institute a trial), "*dico*" (when they pronounced sentence), and "*addico*" (when they give the goods of a debtor to a creditor). Prætôrs were also sent to govern provinces subject to the Romans.

PRO-CONSUL, B.C. 327, a magistrate sent to govern a province with Consular power. It was usual for Consuls, on the expiration of their Consulship at Rome, formally to obtain leave of the people, and get a decree of the Senate for permission to govern a province. The command lasted one year, at the end of which the Pro-Consul made up his accounts, left them in writing in the two chief cities of the province, and returned to Rome. The insignia were the same as the Consuls, but only six lictors.

PROCURATOR, an officer of the Imperial provinces, who discharged the same duties as the Quæstors in other provinces.

PRO-PRÆTOR, an officer who had all the authority of a Prætor. The name was assumed by those who, as Prætors, had continued in power beyond the time fixed.

QUÆSTORES, magistrates, at first two in number; increased B.C. 421 to four, B.C. 265 to eight, by Sulla, B.C. 82, to twenty, by Cæsar to forty. They had the management of the public treasury. Two Quæstors accompanied the Consuls in all their expeditions; they received the name "Peregrini," the other two "Urbani." When the number was augmented, certain Quæstors were sent to collect the taxes in various provinces. No person was eligible to this office under the age of twenty-two years.

TRIBUNI PLEBIS, B.C. 494, certain Roman magistrates, elected from among the Commons to defend their liberties; they were at first only two in number, afterwards increased to five, and lastly to ten. Though at first only redressers of public wrongs, they afterwards assumed great power. They made decrees, and carried laws, which they executed on magistrates themselves, ordering even Consuls to prison; they possessed the right of "*intercessio*," and their persons were "*sacrosancti*." Nothing could be concluded without their consent, which was signified by affixing the letter T to the decree. They could prevent the passing of any measure by standing up, and pronouncing the simple word "*veto*" (called intercessio). They kept open houses, and were never allowed to leave the city, except at the festival "Feriæ Latinæ," held on the Alban Mount.

TRIBUNI MILITUM, B.C. 445, elected with *Consular power*. They were three in number, but in B.C. 405 increased to six. For many years the number of these tribunes was very irregular. The office was abolished B.C. 367.

JUDICIAL PROCEEDINGS, PUNISHMENTS, &c.

The judicial proceedings (*judicia*) of the Romans were either public or private. The *judicia privata*, or civil trials had reference to the rights of private persons, &c, in which at first the Kings, and afterwards the Consuls and Praetors decided. The *judicia publica*, or criminal trials, were originally conducted by *Quæsitores* (subject to the Kings), and after the expulsion of the kings by the Consuls and Prætors. Capital offenders were tried before the Comitia Centuriata, at which it was necessary that the accuser should be a magistrate.

The chief punishments among the Romans were: 1. *mulcta* or *damnum*, a fine; 2. *vincula*, bonds, imprisonment; 3. *verbera*, beating or scourging; 4. *talio*, retaliation, as an eye for an eye; 5. *ignominia* or *infamia*, disgrace inflicted by the Censors, or by edict of the Prætor; 6. *exilium*, banishment; 7. *servitus*, slavery; 8. *mors*, death, either by decapitation, hanging, throwing from the Tarpeian Rock, strangling, burning, crucifying, &c.

PRIESTS.

The ministers of religion among the Romans were divided into two orders: I. Those appointed to the common service of all the gods; and, II. Those devoted to the service of particular deities. Among the former were —

THE PONTIFICES, a college of priests, presided over by the *Pontifex Maximus*. They were first appointed by Numa. The Collegium consisted of four members, elected from the Patricians until B.C. 300, when an equal number of Plebeians were admitted. They administered the ecclesiastical laws, prescribed the ceremonial of any new public or private worship, prepared the forms for public prayers and vows, composed the annals, and regulated the fasti, interpreted prodigies, inaugurated magistrates, and punished persons guilty of offences against religion. The insignia of the Pontifices were the *toga prætexta* and a woollen cap, *pileus*. The Pontifex Maximus chiefly superintended the service of *Vesta*.

THE AUGURES or AUSPICES were originally three or four in number, Patricians, presided over by a *Magister Collegii*; but in B.C. 300 five Plebeians were added, and under Sulla the Augurs were increased to fifteen. The word Augur or Auspex at first meant a diviner by birds (*aves*); but in time the name was applied in a much wider sense. The art was called *Augurium* or *Auspicium*. In ancient times no transaction, either public or private, took place without consulting the auspices, which were divided into five kinds: 1. Those derived from the sky (*ex cœlo*), particularly from lightning and thunder; 2. From birds (*ex avibus*), which were either *oscines*, which gave auguries by singing, or *alites*, by flying; 3. From the feeding of chickens (*ex tripudiis*), chiefly war auguries; 4. From four-footed animals (*ex quadrupedibus*); 5. *Ex diris signis*, which included every other kind of augury, as sneezing, stumbling, &c. The Augurs, when about taking the auspices, stationed themselves on some open ground, and, after offering sacrifices, proceeded, with veiled heads, to mark out with the *lituus*, or curved wand, a particular division, *templum*, in the heavens, in which they intended to make their observations. The *spectio*, or right of taking the auspices of the State, was conducted by a magistrate, assisted by an Augur, who interpreted the signs. The auspices taken by the magistrates were divided into *auspicia majora* and *minora*, the former being taken by the Consuls and superior magistrates, the latter by the Quæstors and Curule Ædiles. The right of self-election, *co-ōptatio*, was possessed by the Augurs until B.C. 103. The insignia of the order were the *trabea* and *lituus*.

THE FETIALES were a college of priests, instituted by Numa. They were twenty in number, and their president was styled *Pater Patratus*. The Fetiales acted as the guardians of the public faith, and it was their office, when disputes arose with foreign states, to demand restitution, conclude treaties, and perform the rites attendant on the declaration of war, &c.

THE HARUSPICES were soothsayers, who interpreted the will of the gods from the appearance of the entrails (*exta*), whence they are sometimes called *Extispices*. The art was called *Haruspicīna*, and much taught in Etruria.

THE DECEMVIRI SACRIS FACIUNDIS or SACRORUM were the priests appointed to take charge of the three Sibylline Books (which Tarquin received from the Sibyl), and offer the sacrifices prescribed by them. At first they were two in number, then ten (five Patrician and five Plebeian), and afterwards fifteen. The term *Decemviri* was also applied to the ten officers who were appointed to draw up a code of laws, B.C. 451 (vide Chronology).

THE CURIONES were priests for the Curiæ, under a Curio Maximus.

THE REX SACRIFICULUS was a priest appointed after the expulsion of the Kings to superintend the religious rites formerly performed by them.

The priests for the services of particular deities.

THE FLAMINES were appointed to the temple-service of certain gods; they were fifteen in number, the chief of whom were *Flamen Dialis*, the priest of Jupiter; *Flamen Martialis*, the priest of Mars; *Flamen Quirinalis*, the priest of Romulus. They wore a purple robe, *læna*, and conical cap, *apex*.

THE VIRGINES VESTALES were appointed by Numa to feed the sacred fire, and guard the relics in the temple of Vesta; they were at first four in number, two more were subsequently added. They were originally chosen by the Kings, afterwards by the Pontifex Maximus, and were required not to be under six nor above ten years of age, and free from bodily defects. The period of service lasted thirty years, at the end of which they were allowed to marry. While in the service of the goddess, they enjoyed many privileges, such as freedom from parental control, a particular seat at shows, the right of liberating any criminal whom they accidentally met, the attendance of a lictor, &c. They were subject to the Pontifex Maximus, who severely punished them for letting out the sacred fire, and for unchastity ordered them to be buried alive. The Vestals were clad in a white robe, and their heads were adorned with fillets (*infŭlæ*).

THE SALII were priests of Mars Gradivus, twelve in number, Patricians, appointed by Numa to guard the *Ancīle*, or sacred shield, which fell from heaven, and the eleven others of similar make which were kept in the temple of Mars, and carried in procession, with dancing and singing, by the Salii, annually on the first of March.

THE LUPERCI were priests of Pan; they went in procession, dressed in goat-skins, on the *Lupercalia* or festivals of Pan, to the Palatine, where they sacrificed to the god.

THE GALLI were the eunuch priests of Cybĕle, whose worship was introduced at Rome from Phrygia, B.C. 204.

THE FRATRES ARVALES were twelve in number, who superintended the yearly rural sacrifice of purification.

PRAYERS, SACRIFICES, FESTIVALS, &c.

The worship of the gods consisted of prayers, vows, and sacrifices. Public prayers were offered by the chief magistrates after a form prepared and recited by the priests; these prayers were often accompanied by vows (*vota*). It was usual for persons who had been in great danger during a voyage, on landing, to hang up their clothes in the temple of Neptune, with a tablet (*votiva tabula*), on which was depicted a representation of the event.

Sacrifices (*sacrificia*) formed the chief part of the public worship of the Romans, whose customs were in this matter much the same as those of the Greeks. The victim (*hostia, victima*), without blemish before being sacrificed, was decorated with garlands (*vittæ, infulæ*), and sometimes its horns were gilded; it was then led to the altar by the *popa*, or attendant, where the animal's head was sprinkled with roast barley meal, mixed with salt (*mola salsa*), and afterwards slaughtered, and its entrails (*exta*) inspected by the *haruspices*, the better parts strewed with meal, wine, and incense, and burnt on the altar, and a solemn banquet prepared. The *lustratio* was a purification in which the victim was lead round the object intended to be purified. (For *libatio*, vide page 104.) The most common sacrifices at Rome were the *suovetaurilia*, consisting of a pig, a sheep, and an ox.

The places dedicated to the worship of the Romans were either buildings, or sacred spots consecrated by the Augurs: e. g. *templa, ædes sacræ, fana, delubra, sacella, ædiculæ; luci.*

Days among the Romans were either devoted to religious observances, *dies festi*, or to business, *dies profesti*. The *feriæ* or festivals, in which the Romans ceased from political transactions, law-suits, &c., were divided into *publicæ* and *privatæ;* the former being again divided into *feriæ stativæ* or immoveable, *feriæ conceptivæ* or moveable, and *feriæ imperativæ*, fasts held by command of the magistrate: the *feriæ privatæ* were kept by families in commemoration of birthdays, &c.

The chief *feriæ stativæ* were the *Lupercalia* to Pan, 15th of February; *Matronalia*, celebrated by matrons for various causes, 1st of March; *Megalesia*, or feast of *Cybĕle*, mother of the gods, 4th of April; *Parilia* or *Palilia*, in honour of Pales, deity of orchards, 21st of April; feast of the *Bona Dea*, attended by the vestal virgins and women only, 1st of May; feast of *Castor* and *Pollux*, with the *Transvectio Equitum*, an annual procession of the Equites or Knights, 15th of July; *Saturnalia*, feasts of Saturn, the most celebrated of the festivals, when all orders devoted themselves to mirth and revelling; the feast commenced on the 19th, afterwards 17th, of December, and lasted several days.

GAMES.

The games of the Romans were either **stated** (*stati*), and **votive**, or **extraordinary**, which were celebrated in consequence of vows, or at the funerals of private persons. The games were of three kinds: I. **Ludi Circenses**; II. **Gladiatorii**, shows of Gladiators; III. **Scenici**, dramatic entertainments.

The **Ludi Circenses**, so called from being celebrated in the *circus* (*maximus*), were of Etruscan origin. They commenced with a procession, and consisted of: I. *Cursus*, chariot or horse-races; 2. *Ludus Trojæ*, a sham fight or tournament on horseback; 3. *Pugna equestris et pedestris*, a representation of a battle; 4. *Certamen gymnicum*, consisting of the πένταθλον of the Greeks (Lat. *quinquertium*); viz. *saltus*, leaping; *cursus*, running; *lucta*, wrestling; *pugilatus*, boxing; *discus*, throwing the quoit or discus; and the *pancratium;* 5. *Venatio*, hunting, i. e. the combats of wild beasts, either with one another or with men hired for the purpose, or with condemned criminals or captives; 6. *Naumachia*, a representation of a naval engagement; the Naumachiæ were either exhibited in the amphitheatres (sufficient water being brought in to float the ships), or in buildings erected for the purpose.

Gladiatorii. The shows of gladiators were also of Etruscan origin, and were first introduced at Rome in the Forum Boarium, B.C. 264, by order of M. and **Decimus Brutus**, at the funeral of their father. Though at first only confined to funerals, the shows of gladiators afterwards took place at public festivals, and combats were exhibited by the chief Roman magistrates and emperors till the time of Constantine, by whom they were abolished. The combatants were at first either slaves, captives, or condemned criminals, and sometimes free men, who hired themselves out; but during the empire, even **Senators** and **Equites** fought in the *arena*.

The gladiators were instructed by a *lanista* in the use of the various weapons, and previous to the actual combats a *prælusio* or sham battle took place, when the gladiators were matched by pairs, and used blunt wooden swords (*rudes*), which were also given them on their discharge.

The several kinds of gladiators were: 1. *Andabatæ*, who wore helmets which covered the face, and consequently they fought blind-folded; 2. *Catervarii*, who fought in companies; 3. *Essedarii*, who fought from chariots; 4. *Mirmillones* (so named from having the image of a fish (μορμύρος) on their helmets), usually matched with *retiarii* or *Thracians;* 5. *Retiarii*, who fought with a "fuscina," or three-pointed lance (*tridens*), and a net (*rete*), with which they endeavoured to entangle their adversaries, and despatch them with the trident; 6. *Samnites*, who used the oblong shield (*scutum*) and the usual armour of the Samnites; 7. *Thraces*, armed like the Thracians, with a round shield and short dagger (*sica*). When a gladiator was wounded, the people shouted *habet*, "he has got it," and the vanquished one lowered his arms in token of submission; but his fate depended on the people, who pressed down their thumbs (*pollicem premere*), if they wished his life to be spared, and turned them up (*vertere*) as a signal for death. The combats usually took place in the Amphitheatrum, a large building, in form a complete oval, the centre space of which was called the *arena*, from being sprinkled with sand; the most celebrated was the Amph. Flavium or Coliseum, built by Vespasian and Titus, which had raised seats, capable of containing 87,000 spectators.

The Scenici, or stage plays, were introduced from Etruria, about B.C. 364. They were performed in theatres (*theatra*), large semicircular buildings, fitted up with benches or seats (*cunei*), which rose one above another; the fourteen foremost rows next the stage being occupied by the Equites; the whole of the space for the public was called *cavea*. The *orchestra* was a semicircular space in front of the spectators, assigned to the Senators, foreign ambassadors, &c. The Scenici were of three kinds: *Comœdia*, Comedy; *Tragœdia*, Tragedy; *Mimus*, Pantomime. The dramatic pieces were purchased by the Ædiles, and the recitation was accompanied by flutes, and the actors usually wore masks, *personæ*. Vide Greek Theatre (page 116), to which, on the whole, the Roman corresponded.

MILITARY AFFAIRS.

CONSCRIPTION AND PERIOD OF SERVICE, &C.

The Romans were a nation of warriors, and thus from the earliest period they had an organized military establishment. In the early times, the army consisted of 3000 infantry and three centuries of cavalry (*Equites*). When Servius Tullius divided the people, he formed the better class of citizens into eighteen centuries of *Equites*. The infantry then consisted of five classes, and were divided into *seniores*, for the defence of the city, and *juniores*, for service abroad.

Every citizen was compelled to enlist when the public service required: the age of enlisting was from *seventeen* to *forty-six*, and the time of service twenty campaigns of one year for the infantry, and ten for the cavalry; these services were looked upon as honourable, and ten years of either infantry or cavalry service was a qualification for the magistracy. At first, none of the poorest citizens (*proletarii*) or freedmen performed military service, except on urgent occasions. Marius, B.C. 107, first chose soldiers without reference to property, in still later times citizens were exempted from compulsory service, and under the Emperors the army consisted chiefly of foreigners. In the times of the Republic, four legions of soldiers were raised, two for each Consul; but this number gradually increased, and was greatly augmented by allies.

The Consuls, at the yearly conscription, required all those who had reached the military age to appear on the *Campus Martius*, or at the *Capitolium*, for the purpose of enrolling their names. The selection was made by the Military Tribunes, after which an oath (*sacramentum*) was administered. Persons suffering from bodily infirmity were exempted from service; but soldiers conscribed on a sudden emergency (*tumultuarii* or *subitarii*) were allowed no exemption. Soldiers who had served their time were called *emeriti*, and received a discharge, *missio*, but sometimes were again called out or induced to re-enlist, and were then termed *evocati*. The pay of the common soldiers was ⅓ denarius a day; the centurion received double this sum; the Equites were allowed a horse at the public expense, and an annual sum for its keep (Vide page 118).

Divisions of the Army.

After the levy was completed, and the oath administered, the troops were formed into l e g i o n s; each *legio* was divided into ten *cohortes*, each cohort into three *manipuli*, and each manipulus into two *centuriæ*. To each legion belonged a body of cavalry (300 in number), divided into ten *turmæ* or troops, each turma containing three *decuriæ*. The number of men in a legion varied at different times, generally from 4000 to 6000 infantry, and from 300 to 400 cavalry. The soldiers were divided into the h a s t a t i (forming the first line, so called from bearing the hasta, a long spear, which was afterwards laid aside, and the pilum used instead), the p r i n- c i p e s (men of middle age in the vigour of life, who formed the second line, originally the first), the t r i a r i i, old soldiers, who formed the third line; they were also called p i l a n i, from the pilum or javelin they used. The other kinds of soldiers were: 1. *Velites*, swift and light-armed soldiers, employed in outpost duty when the Romans were encamped; 2. *Funditores*, slingers; 3. *Sagittarii*, archers; 4. *Ferentarii* and *Rorarii*, light-armed soldiers.

Arms.

The defensive arms were: 1. *scutum*, an oblong shield, made of wicker-work or wood, joined together with iron and covered with hide, and having an iron boss in the centre; 2. *clipeus*, a large shield of a circular form; 3. *galea*, the helmet, made of brass or iron, and surmounted by a *crista* or crest; 4. *lorica*, a coat of mail or cuirass, generally made of leather, covered with plates of iron or of chain; 5. *thorax*, a breast-plate (more in use than the lorica); 6. *ocreæ*, the greaves for the legs, made of metal lined with leather.

MILITARY AFFAIRS.

The offensive arms were: 1. *gladius* or *ensis*, a sword, generally straight, with a two-edged blade; 2. *pila*, javelins pointed with iron; 3. *hastæ*, long spears.

The light-armed soldiers, *velites*, mentioned above, used a small shield called *parma*.

Officers.

The command (*imperium*) of the army was intrusted to the chief magistrates; first to the Kings, and afterwards to the Consuls, Prætors, and Dictators. The principal officers under these were: 1. *Legati*, nominated by the Consul or Dictator, and approved of by the Senate. 2. *Tribuni Militum*, elected by the Consul or Dictator; latterly, B.C. 362, partly by the people; to each *legio* there were at first three, but afterwards six Tribunes, who were relieved every two months. 3. *Centuriones*, chosen by the Tribunes according to merit from the common soldiers; each maniple had two, a *prior* and *posterior*. The Centurions had under them *Optiones*, or *Succenturiones*, and *Signiferi*, or standard-bearers.

The troops of allies (*auxilia*) were commanded by *Præfecti*.

The cavalry was commanded by a *Præfectus alæ*, and the *turmæ* had each three *Decuriones* (or officers of ten), who had under them *Optiones* or deputies.

The military cloak of the General was called *paludamentum* or *chlamys*, and was of a scarlet colour (the latter was also a travelling-dress). The *sagum* was the common military cloak of the soldiers.

The Romans, when on a march, every night constructed an encampment, which they fortified with a palisade (*vallum*), trench (*fossa*), and mound (*agger*). The camp was generally a parallelogram, and had four gates, *prætoria*, *decumana*, *principalis dextra*, and *sinistra*.

The signals were given by wind-instruments: *buccĭna* (a trumpet, bent almost round), *cornu* (a horn similar to the buccĭna), *tuba* (a straight trumpet) in the infantry, and *lituus* (the clarion) in the cavalry.

The Order of Battle.

The army was usually drawn up in three lines, *hastati*, *principes*, and *triarii*, placed at certain distances, and divided into maniples or cohorts, the open spaces being occupied by (*velites*) light troops. The legions were in the centre (*media acies*), and the cavalry and allies formed the wings (*cornua*). Sometimes a different order of battle was necessary, and the troops were formed into the *cuneus* or wedge, the *orbis* or *globus*, a round body, and the *testudo*, a compact body employed in sieges, the whole of the men being covered with their shields, as with a roof.

The standards, *signa*, gave the signals for the movements of the army; each maniple had one, the ancient signal of which was a handful of hay on a pole. The standard of the *legio* was a spear, *hasta*, with the figure of an animal upon it: from the consulship of Marius, B.C. 104, a silver eagle with extended wings became the standard of the *legio*.

The engines used in storming towns, &c., were: 1. *Aries*, a battering ram, consisting of a beam, to one end of which was fixed a mass of iron, in the form of a ram's head; 2. *Ballista*, an engine for projecting stones, &c.; 3. *Catapulta*, used for throwing darts; 4. *Vinea*, a shed (pushed forward on wheels), under which generally hung the aries; 5. *Turris*, a wooden tower, lofty enough to overtop the walls of the city, against which it was usually wheeled upon an artificial mound (*agger*). It was faced with iron or wet hides, to protect it from fire, and consisted of several stories (*tabulata*), on which slingers, catapults, &c., were placed.

MILITARY REWARDS AND PUNISHMENTS. TRIUMPH. OVATION.

Besides a share in the booty taken from an enemy, the Roman soldiers received as rewards garlands of leaves or flowers. The principal were: 1. *Corona civica*, a crown of oak-leaves, presented to one who saved the life of a citizen; 2. *Corona castrensis*, given to the soldier who first forced an entrance into an enemy's camp; 3. *Corona muralis*, for him who first scaled the walls of a besieged city; 4. *Corona obsidionalis* or *graminea* (grass), given to the commander who had relieved a besieged city, or an army surrounded by an enemy; 5. *Corona oleagina* (olive-leaves), presented by their commanders to soldiers who had distinguished themselves. The other rewards were weapons of honour, *hasta pura; vexilla*, standards; *phaleræ*, trappings; *aureæ torques*, gold chains; *armillæ*, bracelets, &c., &c. The military punishments were deprivation of pay, degradation of rank, to be beaten with rods, to be scourged and sold as a slave, to be stoned, to be beheaded, &c., &c.

The highest honour a general could obtain was a triumph, and to be saluted as *Imperator* by his army. To be honoured with a triumph, it was necessary that the general should in a just war have extended the bounds of the empire, and destroyed more than 5000 enemies in one battle. On a triumph being decreed, the procession proceeded from the Campus Martius to the Capitolium, and consisted of musicians, oxen for sacrifice, the spoils taken in war, models of the captured cities, the captives, the lictors (their fasces being wreathed with laurel), and the general (*dux*) dressed in purple embroidered with gold (*togâ pictâ et tunicâ palmatâ*), crowned with a laurel wreath, and in an ornamented chariot drawn by four white horses, followed by the victorious army. There was also an inferior sort of triumph, *ovatio*, in which the general entered the city on foot, crowned with a wreath of myrtle, and sacrificed a sheep.

NAVAL AFFAIRS.

For the names of the various parts of a ship, tackling, &c., the reader is referred to Greek Antiq., "Naval Affairs," page 12*

113, where the corresponding Latin names are given. The Roman navy consisted of *naves longæ, trirēmes, quadrirēmes, quinquerēmes;* lighter vessels, *actuariæ, liburnæ,* vide page 113; *onerariæ,* ships of burden or transports. The Romans in their engagements attempted to set fire to the enemy's ships, or seize and board them by means of *corvi, ferreæ manus,* and *harpagōnes,* grappling irons, &c. Sometimes towers or castles were built on their vessels, from which arrows and other missiles were discharged. The vessels were often manned by slaves, freedmen, and the lowest class of citizens. The admiral, *dux, præfectus classi,* was usually a Consul, and his ship was called *navis prætoria.*

PRIVATE LIFE OF THE ROMANS.

Dress.

The dress of the Romans consisted of the *tunica,* a woollen garment, which was generally without sleeves, and reached a little below the knees. A long tunic with sleeves was considered effeminate. The tunic was fastened round the waist by a belt, *cingulum.* The Senators wore a *tunica laticlavia,* with a broad purple stripe wrought in the cloth; and the Equites or Knights a tunic with a narrow stripe, *tunica angusticlavia.* A dress called *subucula* was generally worn under the *tunica.* The *toga,* the distinguishing part of the Roman dress, was an outer gown or mantle, thrown round the body so as to cover the left arm, and leave the right partly exposed, and forming a fold, *sinus,* on the breast; these folds, when collected in a knot or centre, being called *umbo.* The colour of the *toga* was white (*alba, pura*). Candidates for office wore a *toga* whitened by the fuller (*toga candida*).

Magistrates wore the *toga prætexta*, bordered with purple; and generals in a triumph an embroidered *toga, picta* or *palmata*, having palm-leaves worked on it. The toga prætexta was worn by young women until they were married, and young men till they were seventeen years of age, when the latter assumed the *toga virilis;* this ceremony was performed with great solemnity in the *Forum*. The *pœnula* was a garment used chiefly as a travelling-cloak. In later times, the *lacerna*, a kind of great-coat, was worn above the *toga*, with the *cucullus*, a cowl or hood; similar to the *lacerna* was the *læna*. The *stola* was a female dress worn over the *tunica*, and fastened by a girdle; over the *stola* was worn the *palla*, corresponding to the *toga* of the male sex.

The coverings of the feet were *calcei*, shoes, when abroad, and *soleæ*, sandals, which only covered the sole of the foot. The shoes of the soldiers were called *caligæ*, of comedians, *socci*, and of tragedians, *cothurni*.

The head was uncovered, except in bad weather or when on a journey, when the *pileus*, hat, or *galērus*, cap, was worn.

Rings (*annuli*), set with precious stones, were very much worn by the Romans; the Senators and Equites used golden rings, the Plebeians iron ones.

MEALS.

The first meal taken was the *jentaculum*, or breakfast; to this followed the *prandium*, or luncheon, taken about noon· *cœna*, or dinner, was the next and the principal meal of the Romans; it was taken in the evening, and consisted of three courses, the first *gustatio, antecœna*, or *promulsis*, the second or principal course *caput cœnæ*, and the dessert *mensæ secundæ* or *bellaria*. The guests reclined, according to their rank, on couches (*lecti*), generally three, *summus, medius, imus*, at each table, thus:—

```
                lectus medius
        ┌─────────────────────┐
        │  imus  medius summus│
        │                     │
   ┌────┼──6────5────4────────┼────┐
   │ summus │7│         │3│ imus  │
 l │        │ │         │ │       │ l
 e │ medius │8│  mensa  │2│ medius│ e
 c │        │ │         │ │       │ c
 t │ imus   │9│         │1│ summus│ t
 u │        │ │         │ │       │ u
 s │        └─┴─────────┴─┘       │ s
 i │                              │ 
 m │                              │ s
 u │                              │ u
 s │                              │ m
   └──────────────────────────────┘ m
                                    u
                                    s
```

A supper, *commissatio*, was sometimes taken after the *cœna*. Wine, though rarely drunk in early times, came afterwards into general use, but was sometimes mingled with water or cooled with snow. The best Italian wines were *vinum Cæcubum, Falernum, Massicum, Calēnum, Albānum, Surrentinum, Selīnum,* &c.; the foreign were *vinum Chium, Lesbium, Leucadium, Coum, Rhodium, Naxium, Mæonium,* &c. The wines were brought to table in jars, *amphoræ*, and mixed with water in a bowl, *crater*, whence it was poured into *pocula*, cups.

PRIVATE HOUSES. BATHS.

Though at first mere cottages, the houses of the Romans in after-times were built in a style of great elegance, and ornamented with marble pillars, elegant furniture, pictures, vases, candelabra, &c.

The principal parts of the Roman houses were: 1. *Vestibulum*, an open space before the doors, enclosed on three sides by the building; 2. *Ostium* or *janua*, the door or entrance, with the *limen*, threshold, *postes*, door-posts, *fores* or *valvæ*, the actual doors; 3. *Atrium* or *cavum ædium*, the principal apartment: in the centre of the roof was an opening, *compluvium*, from which the rain-water fell into a cistern

PRIVATE LIFE OF THE ROMANS. 141

(*impluvium*) in the floor; this *impluvium*, which also denoted the aperture in the roof, was ornamented with statues, &c.; 4. *Alæ*, the wings or small apartments on each side of the *atrium*; 5. *Peristylium*, adjoining the *œdium*, a partially open court-yard surrounded by columns, and ornamented with shrubs and flowers; 6. *Cubicula* or *dormitoria*, bed-chambers; 7. *Triclinia*, dining-rooms; 8. *Œci* and *exedræ*, saloons; 9. *Pinacothĕca*, or picture-gallery; 10. *Bibliothĕca*, library; 11. *Cœnacula*, rooms on the second story. The floors, *sola*, were frequently laid in mosaic, and the inner walls, *parietes*, lined with slabs of marble and pictures. The windows, *fenestræ*, were closed with wooden shutters; and in the time of the Emperors with transparent stone (*lapis specularis*, mica) and glass (*vitrum*). The ceilings were flat, and divided by the intersection of the beams and planks into hollows (*lacunaria*, *laquearia*), which were often carved and gilt.

Baths, *balneæ*, *thermæ*. The Romans at first used baths but seldom, and only for health and cleanliness; but afterwards as a luxury. They were taken after exercise, and previous to the principal meal, *cœna*, and sometimes after eating, to promote digestion. The principal parts of the public *thermæ* were: 1. *Vestibulum*, in which the servants waited, and the *balneator*, or keeper, received the *quadrans* paid by each visitor; 2. *Apodyterium*, or undressing-room; 3. *Frigidarium*, the cold-bath; 4. *Tepidarium*, the tepid-bath, or a chamber heated with air; 5. *Caldarium*, the warm-bath, warmed by *hypocausta*, heating-apparatus. After bathing, the Romans made use of instruments called *strigiles*, or scrapers, for removing the oil with which they were anointed, and the impurities of the skin, and *lintea*, towels.

AMUSEMENTS.

The Romans before bathing took various kinds of exercise, one of which was tennis, played with a small ball, *pila*, or with the *follis*, an inflated ball of leather. During the intervals of drinking, they played at various games of chance, among which were alea, dice, played with *tali* (huckle-bones) sometimes numbered on four sides (1, 3, 4, 6) and the ends left blank, or with *tesserœ*, dice made of ivory, bone, or wood, and numbered on six sides, as with us; at first three dice were used, but afterwards two. The dice-box was called *fritillus*. The board, *alveus, alveŏlus*, or *abăcus*, was divided by twelve lines, and was frequently used for playing with two sets of *latrunculi* or draughtsmen, fifteen on each side; this game, *ludus duodecim scriptorum*, nearly agreed with our backgammon, and the *ludus calculorum* was similar to chess.

At drinking-bouts (*commissationes*) a president was chosen by throwing the dice, named *magister* vel *arbiter bibendi*, or *rex convivii*.

Funerals.

The Romans, like the Greeks, paid great attention to funeral rites, as they believed the souls of the unburied could not enter the abodes of the dead. On the death of a friend, the nearest relative closed the eyes and mouth of the deceased, and called on him by name (*conclamare*), exclaiming *have* or *vale;* the corpse was then washed and anointed with oil and perfumes by slaves, who belonged to the undertakers, *libitinarii*, and a small coin was placed in the mouth of the corpse to pay the ferryman of Hades (Charon); the body was then clothed in its shroud (the best toga the deceased had worn when alive; magistrates in the prætexta), and laid out in the vestibule, with feet towards the door, and a branch of cypress was placed in front of the house. The corpse was usually carried out for burial on the eighth day after death. The funeral procession was formed of musicians (*cornicines*, &c.), mourning women (*prœficœ*), who sang a dirge (*mimi* sometimes attended), slaves; and persons bearing the *imagines* (representing the ancestors of the deceased) preceded the corpse, which was carried on a couch (*lectīca* or *feretrum*), followed by the relatives of the deceased. If the deceased were a noble, the procession stopped at the Forum, where a *laudatio* was delivered. The corpse was then carried off and buried (*humare, sepelire*), or burned (*cremare*) on a pile of wood (*pyra* or *rogus*), sprinkled, when burning, with in-

PRIVATE LIFE OF THE ROMANS. 143

cense, &c. When burnt down, the embers were soaked with wine, and the bones and ashes of the deceased collected and placed in an urn (*urna*), which was deposited in a tomb (*sepulchrum*). The mourning and solemnities continued for nine days, at the end of which a sacrifice, *Novendiale*, took place, and games and shows of gladiators were sometimes held in honour of the deceased.

NAMES.

To mark the different gentes and familiæ, and to distinguish individuals of the same family, the Roman citizens had three names: the first (*prænomen*), as Quintus, indicated the individual; the second (*nomen*), as Horatius, the *gens* or clan; the third (*cognomen*), as Flaccus, the *stirps* or *familia*, family. A fourth name (*agnomen*) was sometimes added, for some illustrious action or remarkable event, e. g. Scipio was called *Africanus*, from the conquest of Carthage and Africa. The daughters bore the name of the *gens*, Cornelia, Julia, Livia, Tullia, &c. The following are some of the contractions used for the prænomina: Ap., Appius; A., Aulus; C., Caius; Cn., Cneius; D., Decimus; K., Kæso; L., Lucius; M., Marcus; M'., Manius; N., Numerius; P., Publius; Q., Quintus; Ser., Servius; Sex., Sextus; Sp., Spurius; T., Titus; Ti., Tiberius.

ANCIENT GREEK WRITERS.

POETS.

Epic.

HOMER flourished about b.c. 900. Birth-place uncertain, seven cities contended for the honour.[1] Works: *Iliad*, twenty-four books; *Odyssey*, twenty-four books.

HESIOD, born at Ascra, in Bœotia. Flourished about B.C. 800. Works extant: Θεογονία, Theogony; 'Ασπὶς 'Ηρακλέους, Shield of Hercules; and "Εργα καὶ 'Ημέραι, Works and Days.

Tragic.[2]

ÆSCHYLUS, born at Eleusis, in Attica, B.C. 525; died at Gela, in Sicily, B.C. 456, aged sixty-nine. Works: seventy tragedies, of which only seven are extant, viz.: *Prometheus Chained, Seven Chiefs against Thebes, The Persians, The Suppliants, Agamemnon, The Choëphoræ, The Eumenides.*

SOPHOCLES, born at Athens, B.C. 495; died in his ninetieth year, B.C. 406. Works: 130 plays, of which only seven are extant, viz.: *Antigone, Electra, Trachiniæ, Ajax, Philoctetes, Œdipus Tyrannus, Œdipus in Colonus.*

---

[1] "Septem urbes certant de stirpe insignis Homeri,
   Smyrna, Chios, Colophon, Salamis, Rhodos, Argos, Athenæ."

[2] The Dithyrambs, or choral hymns chanted at the Dionysia (vide Antiq.), first assumed the form of Tragedy, when Thespis, about B. C. 535, introduced between them the representation δρᾶμα ἐπισόδιον, of a story or plot by a single actor (ὑποκριτής), who was separated from the chorus, and played many parts in succession. Æschylus added a *second* actor, and thus founded the dialogue. Sophocles introduced a *third* actor.

ANCIENT GREEK WRITERS.

EURIPIDES, born at Salamis, B.C. 480; died at Macedonia, B.C. 406, in his seventy-fifth year. He is said to have written ninety-two plays, by some; by others, seventy-five, nineteen of which have reached us, viz.: *Medea, Electra, Orestes, Iphigenia in Aulis, Iphigenia in Tauris, Andromache, Trojan Captives, Hecuba, Ion, The Suppliants, Children of Hercules, Phœnician Damsels, Raging Hercules, Alcestis, Hippolytus, Rhesus, The Bacchanalians, Helen, The Cyclops.*

Comic.

ARISTOPHANES, born at Athens, about B.C. 444; died about B.C. 380. Works: fifty-four plays, of which eleven remain perfect: *Acharnians, Knights, Clouds, Wasps, Peace, Birds, Thesmophoriazusæ,* or Feasts of Ceres, *Lysistrata, Frogs, Ecclesiazusæ,* or Female Orators, *Plutus.*

The other writers of the "Old Comedy of Greece" were Epicharmus, born B.C. 540; Phormus, about B.C. 480; Crates, B.C. 450; Cratinus, B.C. 445; Eupolis, B.C. 434.

The poets of the "Middle Comedy" were Antiphanes, B.C. 380; Eubulus, Alexis, Anaxandrides, and Araros, B.C. 375; Timocles, B.C. 336. Of the "New Comedy" were,

MENANDER, born at Athens, B.C. 342, educated under Theophrastus; died B.C. 291. Works: upwards of 100 comedies, of which only fragments remain.

PHILEMON, born at Soli or Syracuse, flourished about B.C. 330. Works: ninety-seven comedies, of which only fragments are extant; the other writers were Philippides, Diphilus, Apollodorus flourished B.C. 336 to 300; Posidippus, B.C. 289.

Lyric.

ANACREON, born at Teos, in Ionia, about B.C. 563; died, aged eighty-five, about B.C. 478. Works: Of five books, sixty-eight poems and fragments are extant; many of the odes are considered spurious.

SAPPHO, born at Mitylene, in Lesbos, flourished about B.C. 610. Her poems formed nine books, of which only fragments are extant.

ALCÆUS, born at Mitylene, in Lesbos, flourished about B.C. 604. He is said to have been the inventor of the "barbiton," or harp. Of his works, only a few fragments of war-songs remain to us.

PINDAR, born at Thebes, in Bœotia, B.C. 522; died, probably in his eightieth year, B.C. 442. Works: *Epinicia*, or triumphal odes describing the four national games of the Greeks; four books entire, and numerous fragments, remain.

The other lyric poets, fragments of some of whose works we have, are Alcman, B.C. 670; Stesichorus, B.C. 612; Simonides, B.C. 540; Bacchylides, B.C. 452.

PASTORAL.

THEOCRITUS, born at Syracuse, flourished B.C. 284–280. Works: Thirty poems known as Idyls, twenty-two epigrams, and a few fragments, are extant, which may be divided into pastoral, lyric, epic, mimetic, and epigrammatic.

BION, born near Smyrna, flourished about B.C. 280. Of his works, fragments are alone extant.

MOSCHUS, born at Syracuse, flourished about B.C. 250. Of his works, only four of his Idyls, an epigram, and three small fragments, are extant.

PROSE WRITERS.

HISTORIANS.

HERODOTUS, born at Halicarnassus, in Caria, B.C 484; died subsequent to B.C. 408, exact period unknown. His history, which embraces a period of about 240 years (from the time of Cyrus), is divided into nine books, called by the names of the Muses.

THUCYDIDES, born at Athens, B.C. 471; died in exile, probably at Scaptesyle, in Thrace, B.C. 391, aged eighty. Works: History of the Peloponnesian War, in eight books, which he brought down to the twenty-first year, and Xenophon concluded to the twenty-eighth.

ANCIENT GREEK WRITERS.

XENOPHON, born about B.C. 445, educated in the school of Socrates; died about B.C. 359, beyond ninety years of age, probably at Corinth. Works: *Anabasis*, in seven books; *Hellenica* (the continuation of the history of Thucydides), in seven books; *Cyropædia* (memoirs of Cyrus), in eight books; *Memorabilia*, in four books; *Agesilaus*; *The Athenian Republic*; *The Lacedæmonian Republic*; *De re Equestri*; *Hipparchicus*; *Cynegeticus*; *Hiero*; *Apology of Socrates*; *Symposium*; *Œconomicus*.

POLYBIUS, born at Megalopolis, in Arcadia, about B.C. 203; died B.C. 121, in his eighty-second year. Work: *A Universal History*, in forty books (of which only five remain entire), commencing B.C. 220.

DIODORUS SICULUS, born at Agyrium, in Sicily, flourished B.C. 60–30. Work: *A History of Egypt, Persia, Syria, Media, Greece, Rome*, and *Carthage*, in forty books, of which fifteen and some fragments are extant.

DIONYSIUS OF HALICARNASSUS flourished B.C. 29–7. Work: *Antiquities of Rome*, in twenty-two books (of which eleven now remain), comprising the History of Rome for 312 years down to B.C. 264.

PLUTARCH, born at Chæronea, in Bœotia; died about A.D. 140. He was sent on an embassy to Rome, where he opened a school. He was honoured by Trajan with the appointment of governor of Illyricum. Works: *Lives of Illustrious Men*, *Moralia*.

ORATORS.

PERICLES, born at Athens, about B.C. 499; died B.C. 429. The first Greek orator, surnamed, from the grandeur of his style, the Olympian.

LYSIAS, born at Athens, B.C. 458; died B.C. 378, aged eighty. Of his orations, thirty-four are extant, remarkable for their purity of style.

ISOCRATES, born at Athens, B.C. 436; died B.C. 338, in his ninety-eighth year, being unable to survive the blow the liberty of his country received at the battle of Chæronea.

As Isocrates was prevented by timidity from addressing the national assemblies, he opened a school in Athens, where he distinguished himself by the number, character, and fame of his pupils. Only twenty-one of his orations have come down to us; he is said to have written sixty.

DEMOSTHENES, born at Athens, B.C. 382: died at Calauria, by poison, B.C. 322. Of his orations, which have been always celebrated as the most perfect models of eloquence, sixty-one are extant, viz.: seventeen political orations, forty-two judicial, and two show speeches.

ISÆUS flourished about B.C. 360. He was the instructor of Demosthenes. Works: sixty-four orations, of which eleven are now remaining.

ÆSCHINES, born B.C. 389; died at Samos or Rhodes, B.C. 314. Works: nine epistles and three orations, of which the orations alone are extant.

The other Greek orators are Demades and Hyperides; they flourished about B.C. 335.

Medical Writers.

HIPPOCRATES, born in the island of Cos, about B.C. 460; died at Larissa, in Thessaly, B.C. 357, in his 104th year. Of his works, more than sixty in number, the majority being written by his disciples and followers, only a few are genuine: *Prænotiones,* or *Prognosticon;* *Aphorismi;* *De Morbis Popularibus,* or *Epidemiorum;* *De Ratione Victûs in Morbis Acutis,* or *De Diæta Acutorum;* *De Aëre, Aquis, et Locis;* *De Capitis Vulneribus.*

GALEN, born at Pergamum, A.D. 130; died about A.D. 200. Works, under the name of Galen: eighty-three Treatises (*genuine*); nineteen, *genuineness doubted;* forty-five *spurious,* nineteen *Fragments;* fifteen Commentaries on the works of Hippocrates.

MATHEMATICIANS.

EUCLID flourished at Alexandria, in the time of the first Ptolemy, B.C. 323-283, and was the founder of the Alexandrine Mathematical School. Works extant: *The Elements*, in thirteen books, the fourteenth and fifteenth being added by Hypsicles; *The Data*, containing 100 propositions; *The Division of the Scale;* a Treatise on *Optics*, &c.

ARCHIMEDES, born at Syracuse, B.C. 287; slain at the taking of Syracuse, B.C. 212. Works extant: *On Æquiponderants and Centres of Gravity; The Quadrature of the Parabola; On the Sphere and Cylinder; The Dimension of the Circle; Spirals; Conoids and Spheroids; The Arenarius; On Floating Bodies; Lemmata*. Archimedes is said to have constructed engines used for military and naval purposes, and many machines, among which was the water-screw; but his most famous invention was a kind of orrery, representing the movements of the heavenly bodies.

GEOGRAPHERS.

STRÅBO, born at Amasia, in Pontus, about B.C. 54; died about A.D. 24. Works: a work on *Geography*, in seventeen books; this is entire, with the exception of the seventh book. Strabo wrote a history, in forty-three books (in continuation of that of Polybius), which is lost.

PAUSANIAS, born in Lydia (?), flourished about A.D. 170. Works: *Periēgēsis*, or *Itinerary of Greece*, in ten books.

FABULIST.

ÆSOP flourished about B.C. 570. He was originally a slave, but received his freedom from Iadmon, his master. *The Fables* now extant in prose, attributed to Æsop, are said to be spurious.

SATIRIC WRITER.

LUCIAN, born at Samosata, in Syria, about A.D. 120; died about the end of the century. Works: *Dialogues*, comprising *The Dialogues of the Gods*, twenty-six in number; *Jupiter Convicted; Vitarum Auctio,* or *Sale of Philosophers; The Fishermen*, &c.; *The Dialogues of the Dead*, comprising *Icaro Menippus, Charon*, &c.

CRITIC.

LONGINUS flourished about A.D. 250. He opened a school at Athens, in which he taught philosophy, criticism, rhetoric, and grammar; but afterwards went to the East, where he became the tutor of Zenobia, queen of Palmyra, on whose capture he was put to death, A.D. 273. Work: *On the Sublime*, Περὶ Ὕψους, a great part of which is extant.

PHILOSOPHERS.

THALES, *the Ionic Philosopher*, born at Miletus, B.C. 636; died about B.C. 546. One of the founders in Greece of the study of philosophy. He maintained water was the first principle of all things.

PYTHAGORAS, born at Samos; flourished B.C. 540-510. He travelled in Egypt and the East, and finally settled at Crotona, in Italy, whence he is called *the Italic Philosopher*. The whole discipline of his sect is represented as tending to a lofty serenity and self-possession. They believed in the transmigration of souls; and it was one of their maxims, that "every thing should not be told to every body;" hence all that was done and taught by the members was kept a profound secret to all but themselves.

SOCRATES, born near Athens, B.C. 469; died B.C. 399. Socrates was the first who turned his thoughts to the subject of Ethics; in discussing which, he employed the *dialectic* or interrogative system, termed from him the Socratic. Notwithstanding his efforts to promote the welfare of mankind, he was accused of corrupting the Athenian youth, and was sentenced to drink poison.

PLATO, born at Athens, B.C. 429 or 428; died B.C. 347. He was the founder of the Academic School, and in his writings are preserved the doctrines of Socrates, whose disciple he was. The *writings* of Plato have come down to us complete; they are in the form of *dialogues*, which are closely connected with one another, and may be divided into three series.

ARISTOTLE, born at Stagīra, in Macedonia, B.C. 384; died B.C. 322, at Chalcis, in Euboea. He was the founder of the Peripatetic School, so called, either from his delivering his lectures in the shady walks (περίπατοι) surrounding the Lycēum, or while walking up and down (περιπατῶν). His numerous writings comprise works on, 1. *Dialectics* and *Logic*; 2. *Theoretical Philosophy, Mathematics, Natural History*, &c.; 3. *Practical Philosophy* or *Politics, Ethics*, &c.; 4. *Works on Art.*

ZENO, the founder of Stoic Philosophy, born at Citium, in Cyprus. Birth and death uncertain. Flourished about B.C. 280. After many years' study, and having sufficiently developed his peculiar philosophical system, he opened his school in one of the Porticoes at Athens (*Stoa Poecile*), and hence his disciples were called Stoics. The Stoic philosophy recognised real good only in virtue, and enjoined a life in accordance with nature.

EPICURUS, the founder of the Epicurean School, born in the island of Samos, B.C. 342; died B.C. 270. He is said to have written 300 volumes, of which the principal was a work on Nature, in thirty-seven books. The theory of the Epicureans represented pleasure as constituting the greatest happiness, and must therefore be the chief end of man.

ANCIENT ROMAN WRITERS.

POETS.

N. B.—The chief works of the writers are mentioned, though all may not come under the same *classified* heads.

Epic.

ENNIUS (Quintus Ennius), born at Rudiæ, in Calabria, B.C. 239. He lived on intimate terms with Scipio Africanus, and died B.C. 169, aged seventy. The Romans regarded Ennius as the "father of their poetry." Work: Fragments only extant, though Ennius wrote *Annales* (i. e. a history of Rome, from its foundation to his own times), an epic poem, in eighteen books.

VIRGIL (Pub. Virgilius Maro), born 15th of Oct., B.C. 70, at Andes, a small village near Mantua; educated at Cremona and Mediolanum (*Milan*); died 22d of Sept., B.C. 19, in his fifty-first year, at Brundusium (*Brindisi*). Works: *Æneid*, in twelve books; *Bucolics*, ten short poems (Pastorals); *Georgics*, an agricultural poem, in four books.

SILIUS (C. S. Italicus), born about A.D. 25; died about his seventy-fifth year. Work: *Punica*, in seventeen books.

LUCAN (M. Annæus Lucanus), born at Corduba, in Spain, A.D. 39; died A.D. 65, in his twenty-sixth year. Work: *The Pharsalia*, in ten books, alone extant.

VALERIUS FLACCUS flourished in the reign of Vespasian; he was a native of Padua, and died A.D. 88. Work: *Argonautica*, an unfinished poem, in eight books.

STATIUS (P. Papinius), born at Neapolis, about A.D. 61; died about A.D. 96. Works: *Thebaid*, in twelve books; *Silvæ*, a collection of occasional poems, in five books.

Elegiac.

OVID (P. Ovidius Naso), born at Sulmo, in the country of the Peligni, 20th of March, B.C. 43. He was descended from an ancient family, and enjoyed the favour of Augustus, by whose edict (A.D. 9) he was suddenly exiled, without even a trial, to Tomi, a town near the mouths of the Danube, where he died, in the sixtieth year of his age, A.D. 18. Works: *Amores*, three books; *Epistles*, twenty-one in number; *Ars Amatoria*; *Remedia Amoris*, one book; *Metamorphoses*, fifteen books; *Fasti* or *Roman Calendar*, twelve books, six only extant; *Tristia*, five books (written at Tomi); *Epistolæ ex Ponto*, four books; *Minor Poems*; *Nux*, or *The Complaint of the Nut-tree*; *Ibis*, a satire, &c.

TIBULLUS (Albius Tibullus), born about B.C. 54; died about B.C. 18; was of the Equestrian order: his patron was Messala. Work: *Elegies*, four books; the genuineness of several poems in the third and fourth books is doubted.

PROPERTIUS (Sex. Aurelius), born about B.C. 51; year of death unknown. He enjoyed the friendship of Mæcenas, Virgil, and Ovid. Work: *Elegies*, four books.

Lyric.

HORACE (Q. Horatius Flaccus), born at Venusia, in Apulia, Dec. 8, B.C. 65. His father was a collector of taxes, and paid the greatest attention to his son's education, who frequented the best schools at Rome, and visited Athens to complete his education. He lived on most intimate terms with Mæcenas, a Roman knight, and obtained the patronage of Augustus. Horace died Nov. 17, B.C. 8, aged fifty-six. Works: *Odes*, five books; *Satires*, two books; *Epistles*, two books; a poem, *De Arte Poetica*.

CATULLUS (Valerius Catullus), born at Verona, B.C. 87; died about B.C. 47. Works extant: 116 poems, on various topics, composed in different styles and metres.

Tragic.

LIVIUS ANDRONICUS, the earliest Roman poet. Fragments of his work are extant.

SENECA (L. Annæus, vide infr.). Ten of his tragedies are extant; they are written in iambic senarii, interspersed with choral parts.

Comic.

PLAUTUS (T. Accius Plautus), born at Sarsina, a village in Umbria, about B.C. 254; died B.C. 184, aged seventy. Works: twenty-one *Comedies*, of which twenty are extant.

TERENCE (P. Terentius Afer), born at Carthage, B.C. 195; died B.C. 159, in his thirty-sixth year. Works: six Comedies, viz.: 1. *Andria;* 2. *Hecyra;* 3. *Heauton-timoroumenos,* or "the Self-tormentor;" 4. *Eunuchus;* 5. *Phormio;* 6. *Adelphi,* i. e. "the Brothers." He is said to have translated 108 of Menander's Comedies when he went to Greece.

Didactic.

LUCRETIUS (T. Lucretius Carus), born at Rome, B.C. 95; perished by his own hand, B.C. 51, in his forty-fourth year Work: *De Rerum Naturâ,* in six books, containing upwards of 7400 lines.

SATIRISTS.

HORACE, vide supra.

PERSIUS (A. Persius Flaccus), born at Volaterræ, in Etruria, 4th of Dec., A.D. 34; died 24th of Nov., A.D. 62, aged twenty-seven. Work extant: six Satires.

JUVENAL (Decimus Junius Juvĕnālis), born at Aquinum, in the reign of Claudius. Works extant: fifteen Satires.

EPIGRAMMATIST.

MARTIAL (Marcus Valerius Martiālis), born at Bilbilis, in Spain, A.D. 43. He resided for thirty-five years at Rome, where he obtained the patronage of the Emperors Titus and Domitian. He died at Bilbilis, about A.D. 104. Work: *Epigrammata*, fourteen books.

FABULIST.

PHÆDRUS, originally a slave, brought from Thrace or Macedonia to Rome, but eventually became a freedman of Augustus. Work: *The Fables of Æsop*, translated, with some alterations, into Latin iambics.

HISTORIANS.

CÆSAR (Caius Julius Cæsar), born 12th of July, B.C. 100; murdered 15th of March, B.C. 44, being stabbed, in the Senate-house, with twenty-three wounds: among the conspirators was his intimate friend Brutus. Works: *Commentarii de Bello Gallico*, in seven books (an eighth is added by another hand); and *Commentarii de Bello Civili*, in three books. The books *De Bello Alexandrino, Africano*, and *Hispaniensi*, are spurious.

CORNELIUS NEPOS flourished in the time of Julius Cæsar. Work extant: *Vitæ Excellentium Imperatorum*, a short biography of twenty-two Grecian and two Carthaginian generals.

SALLUST (C. Sallustius Crispus), born B.C. 86, at Amiternum, in the Sabini; died B.C. 34. Works: *Catilina*, a history of Catiline's conspiracy; *Jugurtha*, a history of the wars of the King of Numidia; *Historiæ*, fragments alone extant.

LIVY (Titus Livius), born at Patavium, B.C. 59; died A.D. 17. Work: *History of Rome, from its foundation to the death of Drusus*, B.C. 9, in 142 books, of which thirty-five are extant, viz., books 1–10, and 21–45, besides fragments and notices of contents (*Epitomæ*).

VALERIUS MAXIMUS flourished during the time of Tiberius. Work: *Factorum Dictorumque Memorabilium libri ix.*, a collection of facts and anecdotes, &c.

TACITUS (Caius Cornelius Tacitus), born A.D. 57, at Interamna (?). Works: *De Situ, Moribus, Populisque Germaniæ; Agricola*, a biography of his father-in-law; *Historiæ; Annales*, a history of Rome, from the death of Augustus to that of Nero; *Dialogus de Oratoribus* (?).

CURTIUS (Quintus Curtius Rufus) flourished in the reign of Vespasian (?). Work: *De Rebus Gestis Alexandri Magni*, in ten books, of which two books are wanting.

SUETONIUS (Caius Suetonius Tranquillus) flourished during the reigns of Trajan and Hadrian. Works extant: *Vitæ* xii. *Imperatorum; De Illustribus Grammaticis; De Claris Rhetoribus*.

FLORUS (Lucius Annæus Florus) flourished in the time of Trajan (?). Work: *Epitōme de Rebus Gestis Romanorum*, four books.

JUSTIN (M. Junianus Justinus) flourished under the Antonines. Work: An abridgment of the *Historiæ Philippicæ* of Trogus Pompeius, in forty-four books.

EUTROPIUS flourished under Constantine and Valens. Work: *Breviarium Historiæ Romanæ*, in ten books.

ORATOR, &c.

CICERO (Marcus Tullius Cicero), born B.C. 106; murdered B.C. 43, at the instigation of the Triumviri. Works: of Orations, fifty-six are extant. Rhetorical works: *De Inventione*, or *Rhetorica; De Oratore*, three books; *Brutus*, or *De Claris Oratoribus; Orator ad Brutum*, or *De Optimo Genere Dicendi; Topica*, a work on evidence; *De Partione Oratoria; De Optimo Genere Oratorum*. Philosophical works: *De Republica*, in six books, of which *Somnium Scipionis* has been preserved; *De Legibus*, three books; *Academica*, divided first into two, and afterwards into four books, one of which, and a fragment of the second, we possess; *De Finibus Bonorum et Malorum*, five books; *Disputationes Tusculanæ*, five books; *De Natura Deorum*, three books; *De Divinatione*, two books; *De Fato*, a fragment; *Cato Major sive de Senectute*; *Lælius sive de Amicitia*; *Paradoxa Stoicorum*; *De Officiis*, three books. Epistolary writings: *Epistolæ ad Diversos*, sixteen books; *Epistolæ ad T. Pomponium Atticum*, sixteen books; *Epistolæ ad Quintum Fratrem*, three books.

EPISTOLARY WRITERS.

ATTICUS (Titus Pomponius Atticus), born B.C. 109; died in his seventy-seventh year, B.C. 32. He corresponded with CICERO (vide supra).

PLINY (Caius Plinius Cæcilius Secundus, surnamed the Younger), born A.D. 61; died A.D. 114. Work: *Epistolæ*, in ten books. Of his Orations, the *Panegyricus* on Trajan is alone extant.

WRITERS ON PHILOSOPHICAL SUBJECTS, &c.

SENECA (Lucius Annæus Seneca), born about A.D. 1; died A.D. 65, in the reign of Nero. Works: 124 *Letters on Philosophical Subjects*; *Quæstiones Naturales*, seven books.

CICERO (vide supra).

Natural History.

PLINY (Caius Plinius Secundus Major, the Elder), born A.D. 23; died in the eruption of Vesuvius, A.D. 79, aged fifty-six. Work: *Historia Naturalis*, in thirty-seven books, alone remains of his numerous writings.

Agriculture.

CATO (Marcus Porcius Cato Censorius), born B.C. 234, died B.C. 149, aged eighty-five. Works: *A Treatise on Agriculture*, the most ancient Latin prose work extant; *Origines*, a history of Rome from B.C. 753–151.

VARRO (Marcus Terentius Varro), born B.C. 116; died B.C. 28. Works: *De Lingua Latina*, a fragment; *De Re Rustica*, a fragment alone extant.

COLUMELLA (Lucius Junius Moderatus Columella), contemporary of Seneca. Work: *De Re Rustica*.

Architecture.

VITRUVIUS (Marcus Vitruvius Pollio), born at Verona; flourished in the time of Cæsar and Augustus. Work: *De Architectura*, in ten books.

Medicine.

CELSUS (Aulus Cornelius Celsus) flourished in the reigns of Augustus and Tiberius. Work: *De Medicina*, in eight books.

Grammar and Criticism.

QUINTILIAN (Marcus Fabius Quintilianus), born A.D. 40; died about A.D. 118. Works: *Institutiones Oratoriæ*, in twelve books; a collection of *Declamations* is by some also ascribed to Quintilian.

AULUS GELLIUS flourished in the time of the Antonines. Work: *Noctes Atticæ*, in twenty books, of which the eighth is wanting.

SCHOOLS OF ANCIENT PHILOSOPHY.

I. The IONIC SCHOOL, FOUNDED BY THALES, FROM WHICH SPRUNG:

1. THE SOCRATIC SCHOOL, founded by Socrates. Disciples: Xenophon, Æschines, Phædo, Euclid, Plato, Alcibiades, &c.
2. CYRENAIC SECT, founded by Aristippus. Flourished about B.C. 370.
3. MEGARIC or ERISTIC SCHOOL, founded by Euclid of Megara, B.C. 399.
4. ELIAC or ERETRIAC SCHOOL, founded about B.C. 395, by Phædo of Elis, whose doctrines were similar to those of Socrates.
5. THE ACADEMIC SECT, founded by Plato.
6. THE PERIPATETIC SECT, founded by Aristotle, succeeded by Theophrastus, Straton, Lycon, Ariston, &c.
7. THE CYNIC SECT, founded by Antisthenes. Disciples: Diogenes Crates, and Hipparchia, his wife.
8. THE STOIC SECT, founded by Zeno, succeeded by Cleanthes, Ariston, Antipater, &c.

II. The ITALIC SCHOOL, FOUNDED BY PYTHAGORAS, FROM WHICH SPRUNG:

1. THE ELEATIC SCHOOL, founded by Xenophanes. Flourished B.C. 540-500. Disciples: Parmenides, Zeno, both of Elea, in Italy, Democritus, Protagoras, &c.
2. THE HERACLITEAN SECT, founded by Heraclitus. Flourished B.C. 513.
3. THE EPICUREAN SECT, four led by Epicurus.
4. THE SCEPTIC SECT, founded by Pyrrhon.

TOPOGRAPHY OF ATHENS.

ATHENÆ, the Capital of Attica, is said to have been founded by Cecrops, about B.C. 1556; it was called from its founder Cecropia, and afterwards Athenæ (αἱ 'Αθῆναι), in honour of Minerva ('Αθήνη), the protectress of the city. It was divided into two parts, 1. THE ACROPOLIS, or UPPER CITY (ἀκρόπολις, Κεκροπία, ἡ ἄνω πόλις), and THE LOWER CITY (ἡ κάτω πόλις). The Acropolis or Citadel was a steep rock, about 150 feet high, 1150 feet long, and 500 feet broad, surrounded by a wall, and approached from the W. by the Propylæa (προπύλαια), a colonnade of Pentelic marble. The summit was covered with temples, statues, &c. The most beautiful of the temples were, 1. the Parthĕnon, sacred to Athēne, with a statue of the goddess by Phidiăs, thirty-seven feet high, and carved in gold and ivory. 2. Erechthēum, or temple of Neptune, with the temple of Athene Polias and the Pandroseum. Between the Parthenon and Erechtheum stood the colossal bronze statue of Athene Promăchos (seventy feet high, whose helmet and spear were first visible from the sea), cast by Phidias.

THE LOWER CITY was built in the plain round the Acropolis, and was surrounded by walls; the chief gates of which were: the Thriasian or Dipȳlon, leading from the inner to the outer Ceramicus and the Academia; and the Piræan gate, leading to the Piræeus. The chief districts: Colyttus, on the N. of the Acropolis; Melĭte, on the E.; Limnæ, on the S.; Ceramīcus (Κεραμεικός, or the "Potter's Quarter"); in the W.

HILLS: Areiopagus, W., and Pnyx, S.W., of the Acropolis.

(160)

TOPOGRAPHY OF ATHENS.

The chief buildings of the Lower City were: 1. The Temple of Olympian Zeus ('Ολυμπίειον), founded by Pisistratus; 2. The Temple of Theseus (Θησεῖον), erected by Conon, and was used as a sanctuary for slaves; 3. Πάνθεον, a temple dedicated to all the gods, a magnificent building, supported by 120 marble pillars; 4. The Temple of the Eight Winds (vide page 172), surmounted by a weather-cock; 5. The Odēum ('Ωδεῖον), built by Pericles, and originally intended for musical festivals, but afterwards used as a court of justice; 6. The Bouleuterion, Βουλευτήριον, or Senate-house; 7. The Prytanēum, Πρυτανεῖον, or place of assembly of the Prytanes (vide Gr. Antiq.); 8. The Great Theatre of Dionysus, S.E. of the Acropolis; 9. Porticoes (Στοαί), or covered walks, in which seats (ἐξέδραι) were placed. The Porticoes were sometimes adorned with paintings by the best masters, as, 10. The Pœcile (στοὰ ποικίλη), N.W. of the Acropolis, adorned with frescoes of the battle of Marathon; 11. Ἀγοραί, corresponding to the Fora at Rome, places both for public assembly and all matters of traffic and public business; 12. The Pnyx (Πνύξ), W. of the Acropolis, the place in which the ancient assemblies were held.

WITHOUT THE CITY: The Academia, where Plato taught; The Cynosarges, where Antisthenes taught; The Lyceum, where Aristotle instructed his disciples, the Peripatetics; The Stadium, for public games.

TOPOGRAPHY OF ROME.

ROMA, the Capital of Italy, is said to have been a colony from Alba Longa, and to have been founded by Romulus, B.C. 753. The original city comprised only the Mons Palatinus; it was surrounded by walls, which followed the line of the Pomœrium, a kind of symbolical wall, the course of which was marked by stone pillars. On the increase of the inhabitants of the city, one hill after another was occupied, to the number of seven (vide pages 28, 168). Servius Tullius divided the city into four regiones or districts, which remained unchanged till the time of Augustus, who divided the city into fourteen regiones.

THE FORA AND CAMPI. The Forum was an open space of ground of an oblong form, in which the people met for the transaction of business, or used for markets. The principal Fora at Rome were: 1. Forum Romanum, or simply the Forum (the narrow or upper end of which was occupied by the Comitium); it was surrounded by public buildings, and adorned with statues of celebrated men, &c. 2. Forum Julii or Cæsaris. 3. Forum Augusti. 4. Forum Trajani. The CAMPI were large open spaces of ground covered with grass, planted with trees, and adorned with works of art. The chief was the Campus Martius, or "Plain of Mars," where the Roman youth exercised.

There are said to have been 215 streets in Rome; Viæ and Vici were the broad streets, and Angiportus the narrow streets. The finest street was the Via Sacra, from the Colosseum to the Forum. The Suburra was a crowded district, between the Esquiline, Quirinal, and Viminal.

TEMPLES. Of these, there are said to have been 400 in Rome, the chief of which were: 1. Templum Jovis, or Capitolium, built on the *Capitoline Hill.* It was commenced by Tarq. Priscus, and dedicated B.C. 507. Three times was it burnt down, and as often rebuilt, but with far greater splendour than before, by Domitian, about A.D. 81. The building was in the form of a square, 200 feet each side; it was approached by 100 steps, and contained *three* temples (*cellæ*), consecrated to Juno, Jupiter, and Minerva. In the building were kept the Sibylline Books, and there the Consuls, upon entering office, sacrificed, and took their vows. THE ARX, or Citadel of Rome, was situated near the Capitol, on the N. summit of the Capitoline Hill. 2. The Pantheum, in the Campus Martius, built by Agrippa, B. C. 27; it is still extant, and used as a Christian church (*Santa Maria della Rotonda*). It is the largest circular building of antiquity, and in form resembles the Colosseum, Regent's Park. The numerous temples were dedicated chiefly to Jupiter, Juno, Mars, Janus, Saturn, Fortuna, &c.

The principal of the CIRCI, or places for chariot and horse-racing, was the Circus Maximus, between the Palatine and Aventine Hills; it is said to have contained seats for 385,000 persons.

Among the THEATRES, the chief were: 1. The Theatrum Pompeii, the first stone theatre built in Rome (B.C. 55); 2. Th. Marcelli. Of the AMPHITHEATRES, the Amphiteatrum Flavium, or Colosseum, was the most magnificent; it was commenced by Vespasian and completed by Titus, A.D. 80; it furnished seats capable of containing 87,000 persons.

THERMÆ. These buildings were distinct from the common Balneæ or baths, as, besides baths, they contained places for athletic games and sports, public halls, porticoes, libraries, &c.; the chief were: 1. Thermæ Antonini; 2. Th. Diocletiani; 3. Th. Constantini; 4. Th. Caracallæ.

THE BASILICÆ were numerous at Rome; they were buildings which served as courts of law, or places of meeting for merchants and men of business THE PORTICOES were covered walks, supported by columns, used as places of recreation or of public business.

Of THE CURIÆ or Senate-houses, the chief was Curia Hostilia, in the Forum; it was used as the place of assembly for the senate until the time of Cæsar. The other chief buildings were the Palaces (e.g. *Palatium, Domus Aurea Neronis*); the Triumphal Arches (*Arcus Fabianus, Ar. Titi, Ar. Trajani, Ar. Constantini*); Aqueducts (*Aqua Appia, Aq. Marcia, Aq. Julia, Aq. Claudia*); Monuments (*Mausolēum Augusti, M. Hadriani*). Of the Columns were: Col. Rostrata, in the Forum, in honour of the naval victory of Duilius, B.C. 260; Col. Trajāni, 117 feet high, *now* surmounted by a statue of St. Peter.

Of THE ROADS leading out of Rome, the principal were: 1. Via Appia, from the *Porta Capena* to Brundusium; 2. Via Flaminia, or Great North Road from the *Porta Flaminia;* 3. Via Aurelia, the Great Coast Road through Etruria and Liguria from the *Porta Janiculensis*.

GREEK AND ROMAN DIVISION OF TIME.

GREEK.

In early times, the Greeks divided their years by the recurrence of the seasons, the rising and setting of the constellations Orion, the Pleiades, &c. Afterwards, having adopted the lunar month of about twenty-nine days and thirteen hours as a division of time, they endeavoured to adjust this to the solar year of 365 days five hours and forty-nine minutes, so that the seasons should regularly occur at the same periods of the calendar year, and that the end of the year should not be in the middle of a month. As the twelve lunar months contain only 354 days, intercalary or additional months (μῆνες ἐμβόλιμοι) were inserted to make up the deficiency. The errors of the early calendars of Thales, Solon, and Cleostratus, were rectified by Meton, who, B.C. 432, introduced a cycle of nineteen years, at the end of which period the position of the earth, with reference to the sun and moon, became the same. Calippus, and after him the celebrated Hipparchus (c. B.C. 150), corrected the slight inaccuracies of Meton's system. The cycle of Hipparchus consisted of 304 years, with 112 intercalary months.

The twelve Attic months contained thirty and twenty-nine days alternately; the former termed *full* (πληρεῖς), the latter *hollow* (κοῖλοι), months. Their names, derived from the various festivals held in them, were, Ἑκατομβαιών, Μεταγειτνιών, Βοηδρομιών, Μαιμακτηριών, Πυανεψιών, Ἀνθεστηριών, Ποσειδεών, Γαμηλιών, Ἐλαφηβολιών, Μουνυχιών, Θαργηλιών, Σκιρροφοριών.[1]

---

[1] The following rough memorial lines will aid the memory in remembering the Attic months:—

Ἑκ — Μἕτᾰ — Γεῐτνῐ — Βὅη — Πὔᾰ — Μαῑμᾰκτῆρῐ — Πὅσειδὣν
Γᾰμ — Ἀνθεστ — Ἐλᾰφη ‖ Μοῡνῠχῐ — Θᾰργ — Σκῐρὅφὅρ.

The days of the month were divided into three decades or sets of ten days, numbered from one to ten: thus the first of each decade (i. e. our first, eleventh, and twenty-first) was termed respectively, πρώτη (sc. ἡμέρα), ἱσταμένου or ἀρχομένου (μηνός)—πρώτη ἐπὶ δέκα or μεσοῦντος—πρώτη ἐπ' εἰκάδι, φθίνοντος, λήγοντος, &c. But in the last decade the days were often reckoned backwards; thus the first was called δεκάτη φθίνοντος, &c. The first day of the month was also termed Νουμηνία (*new moon*), the last ἕνη καὶ νέα, as belonging both to the *old and the new* month.

The three Homeric divisions of the day were: 1. ἠώς (morning), afterwards divided into πρωὶ and πληθούσης τῆς ἀγορᾶς; 2. μέσον ἦμαρ or μεσημβρία (midday); 3. δείλη (afternoon), afterwards divided into πρωία and ὀψία.

At Athens the years were called after the chief Archon (ἐπώνυμος), at Sparta after the first Ephor, at Argos after the priestess of Juno. So at Carthage after the Suffetes, at Crete after the Proto-cosmus, and at Rome after the Consuls.

Timæus of Sicily (c. B.C. 260) introduced the calculation by Olympiads, or periods of four years, commencing from B.C. 776 (vide Chronology). Thus, B.C. 775 would be the second year of the first Olympiad, B.C. 772 the second Olympiad, &c. But as the Attic year began at the summer solstice, with the month Hecatombæon (June and July), the first half of the first Olympiad would be the latter half of B.C. 776, and the latter half of the Olympiad the first of B.C. 775.

ROMAN.

The Roman year was *probably* at first divided into ten months, beginning with March. To this division, which is ascribed to Romulus, Numa is said to have added the two months January and February, to have assigned 355 days to the year, and to have adopted a cycle similar to Meton's. Julius Cæsar, B.C. 46, employed Sosigĕnes, of Alexandria, and Flavius, a scribe, to revise the calendar. The intercalary months were set aside, the solar year was composed of 365 days, and a leap-year inserted every four years. But, as this did not provide for the accumulation of the excess of minutes and seconds, Pope Gregory, A.D. 1582, ordered ten days, between Oct. 4 and 15, in that year to be omitted. This "new style" was not recognized in England till A.D. 1752. The "old," or "Julian style," is still used in Russia.

The names of the Roman months are Januarius, Februarius, Martius, Aprilis, Maius, Julius, Quintīlis and Sextīlis (changed to Julius and Augustus, in honour of the two first Cæsars), September, October, November, December. The number of days in each month was the same as our own; but they were divided into Calends, Nones, and Ides. The Calends were the *first* of every month. In March, May, July, and October, the Nones fell on the 7th, in the other months on the 5th. The Ides were always *eight* days after the Nones, i. e. on the 13th or 15th. If the day of the month was not one of these three divisions, it was expressed by its distance from the *following* Calends, Nones, or Ides, as the case might be. Thus, the 31st of December was termed pridie (the day before) Calendas Januarias. But, as the Romans reckoned in *both* the days *to* and *from* which they calculated, Dec. 30 would be the *third* day before the Calends of January, usually expressed ante diem tertium (or a. d. iii.) Kal. Jan. The Romans (as well as the Greeks) used water-clocks (*clepsȳdræ*) and sun-dials (*solaria*) to measure the divisions of the day.

The Consular æra was used in public affairs. In the time of the Cæsars, the æra "ab urbe conditâ" (A. U. C.), from the founding of Rome, dated by Varro B.C. 753 (by Cato, B.C. 752), was employed by historians and others.

MISCELLANEA.

HILLS OF ROME.

1. Palatinus, first occupied by the Latins.
2. Capitolinus, occupied by the Sabines, afterwards united to the Latins.
3. Cœlius, occupied by the Etruscans.
4. Quirinalis, occupied by the Sabines, afterwards united to the Latins.
5. Aventinus, added by Ancus Martius, who also erected a fort on *Janiculum*, on the right bank of the Tiber.
6. Esquilinus, added by Servius Tullius.
7. Viminalis, added by Servius Tullius.

KINGS OF ROME.

		B.C.	B.C.	
1. Romulus,	reigned	753—716,	37	years.
2. Numa Pompilius,	"	715—672,	43	"
3. Tullus Hostilius,	"	672—640,	32	"
4. Ancus Marcius,	"	640—616,	24	"
5. L. Tarquinius Priscus,	"	616—578,	38	"
6. Servius Tullius,	"	578—534,	44	"
7. L. Tarquinius Superbus,	"	534—510,	25	"

TWELVE CÆSARS.

1. Julius,	B.C. 45—	B.C. 44.
2. Augustus,	" 30—	A.D. 14.
3. Tiberius,	A.D. 14—	" 37.
4. Caligula,	" 37—	" 41.
5. Claudius,	" 41—	" 54.
6. Nero,	" 54—	" 68.
7. Galba,	" 68—	" 69.
8. Otho,	Jan. 15, " 69—Apr. 16,	" 69.
9. Vitellius,	Jan. 2, " 69—Dec. 22,	" 69.
10. Vespasian,	Dec. 22, " 69—	" 79.
11. Titus,	" 79—	" 81.
12. Domitian,	" 81—	" 96.

SEVEN WONDERS OF THE WORLD.

1. The Colossus of Rhodes.
2. The Sepulchre of Mausōlus, king of Caria.
3. The Palace of Cyrus.
4. The Pyramids of Egypt.
5. The Statue of Jupiter at Olympia.
6. The Temple of Diana at Ephesus.
7. The Walls and Hanging Gardens of Babylon.

SEVEN SAGES OF GREECE.

1. Thales, of Miletus.
2. Pittacus, of Mitylene.
3. Bias, of Priene.
4. Solon, legislator of Athens.
5. Cleobūlus, of Rhodes.
6. Periander of Corinth (some say Myson), of Laconia.
7 Chilon, of Sparta.

THE TWELVE LABOURS OF HERCULES.

1. The Fight with the Nemean Lion.
2. The Fight with the Hydra of Lerna, near Argos.
3. The Capture of the Brazen-footed Stag of Arcadia.
4. The Destruction of the Erymanthian Wild Boar.
5. Cleansing the Stables of Augeas, king of Elis.
6. The Destruction of the Stymphalian Birds.
7. The Capture of the Cretan Bull.
8. The Capture of the Mares of Diomēdes, king of Thrace.
9. The Seizure of the Girdle of Hippolўte, queen of the Amazons.
10. The Capture of the Oxen of Gerўon.
11. Obtaining the Golden Apples of the Hesperides.
12. Bringing the Three-headed Dog Cerberus from the lower regions.

THE NINE MUSES.

1. Clīo, muse of History.
2. Euterpe, Lyric Poetry.
3. Thălīa, Comedy.
4. Melpŏmĕne, Tragedy.
5. Terpsichŏre, Choral Dance.
6. Erăto, Erōtic, or Amorous Poetry.
7. Pŏlyhymnia, Rhetoric, Eloquence.
8. Urănia, Astronomy.
9. Callĭŏpe, Epic Poetry.

THE THREE GRACES.

Aglaia (Splendour).
Euphrosўne (Joy).
Thalīa (Pleasure).

MISCELLANEA.

THE THREE HORÆ, OR GODDESSES OF THE ORDER OF NATURE, &c. (Hesiod).

Eunŏmĭa (Good Order).
Dīkē (Justice).
Irēnē (Peace).

THE THREE FATES.

Clotho,
Lachĕsis, } for attributes, vide Parcæ.
Atrŏpos,

THE THREE FURIES.

Alecto.
Megæra.
Tisĭphŏne.

THE THREE JUDGES OF HELL.

Minos, formerly king of Crete.
Rhadamanthus, son of Zeus and brother of Minos.
Æăcus, son of Zeus, famed for his Justice and Piety

THE FIVE RIVERS OF HELL.

Styx.
Achĕron.
Cocȳtus.
Phlegethon.
Lēthē.

THE WINDS..

N., 'Απαρκτίας, *Septemtrio.*
N.E., Καικίας, Βορέας (usually N. wind), *Aquilo.*
E., 'Απηλιώτης, *Subsolanus.*
S.E., Εὖρος, *Eurus, Vulturnus.*
S., Νότος (prop. S.W.), *Auster.*
S.W., Λίψ, *Africus.*
W., Ζέφυρος (prop. N.W.), *Zephyrus, Favonius.*
N.W., 'Αργεστής, Σκίρων, *Corus* or *Caurus.*
'Ετησίαι, northerly winds which blew in the summer.
Iapyx, W. or N.W. wind, which blew from Apulia.
Atăbŭlus (Hor.) a scorching wind of Apulia.

THE ROMAN CALENDAR.

For the purposes of administering justice and holding the assemblies, all the days of the year were divided by the Romans into *dies fasti* and *nefasti.* The former (*dies fasti*) were the days on which the prætor was allowed to administer justice; they were marked in the calendar by the letter F.; the latter (*dies nefasti*) were days on which neither the courts of justice nor comitia were allowed to be held. Some days, however, might be partly *fasti* as well as *nefasti,* in which case they were marked in the calendar thus, Fp. (i. e. *fastus primo*), or Np. (i. e. *nefastus primo*).

The *Nundinæ* (ninth days) were originally market-days, on which the country-people came to Rome to sell the produce of their labour. The nundinæ were *feriæ* or sacred days for the *populus,* while they were real business days for the

MISCELLANEA. 173

plebeians (*dies fasti*), for many years, until the dies fasti and nundinæ coincided.

Days of the month	Mar., May, July, Oct., 31 days.	Jan., Aug., Dec., 31 days.	Apr., June, Sep., Nov., 30 days.	Feb. 28 days, in Leap-year 29.
1	Kalendis	Kalendis	Kalendis	Kalendis
2	6 ⎫	4 ⎫ Ante	4 ⎫ Ante	4 ⎫ Ante
3	5 ⎬ Ante	3 ⎭ Nonas	3 ⎭ Nonas	3 ⎭ Nonas
4	4 ⎭ Nonas	Pridie Nonas	Pridie Nonas	Pridie Nonas
5	3 ⎭	Nonis	Nonis	Nonis
6	Pridie Nonas	8 ⎫	8 ⎫	8 ⎫
7	Nonis	7 ⎬	7 ⎬	7 ⎬
8	8 ⎫	6 ⎬ Ante	6 ⎬ Ante	6 ⎬ Ante
9	7 ⎬	5 ⎭ Idus	5 ⎭ Idus	5 ⎭ Idus
10	6 ⎬ Ante	4 ⎬	4 ⎬	4 ⎬
11	5 ⎭ Idus	3 ⎭	3 ⎭	3 ⎭
12	4 ⎬	Pridie Idus	Pridie Idus	Pridie Idus
13	3 ⎭	Idibus	Idibus	Idibus
14	Pridie Idus	19 ⎫	18 ⎫	16 ⎫
15	Idibus	18 ⎬	17 ⎬	15 ⎬
16	17 ⎫	17 ⎬	16 ⎬	14 ⎬
17	16 ⎬	16 ⎬	15 ⎬	13 ⎬
18	15 ⎬	15 ⎬ Ante Kalendas (of the month following).	14 ⎬	12 ⎬
19	14 ⎬ Ante Kalendas (of the month following).	14 ⎬	13 ⎬ Ante Kalendas (of the month following).	11 ⎬ Ante Kalendas Martias.
20	13 ⎬	13 ⎬	12 ⎬	10 ⎬
21	12 ⎬	12 ⎬	11 ⎬	9 ⎬
22	11 ⎬	11 ⎬	10 ⎬	8 ⎬
23	10 ⎬	10 ⎬	9 ⎬	7 ⎬
24	9 ⎬	9 ⎬	8 ⎬	6 ⎬
25	8 ⎬	8 ⎬	7 ⎬	5 ⎬
26	7 ⎬	7 ⎬	6 ⎬	4 ⎬
27	6 ⎬	6 ⎬	5 ⎬	3 ⎭
28	5 ⎬	5 ⎬	4 ⎭	Pridie Kalendas Martias.
29	4 ⎬	4 ⎭	3 ⎭ Pridie Kalendas (of the month following.)	
30	3 ⎭	3 ⎭ Pridie Kalendas (of the month following).		
31	Pridie Kalendas (of the month following).			

GREEK CHRONOLOGY.

B.C.
1856. Foundation of Argos: of Athens, 1556.
1194. Trojan War commences.
1124. Æolic migration: Ionic migration, 1044.
1104. Return of the Heraclidæ.
1045. Death of CODRUS, last king of Athens. MEDON, first Archon.
884. Legislation of LYCURGUS.
776.*Corœbus gains the victory in the foot-race at the Olympian games.
743. First war between the Messenians and Lacedæmonians commences: ends with the defeat of the Messenians, 723.
734. Syracuse founded by Archias of Corinth.
683. Creon, first annual Archon elected at Athens.
668. End of second *Messenian War;* begun 685.
664. *Sea-fight between Corinthians and Corcyræans,* most ancient recorded.
624. Dracon legislates at Athens.
595. CRŒSUS, king of Lydia, born; Cirrhæan or *Sacred War* commenced.
594.*Solon legislates at Athens as Archon.
586. *Cirrhœans vanquished* and Pythian games celebrated.
The Seven sages flourished about this time.
585. Death of PERIANDER.
572. *War* between *Pisa* and *Elis,* ended by subjection of Pisæans.
560.*PISISTRATUS usurps the government of Athens.
559. CYRUS begins to reign in Persia, and the Median empire ends; it had existed 149 years. Death of Solon.
546. Sardis taken by Cyrus.
548. Temple of Apollo at Delphi burnt.
538. *Babylon taken* by Cyrus.
535. Thespis first exhibits tragedy.
531. Pythagoras, the philosopher, flourished.
527. Death of PISISTRATUS.
521. Death of CAMBYSES, and accession of DARIUS to the throne of Persia.

GREEK CHRONOLOGY.

B.C.
- 514. HIPPARCHUS, tyrant of Athens, slain.
- 510.*HIPPIAS flees from Athens. Ten tribes instituted by CLE-ISTHENES.
- 499. *Ionians revolt*, and, assisted by the Athenians, burn Sardis.
- 494. Sixth and last year of the *Ionian revolt*. *Ionians defeated* in a naval engagement near Miletus.
- 493 Persians take the islands Chios, Lesbos, and Tenedos. MILTIADES comes from the Chersonesus to Athens.
- 492. MARDONIUS, the Persian general, invades Europe and unites Macedonia to the Persian empire.
- 491. DARIUS sends heralds to Greece.
- 490.*DATIS and ARTAPHERNES, the Persian generals, invade Europe, take Eretria in Euboea, and land in Attica, but are defeated at *Marathon* by the Athenians, under Miltiades.
- 489. MILTIADES endeavours to conquer Paros, but is repulsed. He is accused, and being unable to pay the fine is thrown into prison, where he dies.
- 485. XERXES, king of Persia, succeeds DARIUS.
- 483. ARISTIDES ostracised.
- 481. THEMISTOCLES (the chief man at Athens) persuades the Athenians to build a fleet of 200 ships to resist the Persians.
- 480. XERXES invades Greece. Battles of *Thermopylæ* and *Artemisium;* *Athens taken* by Xerxes; battle of *Salamis;* Xerxes' fleet destroyed.
- 479. MARDONIUS, the Persian general, winters in Thessaly, in the spring occupies Athens, and is defeated by the Greeks under PAUSANIAS at the *battle of Platæa*, in Sept.; Persian fleet defeated off *Mycale* on the same day.
- 478. Sestos taken by the Greeks. History of Herodotus terminates. THEMISTOCLES fortifies Athens.
- 477.*Commencement of the Athenian ascendency.
- 471. THEMISTOCLES banished by Ostracism for ten years, and goes to Argos. PAUSANIAS convicted of treason and put to death.
- 468. Mycenæ destroyed. ARISTIDES dies.
- 466. CIMON overcomes the Persians at the river *Eurymedon*, in Pamphylia. THEMISTOCLES flies to Persia.
- 465. Death of Xerxes, who is succeeded by ARTAXERXES. Thasos revolts; subdued by Cimon, 463.
- 464. Earthquake at Sparta. Helots and Messenians revolt.
- 461. Cimon marches to assist the Lacedæmonians; his offer of assistance declined; the Athenian troops sent back, and CIMON ostracised, but recalled, 456. PERICLES chief man at Athens.
- 460. First year of *Egyptian war*, which lasts six years, till 455.
- 457. *Battles* between *Athenians* and *Corinthians;* Athenians defeated by Lacedæmonians at *Tanagra*. Longi Muri com-

B.C.

menced by the Athenians completed, 456, in which year battle of *Œnophyta*.

455. Messenians overcome by the Lacedæmonians. Tolmides, the Athenian general, settles the Messenians at Naupactus, and sails round the Peloponnesus, inflicting much injury.

450 Five years' truce between Athenians and Peloponnesians.

449 *War* with *Persia* renewed. CIMON dies. Athenians victorious at Salamis in Cyprus.

448. *Sacred War* between the *Delphians* and *Phocians* for possession of the oracle and temple. The Lacedæmonians assist the Delphians, the Athenians the Phocians.

447. The Athenians defeated at *Coronea* by the Bœotians.

445. Megara and Eubœa revolt from Athens. Lacedæmonians invade Attica. PERICLES recovers Eubœa. Thirty years' truce between Athens and Sparta.

440. Samos revolts from Athens, but is subdued by Pericles.

439.*ATHENS AT THE HEIGHT OF ITS GLORY.

435. Corinthians and Corcyræans carry on war; *Corinthians defeated* in a sea-fight.

432. Corcyræans, assisted by the Athenians, repulse the Corinthians. Potidæa revolts from Athens.

431.**First year of the Peloponnesian War.* The Thebans make an attempt upon Platæa.—430. .Plague rages at Athens.—429. Potidæa surrenders to the Athenians. Platæa besieged. PERICLES dies.—428. Fourth year of the war—Mitylene besieged.—427. Mitylene taken by the Athenians, and Lesbos recovered, which had revolted the year before. Platæa surrendered to the Peloponnesians.—425. Spartans in the island Sphacteria surrendered to Cleon. Demosthenes takes *Pylos.*—424. NICIAS ravages the coast of Laconia, and captures Cythera. BRASIDAS marches into Thrace. *Athenians defeated* by the Thebans at *Delium*, at which SOCRATES and XENOPHON fought.—423. Ninth year of the war—Truce for one year. THUCYDIDES banished in consequence of the loss of Amphipolis.—422. BRASIDAS and CLEON fall in battle.—421. Truce for fifty years between the Athenians and Lacedæmonians.—419. ALCIBIADES marches into the Peloponnesus.—418. Athenians send an army into the Peloponnesus, which is defeated at the battle of *Mantinea.*—415. The Athenians send an expedition against Syracuse, commanded by NICIAS, ALCIBIADES, and LAMACHUS. ALCIBIADES is recalled, but escapes and takes refuge with the Lacedæmonians.—414. Second campaign in Sicily; the Athenians invest Syracuse, to the assistance of which GYLIPPUS, the Lacedæmonian, is sent.—413. Attica invaded and Decelea fortified by the advice of ALCIBIADES. Third

GREEK CHRONOLOGY. 177

B.C

campaign in Sicily—Demosthenes, the Athenian general, sent to the assistance of the Athenians. *The Athenian army and fleet destroyed.* Nicias and Demosthenes surrender and are put to death. — 412. Lesbians and Chians revolt from Athens. Alcibiades sent to Persia to form a treaty. A treaty is formed with Tissaphernes. The Athenians use the 1000 talents deposited in the temple for emergencies. — 411. Twenty-first year of the war. Democracy abolished at Athens, and the council of the Four Hundred appointed. Alcibiades recalled from exile by the army and by the vote of the Athenian people. Mindarus, the Lacedæmonian admiral, defeated at Cynossema.—407. Alcibiades returns to Athens. Lysander, the Lacedæmonian general, defeats Antiochus, the lieutenant of Alcibiades, by sea at *Notium*. Alcibiades banished. — 406. Callicratidas succeeds Lysander, and is defeated by the Athenian fleet off the *Arginussæ islands*. — 405. Lysander defeats the Athenians off *Ægospotami*, and takes or destroys nearly the whole fleet.

404.* *Twenty-eighth and last year of the Peloponnesian War.* Athens taken by Lysander, and the government intrusted to the "Thirty Tyrants," who held their power for eight months. Death of Alcibiades.

403. Thrasybulus and his party obtain the Piræus, whence they carry on war against the "Ten," the successors of the "Thirty," and obtain possession of Athens in July; though the contest was not ended till Boëdromion (September). Thucydides returns to Athens, having been exiled twenty years.

401. Expedition of Cyrus against his brother Artaxerxes II.: Cyrus is slain in the battle of *Cunaxa*. The Greek allies commence their return home, usually called the "Return of the Ten Thousand." First year of the *war* of *Lacedæmon* and *Elis*, which lasted three years.

899 The Lacedæmonians send Thimbron to assist the Greek cities in Asia. Thimbron superseded by Dercyllidas in the autumn.

896. Agesilaus supersedes Dercyllidas. He winters at Ephesus.

895. Second campaign of Agesilaus. He defeats Tissaphernes.

894. Agesilaus recalled from Asia, to march against the Greek states who had declared war against Lacedæmon. He defeats the allied forces at *Coronea*. Conon, the Athenian admiral, gained a victory over Pisander, the Spartan, off Cnidus. Xenophon fights against his country at *Coronea*, and is banished from Athens.

893. Sedition at Corinth. Pharnabazus and Conon ravage the coasts of the Peloponnesus.

178 **GREEK CHRONOLOGY.**

B.C.
392. The Lacedæmonians, under AGESILAUS, lay waste the Corinthian territory.
390. The Persians side with the Lacedæmonians. CONON is imprisoned. THRASYBŪLUS, the Athenian commander, is defeated and slain at Aspendus. Long walls at Athens rebuilt.
387. The peace of ANTALCIDAS.
386. Platæa restored.
385. *Mantinēa* destroyed by AGESIPOLIS.
382. First year of the *Olynthian War:* the Lacedæmonians commanded by TELEUTIAS. PHŒBIDAS, the Spartan general, seizes Cadmea, the citadel of Thebes.
379. Fourth and last year of the *Olynthian War.* The Cadmea recovered.
378. The Athenians form an alliance with Thebes against Sparta. First Expedition of AGESILAUS into Bœotia.
376. The Lacedæmonian fleet overcome off Naxos.
374. The Athenians, jealous of the Thebans, conclude a peace with the Spartans. TIMOTHEUS, the Athenian, takes Corcyra. War with Lacedæmon renewed.
373. Lacedæmonians attempt to take Corcyra, but are defeated.
371. Congress at Sparta, and a general peace concluded, from which the Thebans were excluded. Spartans invade Bœotia, but are defeated by the Thebans under EPAMINONDAS, at the battle of *Leuctra.*
369. First invasion of the Peloponnesus by Thebans. Second invasion, 368. Third invasion, 366.
365. War between Arcadia and Elis. *Battle of Olympia,* 364.
362. Fourth invasion of Peloponnesus by Thebans. Battle of *Mantinēa.* EPAMINONDAS slain.
361. A general peace with all except the Spartans. AGESILAUS goes to Egypt, but dies in the winter while preparing to return home.
360. WAR between the *Olynthians* and *Athenians,* for the possession of Amphipolis.
359. Accession of PHILIP to the throne of Macedonia (æt. twenty-three).
357. Chios, Rhodes, and Byzantium revolt from Athens. First year of the *Social War.* The Phocians seize Delphi. Commencement of the *Sacred War.*
356. Birth of ALEXANDER. Potidæa taken by PHILIP.
355. Third and last year of the *Social War.*
352. PHILIP enters Thessaly, expels the *tyrants* from *Pheræ,* and makes himself master of Thessaly. Attempts to pass *Thermopylæ,* but is prevented by the Athenians.
348. *Olynthian War* continued.
347. *Olynthus* taken, and destroyed by PHILIP.

B.C.
346. PHILIP brings the Sacred War to a close, after it had lasted ten years.
343. TIMOLEON completes the conquest of Syracuse, and expels *Dionysius*, having sailed from Corinth for this purpose in 344.
842. PHILIP's expedition to Thrace. DEMOSTHENES' Orations.
339. War renewed between PHILIP and the Athenians.
338. PHILIP defeats the Athenians and Thebans at the *battle of Chæronēa*, and becomes master of Greece.
336.*Murder of PHILIP, and accession of ALEXANDER (æt. twenty).
335 *Thebes* revolts, and is *destroyed* by ALEXANDER.
334. *War* commenced against *Persia*. ALEXANDER defeats the Persian Satraps at the *Granicus*.
333. ALEXANDER subdues *Lycia*, collects his forces at *Gordium* in the spring, and defeats DARIUS at *Issus* in the autumn.
332. ALEXANDER takes *Tyre* and *Gaza*, and marches into Egypt, and orders Alexandria to be founded. — 331.' Marches through Phœnicia and Syria, crosses the Euphrates, and defeats DARIUS at *Arbēla* or *Gaugamēla*.
330. DARIUS slain by BESSUS.
329. ALEXANDER crosses the Oxus and Jaxartes, *defeats* the *Scythians*, and winters at Bactra.
327. ALEXANDER conquers Sogdiana; marries ROXANA, a Bactrian princess; returns to Bactria, and *invades India*.
326. ALEXANDER returns to Persia, and sends NEARCHUS with a fleet to sail from the mouths of the INDUS to the Persian Gulf.
325. ALEXANDER reaches Susa; and Babylon, 324.
323.*ALEXANDER dies at Babylon in June, after a reign of twelve years and eight months. The Greek states wage war against Macedonia (*Lamian War*).
322. *Battle of Cranon*, and end of the Lamian War.
316. ANTIGONUS becomes master of Asia.
315. SELEUCUS, PTOLEMY, CASSANDER, and LYSIMACHUS wage war against Antigonus.
312. Fourth year of the war. — 311. A general peace. Roxana murdered. Seleucus recovers Babylon. Æra of the Seleucidæ begins.
308. PTOLEMY's expedition to Greece.
306. PTOLEMY defeated by DEMETRIUS, son of Antigonus, in a *sea-fight*, off *Salamis* in Cyprus.
303. War in Greece carried on by Demetrius against Cassander.
301. *Battle of Ipsus* in Phrygia: Lysimachus and Seleucus defeat Antigonus and Demetrius.

180   GREEK CHRONOLOGY.

B.C.
295. DEMETRIUS takes Athens, and, 294, makes an expedition into Peloponnesus. Becomes king of Macedonia.
294. *Civil War* in Macedonia, between ANTIPATER and ALEXANDER.
290. DEMETRIUS takes Thebes, and, 289, carries on war against PYRRHUS.
287. DEMETRIUS driven from Macedonia, and his kingdom divided.
281. LYSIMACHUS defeated and slain at the battle of *Corupedion.*
280.*SELEUCUS murdered. Rise of the Achæan league. PYRRHUS crosses into Italy.
279. The Gauls, under BRENNUS, invade Greece.
273. PYRRHUS invades Macedonia, and expels Antigonus.
272. PYRRHUS dies. ANTIGONUS regains Macedonia.
227. CLEOMENES, king of Sparta, wages war against the Achæan League.
221. ANTIGONUS obtains possession of Sparta.
220. Social War commences. — 217. Third and last year of the war.
211. Treaty between Rome and the Ætolians. — 208. PHILIP marches into the Peloponnesus to assist the Achæans.
200. War between PHILIP and Rome. Philip defeated at the battle of *Cynoscephalæ*, 197.
192. ANTIOCHUS affords assistance to the Ætolians.
167. *One thousand of the principal Achæans sent to Rome.* Romans victorious.
147. *Macedonia becomes a Roman province.*
146.**Corinth destroyed by* MUMMIUS. *Greece becomes a Roman province.*

ROMAN CHRONOLOGY.

B.C.
753.*Foundation of Rome on the Palatine Mount, 21st of April, according to the era of Varro. Cato gives B. C. 752; Polybius, B.C. 750; Fabius Pictor, B.C. 747.
753–716. ROMULUS, the first Roman King, reigned thirty-seven years. Senate consists of 100 "Senatores." *Wars* with *Fidenæ* and *Veii*.
715–672. NUMA POMPILIUS, the second King, reigned forty-three years. Institution of religious ceremonies, and regulation of the year.
672–640. TULLUS HOSTILIUS, third King of Rome, reigned thirty-two years. *Destruction of Alba*, and removal of inhabitants to Rome.
640–616. ANCUS MARTIUS, fourth King of Rome, reigned twenty-four years. Origin of Plebeians, consisting of conquered Latins settled on the Aventine. Ostia founded.
616–578. LUCIUS TARQUINIUS PRISCUS, fifth King, reigned thirty-eight years. Great public works undertaken. The Senate increased to 300.
578–534. SERVIUS TULLIUS, sixth Roman King, reigned forty-four years. Rome surrounded by a stone wall. Institution of thirty Plebeian tribes.
534–510. TARQUINIUS SUPERBUS, seventh and last Roman King. Expulsion of the Tarquins, and establishment of a republic.
509.*Consuls elected. Death of Brutus. First treaty with Carthage.
508. *War with Porsena*, king of Clusium.
501. Institution of Dictatorship and Magister Equitum.
498 *Battle of Lake Regillus:* Latins defeated.
494 Secession of the Plebs to Mons Sacer.
493. War with the Volscians, and *capture of Corioli*.—491. CORIOLANUS goes into exile.
483. War with Veii.
477. *Slaughter* of the 300 *Fabii* at the *Cremera.*
471. Lex Publilia passed.
465. War with the Æquians.

ROMAN CHRONOLOGY.

B.C.
458. Dictatorship of CINCINNATUS, who relieves the Roman army shut in by the Volscians and Æquians.
454. Three Commissioners sent to Greece, to prepare a code of laws.
451. *DECEMVIRI appointed. Laws of ten tables promulgated; increased by two, 450.
449. Death of Virginia. Decemvirs deposed.
445. Lex Canuleia passed, and *connubium* between Patricians and Plebeians permitted.
444. Tribuni Militum with Consular power.
443. Institution of Censorship.
440. Famine at Rome. Præfectus Annonæ appointed.
438. Inhabitants of *Fidenæ* revolt.
426. *War* with *Veii. Fidenæ destroyed.*
421. Number of Quæstors increased from two to four.
407. Truce with Veii (made 425) expires.
406. Pay decreed to the soldiers by the Senate for the first time.
405. *Siege of Veii.* It lasts *ten years;* ends 396, Veii being taken by CAMILLUS.
399. A pestilence at Rome.—398. An embassy sent to consult the Oracle at Delphi.
391. CAMILLUS banished. Gauls enter Etruria.
390. *Rome taken by the Gauls.* Romans defeated at the *battle of Allia.* CAMILLUS recalled, and appointed Dictator.
367. Licinian laws passed. One of the Consuls to be chosen from the Plebeians. CAMILLUS conquers the Gauls.
365. Death of CAMILLUS.
361. *Invasion of the Gauls.* T. MANLIUS kills a Gaul in single combat, and is surnamed *Torquatus.*
356. First Plebeian Dictator elected.— 351. First Plebeian Censor.
348. Treaty with Carthage renewed.
343. *First Samnite War.* VALERIUS defeats the Samnites.
340. *Latin War.*
337. First Plebeian Prætor.
326. *Second Samnite War.*
321. *Roman* army surrendered to the *Samnites* at the *Caudine Forks,* and sent under the yoke.
300. Lex Ogulnia passed, increasing the number of Pontiffs and Augurs.
298. *Third Samnite War. Samnites defeated* at *Bovianum* and at *Volaterræ,* by the *Etruscans.*
295. *Battle of Sentinum;* Samnites, Umbrians, Etruscans, and Gauls defeated.
290. *Conclusion of* the *Samnite War,* which had lasted fifty-three years.

ROMAN CHRONOLOGY. 183

B.C
281. PYRRHUS arrives in Italy to assist the Tarentines against the Romans.
280. Romans defeated by PYRRHUS near *Heracleia;* and, 279, near *Asculum.*
278. PYRRHUS in Sicily. Romans successful in Southern Italy.
275. PYRRHUS *totally defeated* near *Beneventum.*
272. War in Southern Italy concluded.
264.**The First Punic War.* Cons. CLAUDIUS crosses over into Sicily and defeats the Carthaginians and Syracusans.
262. *Agrigentum taken* after a siege of seven months.
260. Fifth year of the First Punic War. DUILIUS, the Consul, gains a *naval victory* over the *Carthaginians.*
256. The Romans victorious in Africa.
255. REGULUS, in Africa, takes Tunis and overcomes the Carthaginians, but is afterwards defeated and taken prisoner.
250. Fifteenth year of the war. — Great *victory* of METELLUS at *Panormus.* Regulus sent to Rome to solicit peace.
247. HAMILCAR appointed to the command of the Carthaginians. HANNIBAL born.
241. *Twenty-fourth and last year* of the *First Punic War.* — Naval victory of C. Lutatius, off the Ægates. Peace made with the Carthaginians. Sicily becomes a Roman province.
229. Death of HAMILCAR in Spain. He is succeeded by HASDRUBAL.
225. *War* with the *Gauls.* Fourth and last year of the war, 222.
219. HANNIBAL takes *Saguntum*, and winters at Carthago Nova.
218.**Second Punic War.* — HANNIBAL reaches Italy from Spain in five months. He defeats the Romans at the *battles* of the *Ticinus* and the *Trebia.* SCIPIO carries on the war in Spain.
217. HANNIBAL defeats FLAMINIUS at the battle of the *Trasymene Lake,* and marches into Apulia.
216. Romans defeated at the *battle* of *Cannæ.*
215. MARCELLUS overcomes HANNIBAL near Nola. The SCIPIOS successful in Spain.
212. Seventh year of the war. — HANNIBAL takes *Tarentum,* and MARCELLUS takes Syracuse. The two SCIPIOS *defeated* in Spain.
208. The two consuls are defeated by HANNIBAL near *Venusia.* HASDRUBAL crosses the Pyrenees and winters in Gaul.
207. HASDRUBAL marches into Italy, is *defeated* on the *Metaurus,* and *slain.*
206. SCIPIO becomes master of Spain. — 204. HANNIBAL worsted near *Croton.* SCIPIO crosses over into Africa.
203. Carthaginians defeated, SYPHAX taken prisoner. HANNIBAL leaves Italy for Africa.
202 SCIPIO defeats HANNIBAL at the decisive *battle of Zama.*

B C.

201.*Eighteenth and last year of the Second Punic War. Peace with Carthage.
200. War renewed with PHILIP of Macedon.
197. PHILIP defeated by FLAMINIUS at the battle of Cynoscephalæ, and peace concluded.
196. Flaminius proclaims the independence of Greece.
191. War with ANTIOCHUS, who is defeated at Thermopylæ.
190. L. Scipio, the consul, crosses into Asia and defeats ANTIOCHUS at the battle of Magnesia.
183. Death of HANNIBAL and of SCIPIO AFRICANUS (exact date not settled).
171. War with PERSEUS.
168. Fourth and last year of the war. PERSEUS defeated by ÆMILIUS PAULUS at the battle of Pydna.
149. Third Punic War. — The Consuls land in Africa.
146.*Fourth and last year of the Third Punic War. — Carthage destroyed by SCIPIO.
143. Numantine War commenced.—140, 138 and 137. Numantines successful.
133. Numantia taken and destroyed by SCIPIO.
129. Death of SCIPIO AFRICANUS (æt. 56). Death of C. GRACCHUS, 121.
111. Jugurthine War. — 106. Sixth and last year, Jugurtha captured, MARIUS commander.
102. Battle of Aquæ Sextiæ.—MARIUS defeats the Teutones. Servile War arises in Sicily.
101. MARIUS and CATULUS, Pro-con., defeat the Cimbri at Campi Raudii.
90. Marsic or Social War. — 89. Romans successful, Asculum taken.
88.*End of the Marsic War. SULLA appointed to command the army against MITHRIDATES, which occasions the civil war of MARIUS and SULLA. Sulla marches upon Rome, proscribes Marius and his party.
87. SULLA crosses into Greece to conduct the war. MARIUS and CINNA, the Consul, enter Rome and murder their opponents.
86. MARIUS dies (æt. seventy). War continued against MITHRIDATES. ARCHELAUS defeated in Bœotia.
84. Mithridates and Sulla conclude a peace.
83. SULLA returns to Italy and continues the civil war against the party of MARIUS. The Capitol burnt.
82. SULLA, victorious, is appointed Dictator. Præneste captured.
78. Death of SULLA (æt. sixty).
75. P. SERVILIUS VATIA, the Pro-consul (sent against the Pirates on the S. coast of Asia Minor, 78), conquers the Isaurians.

ROMAN CHRONOLOGY.

B.C.
74. *War with Mithridates* renewed. Lucullus appointed general.
73. MITHRIDATES defeated by LUCULLUS, *near Cyzicus*. Commencement of the *war* in Italy against the *Gladiators* under SPARTACUS.
71. *Mithridatic War* continued. MITHRIDATES flees into Armenia, to Tigranes. SPARTACUS, the leader of the Gladiators, *defeated*.
69. LUCULLUS invades Armenia, and defeats TIGRANES.
66. Mithridatic War intrusted to CN. POMPEIUS.
65. CATILINE's first *conspiracy*.
63. Death of MITHRIDATES. CATILINE's second *conspiracy* discovered and crushed by CICERO the Consul.
62. CATILINE defeated and slain.
61. POMPEIUS, having returned to Italy, triumphs.
60. C. J. CÆSAR victorious in Spain. CÆSAR, POMPEIUS, and CRASSUS establish the FIRST TRIUMVIRATE.
58. CÆSAR undertakes his first campaign in Gaul. Defeats the Belgæ, 57; *crosses the Rhine*, and *invades Britain*, 55; *second expedition* into *Britain*, 54.
54. CRASSUS marches against the Parthians. — 53. *Defeat* and death of CRASSUS.
51. CÆSAR subjugates Gaul, his ninth campaign.
49. Commencement of the *Civil War* between POMPEIUS and CÆSAR.
48. CÆSAR lands in Greece, and defeats POMPEIUS *at the battle of Pharsalus*. POMPEIUS murdered before Alexandria (æt. 58). Alexandrine War.
47. CÆSAR, Dictator, concludes the *Alexandrine War;* marches into Pontus, and *conquers* PHARNACES.
46. CÆSAR defeats the partisans of POMPEIUS at the *battle of Thapsus*. He reforms the Calendar.
45. *Battle of Munda* in Spain. CÆSAR defeats the sons of POMPEIUS, and is made Consul for ten years, and Dictator for life.
44. CÆSAR ASSASSINATED, on the 15th of March (æt. fifty-six). *Civil War of Mutina* against ANTONY.
43. SECOND TRIUMVIRATE formed by OCTAVIANUS, ANTONIUS, and LEPIDUS.
42. *War in Greece.* Battle of *Philippi*, and death of CASSIUS. Second battle of *Philippi*, and death of BRUTUS.
36. Defeat of SEX. POMPEIUS. LEPIDUS ceases to be a Triumvir.
34. Dalmatians defeated.
33. A rupture takes place between OCTAVIANUS and ANTONIUS, and both prepare for war.
31. ANTONIUS defeated at the *battle of Actium*, 2d of Sept.
30.*Death of ANTONIUS (æt. fifty-one) and Cleopatra. *Egypt becomes a Roman province.* OCTAVIANUS SOLE RULER OF THE

16 *

B.C.

ROMAN EMPIRE. He returns to Rome from the East, and celebrates three triumphs, *Dalmatian, Actian, Alexandrine.*

27. OCTAVIANUS takes the title of AUGUSTUS, and accepts the government for ten years.
25. The Temple of Janus shut a second time.
23. Death of MARCELLUS.
20. Ambassadors sent to Rome from India.
12. Death of AGRIPPA.
10. AUGUSTUS returns to Rome from Gaul, with DRUSUS and TIBERIUS.
9. DRUSUS sent against the Germans. Dies.

A.D.

4. TIBERIUS adopted by Augustus, and sent to carry on *war* against the *Germans.*
12. TIBERIUS returns to Rome from Germany, and triumphs.
14. Census taken, the citizens are 4,197,000. AUGUSTUS dies at *Nola* in *Campania* (æt. seventy-six), and is succeeded by TIBERIUS (æt. fifty-six).
16. GERMANICUS continues the *war* in *Germany*, and triumphs, 17. Returns to Rome.
19. *Germanicus* visits Egypt, and returns to Syria. Dies (æt. thirty-four). The Jews are banished from Italy.
23. Death of DRUSUS, poisoned by Sejanus.
31. Fall and execution of SEJANUS.
33. AGRIPPINA and her son DRUSUS are put to death.
37. Death of TIBERIUS (æt. seventy-eight), having reigned twenty-three years. CALIGULA succeeds (æt. twenty-five).
39. HEROD ANTIPAS, tetrarch of Galilee, deposed, and succeeded by AGRIPPA.
40. CALIGULA in Gaul. His expedition to the ocean. He returns to Rome.
41. CALIGULA slain (æt. twenty-nine). CLAUDIUS succeeds (æt. fifty). Germans defeated by GALBA.
43. *Expedition* of CLAUDIUS into *Britain.* Returns to Rome, and triumphs, 44.
49. CLAUDIUS (his wife Messalina having been put to death in 48) marries AGRIPPINA.
54. CLAUDIUS poisoned (æt. sixty-three); reigned fourteen years. NERO succeeds (æt. seventeen).
59. AGRIPPINA, the mother of Nero, is murdered by his order.
61. Insurrection in *Britain* under *Boadicea.*
62. NERO divorces OCTAVIA, and marries POPPÆA SABINA, the wife of Otho.
64 Great fire at Rome. *First persecution* of the *Christians.*
65. Piso's conspiracy discovered and suppressed.
66. NERO goes to Greece. The Jewish war begins.
67 NERO in Greece. VESPASIAN conducts the Jewish War.

ROMAN CHRONOLOGY. 187

A.D.
68. NERO kills himself (æt. thirty). GALBA succeeds.
69. GALBA slain, Jan. 15 (æt. seventy-three). OTHO succeeds, Jan. 15, and died April 16 (æt. thirty-six). VITELLIUS proclaimed at Cologne, Jan. 2; reigned till his death, Dec. 22 (æt. fifty-four). VESPASIAN (æt. sixty) proclaimed at Alexandria, July 1. On the death of Galba, the Civil War between Otho and Vitellius commenced. The troops of Otho defeated at the *battle of Bedriacum;* the generals of Vespasian meanwhile invade Italy, take Cremona, and march upon Rome. The Capitol burnt. Vitellius slain, 22d of Dec.
70. *VESPASIAN proceeds to Italy, leaving TITUS his son to carry on the Jewish war. *Jerusalem taken,* after a siege of five months.
71. Triumph of VESPASIAN and TITUS. Temple of Janus closed.
78. AGRICOLA in Britain.
79. Death of VESPASIAN, June 23 (æt. sixty-nine). TITUS succeeds (æt. thirty-eight). Second campaign of Agricola in Britain. Eruption of Vesuvius.
80. Great fire at Rome. Colosseum completed. Third campaign of AGRICOLA.
81. Death of TITUS, Sept. 13 (æt. forty). DOMITIAN succeeds (æt. thirty). Fourth campaign of AGRICOLA in Britain. Fifth campaign, 82; sixth, 83; seventh, 84. Agricola recalled to Rome, 85.
96. DOMITIAN slain, Sept. 18 (æt. forty-four). NERVA Emperor (æt. sixty-three); died Jan. 25, 98 (æt. sixty-five).
98. TRAJAN (æt. forty-one); died Aug. 8, 117 (æt. sixty), having reigned nineteen years.
117. HADRIAN (æt. forty-two; died July 10, 138 (æt. sixty-two), having reigned twenty-one years.
138. ANTONIUS PIUS (æt. fifty-one); died Mar. 7, 161 (æt. seventy-four), having reigned twenty-three years.
161. M. AURELIUS (æt. thirty-nine); died Mar. 17, 180 (æt. fifty-eight), having reigned nineteen years.
180. COMMODUS (æt. nineteen); slain Dec. 31, 193 (æt. thirty-one), having reigned thirteen years.
193. PERTINAX (æt. sixty-six); slain Mar. 28, 193, having reigned three months. JULIANUS (æt. fifty-six); reigned from Mar. 28 to June 1. SEPTIMUS SEVERUS (æt. forty-six); died Feb. 4, 211, at Eboracum, *York,* (æt. sixty-four), having reigned eighteen years.

GREEK INDEX.

A.

ἄγκυρα, 113.
ἀγοραί, 161.
ἀγῶνες, 108.
ἄδυτον, 103.
ἀδώνια, 105.
ἀθήναια, 107.
'Αθήνη, 69.
'Αΐδης, 72.
αἰχμή, 112.
ἀκόντιον, 112.
ἀκράτισμα, 114.
ἀκρόπολις, 160.
αλμα, 108.
ἀλτῆρες, 108.
ἀμφικτυονία, 102.
ἀνάρρυσις, 106.
ἀναρρύω, 104.
ἀνθεστήρια, 106.
'Ανθεστηριών, 165.
ἄντλος, 113.
ἀξίνη, 112.
'Απαρκτίας, 172.
ἀπαρχή, 104.
ἀπατούρια, 106.
'Απηλιώτης, 172.
'Αργεστής, 172.
ἀρδάνιον, 115.
ἀρειοπαγεῖται, 101.
"Αρης, 68.
ἀρητῆρες, 103.
ἄριστον, 114.
"Αρτεμις, 70.
ἀρχεῖον, 100.

ἄρχων, 98.
'Ασκλήπιος, 70.
ἀσπίς, 111.
ἀτιμία, 103.
αὐλαία, 116.
αὐλός, 108.
'Αφροδίτη, 70.

B.

βασιλεύς, 98, 99.
βέλη, 112.
Βοηδρομιών, 165.
Βορέας, 172.
Βουλευτήριον, 161.
βουλή, 100.
βρόχος, 103.
βωμός, 103.

Γ.

Γαμηλιών, 165.
γέροντες, 101.
γερουσία, 101.
Γαῖα, 71.
Γῆ, 71.
γραμματεύς, 99.

Δ.

δαφνηφόρια, 106.
δειλινόν, 114.
δεῖπνον, 114.
δελφίν, 114.
δεσμός, 103.
δήμαρχοι, 99.
Δημήτηρ, 69.

δῆμοι, 99.
διαιτηταί, 101.
δίαυλος, 108.
διέκπλους, 114.
διονύσια, 106.
Διόνυσος, 71.
δίσκος, 108.
δοκιμασία, 101.
δόλιχος, 108.
δόμος, 103.
δόρπεια, 106.
δόρπον, 114.
δόρυ, 112.
δουλεία, 103.
δοῦλοι, 98.
δρόμος, 108.

E.

ἔγχος, 112.
ἔγκυκλον, 115.
ἐδώλια, 113.
εἵλωτες, 98.
'Εκατομβαιών, 168.
ἑκατόμβη, 104.
ἑκατονταρχία, 112.
ἐκκλησία, 100.
'Ελαφηβολιών, 165.
ἐλευσίνια, 106.
ἔμβολον, 113.
ἔνδεκα, 99.
ἐπιβάται, 114.
ἐπιστάτης, 100.
ἐπιστολεύς, 114.
ἐπώνυμος, 98.

(189)

ἐρέται, 114.
ἐρετμοί, 113.
Ερμῆς, 69.
Ἔρως, 71.
ἐσθής, 115.
Ἑστία, 69.
εὐθύνη, 101.
Εὐμενίδες, 71.
Ἐτησίαι, 172.
Εὖρος, 172.
ἐφεστρίς, 115.
ἐφέται, 102.
ἐφορεῖον, 100.
ἔφοροι, 99.
Εως, 71.

Z.

Ζεύς, 68.
Ζέφυρος, 172.
ζυγά, 113.
ζυγῖται, 113.

H.

ἡλιαία, 101.
ἡλιασταί, 101.
ἡνίοχοι, 111.
Ἥρα, 69.
Ἥρη, 69.
ἡρῷα, 116.
Ἥφαιστος, 68.

Θ.

θαλαμῖται, 113.
θάλαμος, 113.
θάνατος, 103.
Θαργηλιών, 165.
θέατρον, 116.
θεοπρόποι, 104.
θεσμοθέται, 98, 99.
θεσμοφόρια, 107.
θησαυρός, 103.
θοανῖται, 113.
θρᾶνοι, 113.

θυμέλη, 116.
θυοσκόοι, 103.
θυρεός, 112.
θώραξ, 111.

I.

ἱερεῖς, 103.
ἱερεῖον, 104.
ἱμάτιον, 115.
ἵππαρχοι, 112.
ἱππεῖς, 111, 112.
ἱστίον, 113.
ἱστός, 113.

K.

Καικίας, 172.
καλάθιον, 107.
καταστρώματα, 113.
Κεκρωπία, 160.
κεραῖαι, 113.
Κεραμεικός, 160.
κέρατα, 112, 113.
κέρνα, 104.
κίονες, 116.
κλῖναι, 114, 115.
κνημῖδες, 111.
κόθορνοι, 115.
κοῖλον, 117.
κοντοί, 113.
κόρυς, 111.
κουρεῶτις, 106.
κράνος, 111.
κρηπῖδες, 115.
Κρόνος, 75.
κυβερνήτης, 114.
κυνέη, 111.
κύφων, 103.
κῶπαι, 113.

Λ.

ληξίαρχοι, 99.
λιθοβολία, 103.
Λίψ, 172.

λογεῖον, 116.
λοιβαί, 104.
λόφος, 111.
λόχοι, 112.
λόχος, 112.

Μαιμακτηριών, 165.
μάντιες, 104.
μελιτοῦττα, 115.
μεσόκοιλα, 113.
Μεταγειτνιών, 165.
μέτοικοι, 98.
μέτωπον, 113.
μῆρα, 104.
μόραι, 112.
Μουνυχιών, 165.
μυστήρια, 106.

N.

ναΐδια, 116.
ναός, 103.
ναύαρχος, 114.
ναῦται, 114.
νομοθέται, 99.
Νότος, 172.
νουμηνία, 166.

Ξ.

ξίφος, 103, 112.

O.

ὀβολός, 115.
Ὀδυσσεύς, 94.
οἴαξ, 113.
οἰνωνοπόλοι, 104.
ὀϊστοί, 112.
οἰωνισταί, 104.
ὁλκάδες, 113.
ὁλκοί, 114.
ὀμφαλος, 111.
ὀνειροπόλοι, 104.
ὀπισθόδομυς, 103.

GREEK INDEX. 191

ὁπλῖται, 111.
ὁπλί=ης, 108.
ὀρχήστρα, 116.
ὀστρακισμός, 102.
οὐλοχύται, 104.
οὐρά, 112.

Π.

παγκράτιον, 109.
κάλη, 109.
Πάλλας, 69.
παναθήνα.α, 107.
πεζοί, 111.
πέλανοι, 104.
πελειάδες, 105.
πέλεκυς, 112.
πελτασταί, 111, 112.
πέλτη, 111, 112.
πεμπάς, 112.
πένταθλον, 108.
πεντηκόντοροι, 113.
περικεφαλαία, 111.
περίοικοι, 98.
περίπλους, 114.
πηδάλιον, 113.
πιθοιγία, 106.
πῖλοι, 115.
πλάται, 113.
πλευραί, 113.
πλοῖα, 113.
πνύξ, 161.
πόδες, 113.
ποικίλη, 161.
πολέμαρχος, 98, 112.
πολῖται, 98.
Ποσειδεών, 165.
Ποσειδῶν, 68.
πρόδομος, 103.
πρόεδροι, 100.
πρόθεσις, 115.
πρόναος, 103.
προπύλαια, 160.
προσκήνιον, 116.
πρύμνη, 113.

πρυτανεία, 100.
πρυτανεῖον, 161.
πρυτάνεις, 100.
πρώρα, 113.
Πυανεψιών, 165.
πυγμή, 108.
πυλαία, 101.
πῦρ, 103.

Σ.

σανίς, 103.
σηκός, 103.
σήματα, 104.
σκηνή, 116.
Σκιρροφοριών, 165.
Σκίρων, 172.
σόλος, 108.
Σπαρτιᾶται, 98.
σπείρη, 113.
σπονδαί, 104.
στάδιον, 108.
σταυρός, 103.
στῆλαι, 116.
στήλη, 103.
στίγματα, 103.
στοαί, 161.
στόλαρχος, 114.
στολή. 115.
στρατηγοί, 112.
στρατηγός, 114.
στρατιά, 112.
στρογγύλαι, 113.
σφενδόνη, 112.
σχοινία, 113.

Τ.

ταξίαρχοι, 112.
τάξις, 112.
τέμενος, 103.
τέρπτα, 104.
τεσσαράκοντα, 102.
τοξεύματα, 112.
τόξον, 112.
τοπεῖα, 113.

τράπεζαι, 116.
τράφηξ, 113.
τρίβων, 115.
τριήραρχος, 114.
τρίτα, 116.
τρόπις, 113.
τρόποι, 113.
τροχός, 103.
Τύχη, 71.

Υ.

ὑπέραι, 113.
ὑποβολεύς, 117.
ὑποδήματα, 115.

Φ.

φαινόλης, 115.
φάλαγξ, 112.
φάρμακον, 103.
φάρος, 115.
φορτηγοί, 113.
φυγή, 103.
φυλαί, 102.
φύλαρχοι, 99, 112.

Χ.

χειροτονία, 100.
χιτών, 115.
χιτώνιον, 115.
χλαῖνα, 115.
χλαμύς, 115.
χοαί, 104, 116.
χόες, 106.
χοῖνιξ, 103.
χοραγός, 117.
χύτροι, 106.

Ψ.

ψήφισμα, 100.
ψῆφοι, 100.
ψιλοί, 111.

Ω.

Ὠδεῖον, 161.

INDEX.

A.

Abăcus, 142.
Absyrtus, 86.
Academia, 161.
Academic Sect, 159.
Acarnania, 38.
Accensi, 122.
Acestes, 95.
Achaia, 40.
Acheron, 75.
Achilles, 91.
Actuariæ, 138.
Acropolis, 160.
Admetus, 75.
Adonis, 76.
Adrastus, 87.
Æacus, 76.
Ædium, 140.
Ædiles, 122.
—— Curules, 122.
—— Ccreales, 122.
Æetes, 85.
Ægeon, 77.
Ægyptus, 64, 65.
Aello, 79.
Æneas, 95.
Æolia, 49.
Æolus, 70.
Æolian league, 52.
Ærarium, 120.
Æschines, 148.
Æsɔhylus, 144.
Æsculapius, 70.
Æson, 85.

Æsop, 149.
Ætolia, 38.
Africa, 63.
—— Propria, 66.
Africus, 172.
Agamemnon, 89, 92.
Agenor, 86.
Agger, 135.
Aglaia, 72.
Agora, 144.
Ajax, 92.
Albania, 57.
Alcæus, 129.
Alcestis, 76.
Alcyone, 82.
Alcman, 130.
Alecto, 71.
Alexander, 89, 95.
Alveolus, 126.
Alveus, 126.
Amazones, 76.
Ammon, 70.
Amor, 71.
Amphiaraus, 87.
Amphitrīte, 70.
Amphoræ, 140.
Anacreon, 129.
Anaxandrides, 129.
Anchises, 95.
Ancile, 129.
Andabătæ, 132.
Andromache, 95.
Andronicus (Livius), 154.

Angustus Clavus, 118
Annuli, 139.
Antenor, 95.
Antĭgŏne, 87.
Antilŏchus, 92.
Antiphanes, 129.
Apis, 70.
Apodyterium, 141.
Apollo, 69.
Apparitores, 122.
Apulia, 29.
Aqueducts, 164.
Aquilo, 172.
Aquitani, 17.
Aquitania, 18.
Arabia, 55.
Araros, 145.
Arcadia, 42.
Arches, Triumphal, 164.
Archimedes, 149.
Arena, 131.
Argo, 85.
Argolis, 41.
Argonautæ, 85.
Argus, 80, 85.
Aria, 60.
Ariadne, 76.
Arianus, 60.
Aries, 136.
Aristophanes, 145.
Aristotle, 151.
Armenia, 57.
—— Minor, 51.

(192)

INDEX.

Arx, 163.
Asia, 46.
—— Minor, 47.
—— (Seven Churches of), 52.
Assaracus, 88.
Assyria, 59.
Astræa, 70.
Atăbulus, 172.
Athamas, 85.
Athena, 69.
Atlas, 76.
Atrium, 140.
Atrŏpos, 75.
Attica, 40.
Atticus, 157.
Augures, 127.
Augurium, 127.
Aulæa, 116.
Aurora, 71.
Auspices, 127.
Auspicium, 127.
Ausonia, 23.
Auster, 172.
Automedon, 92.
Auxilia, 135.

B.

Babylonia, 58.
Bacchus, 71.
Bacchylides, 146.
Bactria, 60.
Bactriana, 60.
Bætica, 16.
Ballista, 136.
Balneæ, 141.
Balneator, 141.
Basilicæ, 163.
Batanæa, 55.
Belgæ, 17.
Bellĕrŏphon, 76.
Bellona, 71.

Bion, 146.
Bithynia, 48.
Bœotia, 39.
Bona Dea, 130.
Boreas, 172.
Briareus, 77.
Briseis, 90.
Britannia, 44.
Bruttium, 30.
Buccĭna, 135.

C.

Cadmea, 86.
Cadmus, 86.
Cæsar, 155.
Cæsars, the Twelve, 169.
Calcei, 139.
Calceus lunatus, 120.
Calchas, 89, 92.
Caldarium, 141.
Calends, 167.
Caligæ, 139.
Calliŏpe, 73.
Calypso, 77.
Campania, 29.
Campi, 162.
Campus Martius, 162.
Cappadocia, 51.
Capitolium, 163.
Capăneus, 87.
Caria, 50.
Carina, 113.
Carmania, 61.
Carni, 26.
Cassandra, 89, 95.
Castor, 77.
Castra, 136.
Catapulta, 136.
Cato, 158.
Catullus, 153.
Catervarii, 132.
Caurus, 172.

Cavea, 117, 132.
Celæno, 79, 82.
Celsus, 158.
Celtæ, 17.
Censores, 123.
Centauri, 77.
Centūriæ, 134.
Centuriones, 135.
Ceramīcus, 160.
Cerberus, 77.
Ceres, 69.
Cestus, 108.
Chaldæa, 58.
Charon, 77.
Chimæra, 76.
Chiron, 77.
Chlamys, 135.
Chrysēis, 90.
Chryses, 90.
Cicero, 156, 157.
Cilicia, 50.
Cingulum, 138.
Circe, 77.
Circi, 163.
Circus, 163.
Cistæ, 121.
Clepsȳdræ, 167.
Clio, 73.
Clipeus, 134.
Clotho, 75.
Cocȳtus, 77.
Cognomen, 143.
Cœlus, 75.
Cœna, 139.
Cohortes, 134.
Colchis, 56.
Columella, 158.
Columns, 164.
Colyttus, 160.
Comitia, 121.
—— Curiata, 121.
—— Centuriata, 121.

17

Comitia Tributa, 122.
Comissatio, 140.
Compluvium, 140.
Conscription, 133.
Consules, 123.
Co-öptatio, 128.
Cornu, 135.
Corœbus, 96.
Corinthĭa, 42.
Corona Civica, 136.
——— Castrensis, 137.
——— Muralis, 137.
——— Obsidionalis, 137.
——— Graminea, 137.
——— Oleagina, 137.
Corvi, 138.
Cothurni, 117, 139.
Crater, 140.
Crates, 145.
Cratinus, 145.
Creon, 88.
Cucullus, 139.
Cunei, 132.
Cuneus, 136.
Cupido, 71.
Curatores, 123.
Curiæ (Senate-houses), 164.
Curiæ, 118.
Curio, 118.
Curiones, 128.
Cursus, 131.
Curtius, 156.
Cybĕle, 83.
Cyclades, 43.
Cyclopes, 78.
Cynic Sect, 159.
Cynosarges, 161.
Cyprus, 52.
Cyrenaic Sect, 159.

D.

Dacia, 32.
Dædalus, 78.
Damnum, 126.
Danaides, 84.
Daphne, 78.
Dardănus, 88.
Decemviri, 128.
Decretum, 120.
Decuriæ, 134.
Deiphŏbus, 88, 96.
Delta, 64.
Demosthenes, 148.
Deucalion, 78.
Diana, 70.
Dictator, 124.
Dies Fasti, 172.
——— Festi, 130.
——— Nefasti, 172.
——— Profesti, 130.
Dīke, 72.
Diodorus (Siculus), 147.
Diomēdes, 92.
Dionysius, 147.
Dionysus, 71.
——— Theatre of, 161.
Diphilus, 145.
Diræ, 71.
Dis, 72.
Discessio, 120.
Dithyrambs, 144.
Dormitoria, 141.
Dorian (States), 51.
Doris, 38, 50.
Dryădes, 73.

E.

Eleatic School, 159.
Electra, 82, 93.

Eliac School, 159.
Elis, 40.
Elysĭum, 78.
Emeriti, 133.
Endȳmĭon, 78.
Ennius, 152.
Ensis, 135.
Epaphus, 80.
Epeus, 91.
Epicharmus, 145.
Epicurean Sect, 159.
Epicurus, 151.
Epirus, 38.
Equites, 118, 132.
Erăto, 73.
Erĕbus, 78.
Erechtheum, 160.
Eretriac School, 159.
Ericthonius, 86.
Eristic School, 159
Essedarii, 132.
Eteŏcles, 87.
Etruria, 26.
Eubulus, 145.
Euclid, 149.
Eumenĭdes, 71.
Eunŏmĭa, 72.
Euphrŏsȳne, 72
Eupolis, 145.
Euripides, 145.
Europe, 13.
Eurōpa, 78, 86.
Eurus, 172.
Eurȳăle, 79.
Eurȳdĭce, 81.
Eurȳsăces, 92.
Eurystheus, 79.
Eurȳtion, 82.
Euterpe, 73.
Eutropius, 156.
Evocāti, 134.
Extispices, 128.

www.ingramcontent.com/pod-product-compliance
Lightning Source LLC
Chambersburg PA
CBHW032138160426
43197CB00008B/698